秋田県の教員採用試験過去問シリーズ❺

2025年度版

秋田県の英語科

過去問

協同教育研究会 編

協同出版

本書には，秋田県の教員採用試験の過去問題を収録しています。各問題ごとに，以下のように5段階表記で，難易度，頻出度を示しています。

難　易　度

非常に難しい	☆☆☆☆☆
やや難しい	☆☆☆☆
普通の難易度	☆☆☆
やや易しい	☆☆
非常に易しい	☆

頻　出　度

◎	ほとんど出題されない
◎◎	あまり出題されない
◎◎◎	普通の頻出度
◎◎◎◎	よく出題される
◎◎◎◎◎	非常によく出題される

※本書の過去問題における資料，法令文等の取り扱いについて

本書の過去問題で使用されている資料や法令文の表記や基準は，出題された当時の内容に準拠しているため，解答・解説も当時のものを使用しています。ご了承ください。

はじめに～「過去問」シリーズ利用に際して～

教育を取り巻く環境は変化しつつあり，日本の公教育そのものも，教員免許更新制の廃止やGIGAスクール構想の実現などの改革が進められています。また，現行の学習指導要領では「主体的・対話的で深い学び」を実現するため，指導方法や指導体制の工夫改善により，「個に応じた指導」の充実を図るとともに，コンピュータや情報通信ネットワーク等の情報手段を活用するために必要な環境を整えることが示されています。

一方で，いじめや体罰，不登校，暴力行為など，教育現場の問題もあいかわらず取り沙汰されており，教員に求められるスキルは，今後さらに高いものになっていくことが予想されます。

本書の基本構成としては，出題傾向と対策，過去5年間の出題傾向分析表，過去問題，解答および解説を掲載しています。各自治体や教科によって掲載年数をはじめ，「チェックテスト」や「問題演習」を掲載するなど，内容が異なります。

また原則的には一般受験を対象としております。特別選考等については対応していない場合があります。なお，実際に配布された問題の順番や構成を，編集の都合上，変更している場合があります。あらかじめご了承ください。

最後に，この「過去問」シリーズは，「参考書」シリーズとの併用を前提に編集されております。参考書で要点整理を行い，過去問で実力試しを行う，セットでの活用をおすすめいたします。

みなさまが，この書籍を徹底的に活用し，教員採用試験の合格を勝ち取って，教壇に立っていただければ，それはわたくしたちにとって最上の喜びです。

協同教育研究会

C O N T E N T S

第１部

秋田県の
英語科
出題傾向分析

秋田県の英語科　傾向と対策

近年出題されているのはリスニング問題と読解問題である。秋田県の英語は，中高共通問題，中学校，そして高校学校とに分けられるが，全体の問題構成は例年ほぼ同じである。一部記号選択問題もあるが，全体として日本語での記述の割合が大きい。英文を和訳するだけで解答できる問題もあるが，制限字数がやや厳しい問題も含まれているので，日本語で要約文などを書く学習など，短時間で解答や考えをまとめる学習を日常からすることが必須である。制限字数のある英問英答問題も近年出題されている。

中高共通

リスニング問題も構成は例年と同様，選択式，英問英答式，日本語の質問に日本語で答える形式である。選択肢や質問内容など，問題用紙に情報があるものについては，英語が読まれる前に目を通しておき，聞き取る際はメモをとることが重要である。様々な形式のリスニング問題を学習するためには，TOEIC®や英語検定2級から準1級レベルの学習CDを使用するのも役に立つだろう。全体的に量が多いので，決められた時間でリスニング問題に取り組んで集中力を養う学習が必須である。

読解問題はインディアンリバーラグーンのマナティーをテーマに自然環境系の長文問題が1題出題された。設問は，日本語での内容記述式と空所補充問題であった。いずれも英文の内容が正しく把握できているかどうかを問われる。英文中の代名詞による照応関係や因果関係の一貫した理解に加え，与えられた文字数で内容をまとめる学習が必要である。また，2023年度と同様にTimeやThe New York Timesなどニュース記事が出典となっているのでニュース記事独特の文体や語彙，イディオムに慣れておくこと，話題となりやすい情報も押さえておくとよい。すべて読むのではなく，500語程度の読みやすい記事を選んで読むようにしたい。

中学校

2024年度は，リスニング1(共通)，会話文1，読解2(うち共通1)，文法・語法1，整序1，英作文2の合計8題が出題された。

会話文問題は，日本語による内容記述を中心に，内容に即した語の挿入問題が扱われた。口語表現と隠れた疑問文には注意し，登場人物の誰が欲求，希望，提案をしているのか間違えないようにすること。空所補充問題の練習としては，問題集のコピーに修正テープを貼り付ける方法がおすすめである。

中学校の読解問題は，日本語による記述で解答を求める問題が2問，文脈に応じた選択肢問題が2問であった。共通問題も4問中3問が日本語での内容記述式の問題であった。2024年度の記述問題では部分訳を中心にきちんと日本語化できるかが問われている印象がある。語彙力を向上させ，精読するスキルの練習は欠かせない。

2024年度の文法・語法問題は，選択式の空所補充問題でイディオムや慣用表現を問う問題のみ出題された。問題数は少ないものの，参考書や問題集で頻出の語彙やイディオムは完全に頭に入れておくことが必要である。

英作文問題は整序英作文の3問と実際の授業や学習指導要領に関連した自由英作文の形式で出題されている。整序英作文は日本語が提示されているので，選択肢と元の日本語を見比べ，まず主語と動詞を決定すれば，残りの部分の組み合わせは難しくない。自由英作文は，昨年同様にALTへの依頼を50語程度で書く問題と，「話すこと［やり取り］」のパフォーマンステストを実施する上での留意点を2つ70語程度で書く問題が出題された。2022年度は60語から100語という指定があったため，いろいろな語数の英文で考えをまとめられるように日ごろから学習をしておくことに加え，学習指導要領の内容や，秋田県の指導方針をよく把握したうえで，自分の考えの基礎をしっかり固めておきたい。英作文の練習としてはDeepLのような翻訳ツールに加え，ChatGPTのような対話型AIを活用して，自分の英作文をブラッシュアップしていくとよいだろう。

高等学校

2024年度は，リスニング1(共通)，読解3(うち共通1)，授業に関するもの2，文法・語法2，英作文1の合計8題が出題された。

読解問題は2問出題されていて，いずれも500語程度の英文である。設問形式は空所補充と日本語での内容記述であり，小問数8問のうち6問が日本語での記述である。本文で示されている具体例や何を指しているかを問う問題が多いため，本文を適切に読解できるかが問われている。

文法・語法問題は，空所補充と正誤判断などの形式で出題された。語彙問題は低頻度語彙が対象となっており比較的難易度が上がったため，New JACET 8000 Basic Word List やPHaVE List のような無料で公開されている語彙リストを活用するとよい。おすすめの学習方法は単語カードのスマホアプリである。

英作文問題は，international studentへの支援に関するもので，自分の意見を80語程度で記述するという問題である。何度も書き直しをすることのないように，使用するキーワードやフレーズの選定とともにブレインストーミングを行ってからアウトラインにまとめ上げ，同時に文字量の感覚をつかんでおくことが必要である。様々なトピックで何本も練習し，ChatGPTに“Be an English Teacher. Can you check my essay?”のように添削のメッセージを入れて確認するとよいだろう。役立ちそうな文はストックし，アレンジして利用することを勧める。

英語の授業に関する問題では，言語活動を行う際の留意点や生徒への具体的な支援について記述させる問題があった。学習指導要領については網羅的に理解をしておくことが不可欠であり，英作文問題にも関わることがあるので，日本語，英語にかかわらず，学習指導要領に沿った自分なりの実践方法を考えておく必要がある。その上で，様々な英語教授法を授業の中で具体的にどのように落とし込んでいくかなど自分の考えを簡潔にまとめておくことが必要であろう。

過去5年間の出題傾向分析

中学＝●　高校＝▲　中高共通＝◎

分類	設問形式	2020年度	2021年度	2022年度	2023年度	2024年度
リスニング	内容把握	◎	◎	◎	◎	◎
発音・アクセント	発音					
	アクセント					
	文強勢					
文法・語法	空所補充	●▲	●▲	●▲	●▲	●▲
	正誤判断	▲	▲	▲	▲	▲
	一致語句					
	連立完成					
	その他					
会話文	短文会話					
	長文会話	●	●	●	●	●
文章読解	空所補充	▲	●▲	●▲	●▲◎	●▲◎
	内容一致文					●
	内容一致語句		◎			
	内容記述	●▲	●▲◎	●▲	●▲◎	●▲◎
	英文和訳					
	英問英答					
	その他	●▲	●▲	▲	▲	▲
英作文	整序	●	●	●	●	●
	和文英訳	●	●			
	自由英作	●▲	●▲	●▲	●▲	●▲
	その他					
学習指導要領		●▲	●▲	▲	●▲	●▲

第２部

秋田県の
教員採用試験
実施問題

2024年度　実施問題

【中高共通】

【１】リスニングテスト

Part A

(1) Write your answer on your answer sheet.

(2) Write your answer on your answer sheet.

(3) Write your answer on your answer sheet.

(4) Write your answer on your answer sheet.

(5) Write your answer on your answer sheet.

Part B

(1) (A) He wants to study math.
(B) He wants to help the woman.
(C) He wants to be a math teacher.
(D) He wants the woman to work with him.

(2) (A) Revising a menu.
(B) Taking public transportation.
(C) Asking a coworker to help.
(D) Requesting a refund.

(3) (A) Taking some vaccinations.
(B) Writing a travel guide.
(C) Retiring from office.
(D) Taking a trip overseas.

Part C

(1) Write your answer on your answer sheet.
I should (　　).

(2) Write your answer on your answer sheet.
Because he (　　).

Part D

(1) トマトが発する音を聞くために，研究者たちはどのようなことをしたか。

(2) 実験で，トマトに与えた二つのストレスは何か。

(☆☆☆◎◎◎)

【2】次の英文を読んで，(1)～(4)の設問に答えよ。

INDIAN RIVER LAGOON, Florida—It was (A)<u>an extraordinary experiment</u>: humans dumping leafy greens to feed manatees in the warm waters of the Indian River Lagoon, where decades of pollution have destroyed their delicate sea grass diet.

At first, the manatees stayed away from the lettuce. Eventually, a bold pair approached. With their prehensile lips—they are distantly related to elephants—they grabbed the lettuce and nibbled. More followed.

On the coldest days, hundreds came, and over the three-month feeding period, the hungry mammals ate all of the 92,000 kilograms of lettuce.

Manatees are gentle giants that have long captured the human imagination. But people have failed to care for their environment, putting their survival at risk. Now, as manatees are disappearing in large numbers, humans are trying desperate measures to keep them alive. It may not be enough.

The manatee remains in trouble, and with it, a piece of Florida's identity. For over a century, the state has had a (①) relationship with nature. Its lifestyle is synonymous with outdoor pursuits—but also with sprawling development that damaged the natural flow of Lake Okeechobee and the Everglades, threatened the drinking water supply and left the state gravely vulnerable to climate change.

Manatees had been (B)<u>something of a success story</u>, their status upgraded to threatened from endangered in 2017 after years of educating boaters to avoid deadly strikes. Starvation has again put them in peril.

Along Florida's Atlantic coast, the die-off began last year, after the Indian

River Lagoon, a 252-kilometer estuary that had been a seasonal refuge, turned into a barren underwater desert. Decades of waste from leaky septic tanks and fertilizer runoff from farms and development fueled algal blooms that choked the sea grass that manatees eat.

The feeding experiment, executed by federal and state wildlife officials and funded by $116,000 in public donations, was a gamble. Between January 1 and April 1, the number of confirmed deaths fell to 479, down from 612 in 2021. In 2020, that figure was 205. In all of last year, 1,100 Florida manatees died, a record. About 7,500 are thought to remain in the wild.

This year's dip in deaths does not necessarily mean that feeding has helped. Scientists will spend the summer reviewing environmental conditions, necropsy results and other data to make a more complete assessment, said Dr. Martine de Wit, a veterinarian with the Florida Fish and Wildlife Conservation Commission. "It likely had to do with a later start to winter," she said of the lower preliminary death toll. "And then we had a relatively short winter."

Floridians share a special (　②　) for manatees. "Save the Manatee" is one of the state's most popular specialty license plates. Homes display manatee mailboxes. Small towns like Orange City, home to Blue Spring State Park, hold manatee festivals that draw tourists to places that do not otherwise get many visitors. The most famous is perhaps Crystal River, on the gulf coast, where people can swim with manatees.

【出典　*The New York Times INTERNATIONAL WEEKLY*, May 29, 2022】

(1)　下線部(A)の内容を具体的に日本語で書け。

(2)　下線部(B)の根拠を具体的に日本語で書け。

(3)　(　①　)，(　②　)に入る最も適切な語を，次のア～エからそれぞれ一つずつ選び，その記号を書け。

①　ア　cooperative　　イ　conventional　　ウ　contradictory
　　エ　constructive

② ア bait　　イ hatred　　ウ affection
　エ permission

(4) インディアンリバーラグーンが海底砂漠となった要因について，次の(　　)それぞれに適する日本語を書け。

何十年にもわたる①(　　)によって藻が繁殖し，②(　　)ため。

(☆☆☆☆◎◎◎)

【中学校】

【1】次の会話文を読んで，(1)～(5)の設問に答えよ。

Joan : I am preparing the job ad for the opening in your department. I'm fairly confident that I know generally what you are looking for, but I would like to know about your (①) goals for someone in this role.

Hisato : I'd be happy to explain. I prefer to hire someone with at least five years' experience, rather than [I], as this particular position will be dealing with our highest-priority accounts. I worry that someone who is less skilled might have trouble dealing with [II], which would leave everyone frustrated and unhappy. Without a doubt, I'd also like to find someone with firm (②) of mergers and acquisitions as well as international regulations, who is tech savvy, and so on.

Joan : Would you consider hiring an outside candidate, or do you prefer an internal hire?

Hisato : (A)<u>Either an internal or outside candidate would be fine with me</u>. A much greater (③) of mine is that he or she can begin work without much need for training. Given the fact that our department is so busy, it's imperative to find someone who is confident and up to date in their skills.

Joan : It sounds like (B)<u>yon know just what sort of person you want to hire</u>. I'll get the ad placed right away and be sure to send you

| Ⅲ | as soon as they begin arriving.

Hisato : Thanks for your help with this!

【出典　内藤　由美子，『最強の英語力』，新星出版社】

(1)　(　①　)～(　③　)に入る最も適切な語を，次のア～クから一つずつ選び，その記号を書け。

ア　reiteration　　イ　knowledge　　ウ　substance

エ　hazardous　　オ　concern　　カ　obscure

キ　specific　　ク　meditative

(2)　| Ⅰ |～| Ⅲ |に入る最も適切なものを，次のア～ウから一つずつ選び，その記号を書け。

ア　the complex tasks of the job　　イ　all the resumes

ウ　a new graduate

(3)　次の説明に該当する1語を，本文中から抜き出して書け。

to make something clear or easy to understand by describing or giving imformation about it

(4)　下線部(A)の英語を日本語に直せ。

(5)　下線部(B)について，Hisatoが求めている人材の必須条件を日本語で書け。

(☆☆☆☆◎◎◎)

【２】次の英文を読んで，(1)～(4)の設問に答えよ。

Some approaches to language teaching, which we will call (A)form-based approaches, are based on the belief that we need to take great care, at each stage or learning, that learners produce the language accurately. Usually this involves a focus on form at the very beginning of a teaching sequence. By a focus on form we mean that teachers isolate one or two specific forms, specific grammatical structures or functional realizations, and identify these as the target forms.【ア】Learners know that by the end of the teaching sequence, often contained in a single lesson, they will be expected to produce these forms with an acceptable level of accuracy.

A well known form-focused approach is often known as PPP (Presentation → Practice → Production). This begins by highlighting one or two new forms and illustrating their meaning. It then goes on to practise that form under careful teacher control. This control is gradually relaxed until finally learners are offered the opportunity to produce the target form(s) in a communicative activity. 【イ】 This approach has four main characteristics:

1 A focus on one or two forms, specified by the teacher, which are later to be incorporated in the performance of a communicative activity.

2 This focus on form comes *before* learners engage in communicative activity.

3 Teacher control of learner language. This is imposed strictly in the early stages of the cycle and gradually relaxed.

4 The success of the procedure is judged in terms of whether or not learners do produce the target forms with an acceptable level of accuracy.

Other approaches, which we will call (B)meaning-based approaches, are based on the belief that it is more effective to encourage learners to use the language as much as possible, even if this means that some of the language they produce is inaccurate. Teachers provide learners with opportunities in the classroom to use the language for genuine communication. This involves a focus on *meaning*. Inevitably, in the course of a meaning-focused activity, learners will sometimes naturally focus on language for themselves. 【ウ】 When this happens learners are not simply thinking about forms specified by the teacher and how best to incorporate these forms in their output. They are thinking about language in general and searching their own language repertoire to decide how best to express themselves in a given communicative situation. We will call this (C)a focus on *language*.

【出典　Dave Willis and Jane Willis, *Doing Task-based Teaching*, OXFORD UNIVERSITY PRESS】

(1)　下線部(A)はどのような考え方に基づくか，日本語で書け。

(2)　下線部(B)について，その特徴として正しいものを次のア～オから二つ選び，その記号を書け。

ア　Teachers do not attempt to highlight accuracy at the very beginning of a communicative activity.

イ　Teachers urge learners to pay attention to certain words or phrases for study.

ウ　Learners pause to think how best to utilize the form exemplified by the teacher.

エ　Learners are supposed to understand new sentences before they participate in a communicative activity.

オ　Teachers will help learners to shape and clarify what they want to say.

(3)　次の英文が入る最も適切な箇所を本文中の【ア】～【ウ】から一つ選び，その記号を書け。

They will, for example, stop for a moment to think 'How do I best express this next idea?', 'What's the word for X?', or 'Should I be using the past tense here?'

(4)　下線部(C)が示す内容を，具体的に日本語で書け。

(☆☆☆☆◎◎◎)

【３】次の(1)～(4)について，それぞれの英文の[　　]内に入る最も適切なものを，ア～エから一つずつ選び，その記号を書け。

(1)　He worked so hard in the afternoon, trying to [　　] up his job for a meeting.

ア　build　　イ　bounce　　ウ　stand　　エ　wrap

(2)　If you find [　　] making more mistakes than usual, you should have a break.

ア　it　　イ　yourself　　ウ　your　　エ　itself

(3)　After the school was rebuilt, students were surprised that there was absolutely [　　] left of the original structure.

ア　both　　イ　nothing　　ウ　anything　　エ　another

(4)　Passengers are asked to [　　] updates, which will be announced over the public address system.

ア　come down with　　イ　get on toward　　ウ　stand by for

エ　cut down on

(☆☆☆◎◎◎)

【4】次の(1)～(3)について，それぞれの日本語の内容を表すように，[　　]内の語句を並べかえよ。なお，(4)については，日本語の意味になるように英語で書け。

(1)　自分の予定の遅れを取り戻すために私は頑張らなければならない。

I must [up / my / hard / catch / to / work / on] schedule.

(2)　WHOは1日にティースプーン6杯の砂糖が大人にとって妥当な量であるとしている。

WHO suggests that [an appropriate / sugar / is / six teaspoons / of / amount / for] adults each day.

(3)　私は，他国の文化を学ぶための授業をもっと導入するという考えに賛成です。

I agree with the idea [for learning / cultures / introducing / more lessons / about / of / in] other countries.

(4)　シートへの記入が終わったら，私に提出してください。

(☆☆☆☆◎◎◎)

【5】帰国したALTに，3月に卒業する生徒にメッセージを送ってもらうことにした。次の〈依頼したい内容〉を踏まえ，ALTへのメール文を50語程度の英語で書け。挨拶の英文は省略するものとする。※語数を数えて記入すること。(符号は語数に含めない)

〈依頼したい内容〉

・生徒を激励するメッセージを送ってほしい。

・2月末日までに送ってほしい。

・英語の授業で印象に残っているエピソードがあれば，その内容も書いてほしい。

(☆☆☆☆☆◎◎◎)

【6】「話すこと[やり取り]」のパフォーマンステストを行う上での留意点を二つ挙げ，70語程度の英語で書け。※語数を数えて記入すること。(符号は語数に含めない)

(☆☆☆☆☆◎◎◎)

【高等学校】

【1】次の英文を読んで，(1)～(5)の設問に答えよ。

PULLING FORD'S NEW ALL-ELECTRIC MUSTANG Mach-E out of a Brooklyn garage late this winter, I felt a little $_{(A)}$duped. It seemed more like I was driving a giant motorized iPad than the electrified successor to an iconic American muscle car. Just a few weeks earlier, the company's sound designers told me about the lengths to which they had gone to design and digitally produce the perfect engine noise, experimenting with recordings of electric guitars, Formula E race-car engine sounds and the hum of high-voltage power lines. But inside the loaner car's cabin, I didn't hear anything at all. Then, while messing around on the vehicle's touchscreen, I found — and immediately pressed — an all-too-tempting button to engage "unbridled mode." Next time I hit the accelerator, the car took off, emitting the throaty, electric roar of a cyberpunk spaceship. Now that was more like it.

Because their motors have few moving parts, $_{(B)}$electric vehicles (EVs) are shockingly quiet. That might sound like a blessing for city dwellers and others sick of traffic noise, but it can create added risk for drivers (who rely on engine noise to get a sense of their speed) and pedestrians (who listen for oncoming traffic). For automakers, it also compromises decades of marketing based on the alluring rumble of a revving engine, especially in sports cars and trucks. "As a car person, there are a lot of expectations for what a car should sound like," says Ram Chandrasekaran, a transportation analyst at consultancy Wood Mackenzie. "[Even] for a regular person who doesn't care about V-8 engines or manual transmissions, there's still an innate expectation that when you push the pedal, you hear an auditory response."

So companies like Ford have turned to (C)elite teams of sound designers to create new noises that play from EV's internal and external speakers, making them safer and more marketable. With EVs on the cusp of widespread adoption — analysts predict their share of U.S. auto sales will quadruple to 8.5% in the next four years — these specialists are getting a once-in-a-lifetime chance to create the sounds that will dominate 21st century highways and cities, just as the constant drone of internal-combustion engines dominated those of the 20th.

The sound designers who spoke to TIME for this story, from companies like BMW, Audi and Ford, often framed their work as an effort to encode their brands' (D)ethos into a sound. There's precedent for that kind of auditory corporate soul-searching, from ESPN's six-note fanfare to the Yahoo yodel. But (E)there's greater urgency to the automakers' work: the longer it takes for people to switch to electric vehicles, the more damage internal-combustion engines will do to our planet. While (F)EVs aren't completely green — battery production and electricity generation exact an environmental toll — the scientific consensus is that they're less harmful than gasoline cars. Ninety percent of cars on U.S. roads must be electric by 2050 to meet the Paris Agreement's goals, but right now, only about 2 in every 100 cars sold in the country are nonhybrid EVs. And in order to sell, EVs have to drive well and far enough to meet people's needs — as well as sound good to prospective buyers.

【出典　*TIME*, April 12/April 19, 2021】

(1) 下線部(A)と下線部(D)のそれぞれに関して，ほぼ同じ意味を表す語を，ア～エから一つ選び，その記号を書け。

(A)　ア　thrilled　　イ　deceived　　ウ　frightened

　　エ　delighted
(D)　ア　fame　　　イ　credit　　　ウ　consideration
　　エ　spirit

(2)　下線部(B)であることで，人にどのようなデメリットがあると本文で述べられているか，2点日本語で書け。

(3)　下線部(C)について，自動車メーカーが彼らを起用する理由を，日本語で書け。

(4)　下線部(E)の理由を，日本語で書け。

(5)　下線部(F)の理由として本文に述べられていることを，日本語で書け。

(☆☆☆☆◎◎◎)

【２】次の英文を読んで，(1)～(3)の設問に答えよ。

Flipped learning is mainly designated to grant more autonomy to learners in the learning process and offer an opportunity for the teachers to use class time more efficiently. It also changes the instructional model from a knowledge transmission format to a co-construction of knowledge format. When educators lecture, in many cases, learners expect them to transmit knowledge without the learner needing to do more than grasp a surface-level understanding of the material, remember the material, and restate the material on an assessment. In this model, learning is not necessarily deep, meaningful, or lasting. To allow the material to be learned in a more profound and lasting way, educators can engage learners' brains in the co-construction of knowledge. While learners initially take in different perspectives through readings, videos, podcasts, lectures, etc. prior to the class meeting, when the class convenes educators design learning experiences to prompt learners to enhance their knowledge collaboratively (i.e., co-construct their knowledge) through interaction. This learning perspective is called *social constructivism* or simply *constructivism* (Fosnot, 2005, 2013; Fosnot & Perry, 1996). The links between technology, education, and constructivism have been investigated extensively by Jason Ravitz (https://evalutionbydesign.com).

In moving from teachers (A) to (B) and causing learners to think critically and participate actively in their own learning changes, many facets of the teaching and learning process are transformed. The workload is shared in time and space. Prior to face-to-face meetings, teachers produce and share digitalized content. Learners work toward understandings and thinking about the material. All of these activities are performed in space outside of the classroom.

Benefits of the flipped design

The "flipped" classroom as a pedagogical design increases the time spent on (C), which are key factors in the quality and amount of learning. It also strengthens learners' sense of responsibility and boosts a sense of confidence, such that they attend the lesson with a great deal of knowledge needed to participate in discussions and generate critical ideas during the courses. In this way, class time is no longer used to introduce new knowledge, but discuss how new knowledge can be built, interpreted, and used.

Despite the pedagogical benefits of a "flipped" classroom, there are some practical challenges for both teachers and learners. Flipping classes in this manner requires a different type of preparation for teachers; sometimes this preparation is more time-consuming. Teachers, for example, need to work harder before the course to prepare the whole course and all the materials. They need to prepare the digital course content by scripting and video recording themselves in order to make them available online. The workload increases for both teachers and learners, which necessitate the course credits to be increased for courses delivered in this mode.

【出典　Kate Mastruserio Reynolds, Kenan Dikilitas, Steve Close, *INTRODUCTION TO TESOL BECOMING A LANGUAGE TEACHING PROFESSIONAL*, WILEY Blackwell】

(1)　第1段落では，flipped learningを導入する前後で学習者の姿はどう変わると述べているか。日本語で次の表を埋めよ。

	導入前	導入後
授業前		②
授業中	①	③

(2)　空所(　A　)～(　C　)には次のア～ウのいずれかが入る。その組み合わせとして正しいものを①～⑥から一つ選び，その番号を書け。

ア　guiding the learning process

イ　learning content and engaging in tasks

ウ　having the exclusive role of generator of information

(選択肢)

番号	A	B	C
①	ア	イ	ウ
②	ア	ウ	イ
③	イ	ア	ウ
④	イ	ウ	ア
⑤	ウ	ア	イ
⑥	ウ	イ	ア

(3)　授業者の視点から，本文で挙げられているflipped learningの短所を日本語で書け。

(☆☆☆☆☆◎◎◎)

【３】次の(1)，(2)について，日本語で答えよ。

(1)「高等学校学習指導要領(平成30年3月告示)」において，「話すこと[やり取り]」の指導に関して，「日常的な話題について，使用する語句や文，対話の展開などにおいて，多くの支援を活用すれば，基本的な語句や文を用いて，情報や考え，気持ちなどを話して伝え合うやり取りを続けることができるようにする。」とある。これを踏まえ，生徒の英語でのやり取りを促す具体的な手立ての例を三つ答えよ。

(2)　英語の授業で，教科書のある単元のまとめとして，その内容に基づいたテーマについて，自分の考えなどを英語で書く活動をすることにした。その際，何を書いて良いかわからない生徒に対して，ど

<u>のような支援をするか，具体的な手立ての例を三つ</u>答えよ。

(☆☆☆☆☆◎◎◎)

【4】次の(1)～(5)の(　　)に当てはまる最も適切なものを，それぞれア～エから一つ選び，その記号を書け。

(1) The accused have a fundamental right to be (　　) in a court of law.

ア indicted　イ prosecuted　ウ defended　エ voted

(2) The (　　) of the scientific study revealed groundbreaking findings that could revolutionize the field.

ア contagion　イ conglomerate　ウ conclusion

エ concession

(3) I was eager to start the game, but my coach said, "(　　). You should wait for further instructions."

ア Bite the bullet　イ Break a leg　ウ Hold your horses

エ Cost an arm and a leg

(4) The detective (　　) the mystery by meticulously analyzing the evidence and interrogating the suspects.

ア clenched　イ deduced　ウ thwarted　エ apprehended

(5) The sunset painted the sky with its (　　) colors, casting a warm and enchanting glow over the landscape.

ア vibrant　イ dull　ウ ordinary　エ somber

(☆☆☆☆☆◎◎◎)

【5】a) 次の(1)～(3)の各英文には，それぞれ文法的な誤りが1か所ある。その部分の記号を書き，正しい英語に直せ。

(1) $_A$<u>Besides his achievements</u>, he has a strong passion for the arts. Not only $_B$<u>he excels</u> in academics, but he is also skilled in playing multiple $_C$<u>musical instruments</u>. He has a well-rounded talent $_D$<u>that extends</u> beyond the classroom.

(2) The teacher gave the students a clear explanation, $_A$<u>provided them</u> with

helpful examples, and $_{\text{B}}$assigned to complete the homework $_{\text{C}}$by the end of the week. The students $_{\text{D}}$felt confident and prepared to tackle the assignment with the guidance they received from their teacher.

(3)　Since our $_{\text{A}}$earliest days, our parents have been a source of $_{\text{B}}$unconditional love and support. Their guidance and sacrifices $_{\text{C}}$shape our lives, and it's difficult to express how we are $_{\text{D}}$grate to them for their dedication.

b)　次の(1), (2)は，以下のタイトルで生徒が書いた英文であるが，それぞれ文法的な誤りが1か所ある。その部分に下線を引いて指摘し，下線の下に正しい英語を書け。ただし，タイトルは訂正しないこと。

(1)　Title:　My favorite subject

My favorite subject is math. I like solving problems. Math helps my learning how to count, add, subtract, multiply, and divide. I enjoy figuring out patterns and playing with shapes. It's fun to solve math puzzles and see how things fit together.

(2)　Title:　Abolishing school uniforms

Abolishing school uniforms is a good idea because students can show their own style with their clothes. I would appreciate if the school principal could consider abolishing school uniforms. It would be more enjoyable if everyone had the freedom to look different from one another.

(☆☆☆☆◎◎◎)

【6】次の質問に，80語程度の英語で答えよ。

Suppose you are a high school teacher. What advice would you give to a student from overseas who is having difficulty fitting into his/her class?

(☆☆☆☆☆◎◎◎)

解答・解説

【中高共通】

【1】Part A (1) B (2) C (3) B (4) A (5) A
Part B (1) B (2) C (3) D Part C (1) (I should) approach Gate 10 within the next 30 minutes. (2) (Because he) wanted Mary to come in for an interview. Part D (1) 解答略 (2) ・水を与えないこと ・茎を切ること

〈解説〉スクリプトは非公開である。問題用紙には放送回数や指示等が記載されていないので，開始前の指示を聞き逃さないようにしたい。
Part A 問題用紙には質問文や選択肢などが印字されていない。英文，質問文，選択肢すべて音声のみで解答しなければならないので，集中して臨みたい。TOEIC® ListeningのPart 2のような応答問題形式も想定できるので，リスニングが苦手な人は練習しておくとよいだろう。
Part B 選択肢は問題用紙に印字されているので，放送前に目を通し，どんなことを問われるのか予想しながら聞くこと。 Part C Part Aと同様に，問題用紙に文字情報はない。公開解答からの推測であるが，対話などを聞いて，～は何をすべきか，なぜ～したのか等，5W2H(why, when, where, who, what, how, how much/how many)の情報を聞き取るスキルが必要であろう。 Part D 英文(おそらくshort talkやlectureの類と思われる)を聞き，問題用紙に印字されている日本語の質問文に答える記述問題。先に質問文に目を通し，解答に該当する箇所を探すように聞く。

【2】(1) (解答例) フロリダ州インディアン・リバー・ラグーンでは，マナティーが海草を餌としているが，数十年にわたる汚染によって，環境の影響を受けやすい海草が枯死してしまったため，人間がマナティーの餌として葉物野菜を投与すること。 (2) (解答例) マナティーとの衝突を防ぐように，何年ものあいだ船舶操縦者を教育してきた

結果，2017年にはマナティーの絶滅危惧種としての深刻度が軽減したこと。　(3)　①　ウ　②　ウ　(4)　①　(解答例)　廃棄物や肥料　②　(解答例)　海草が枯れた

〈解説〉(1)　下線部(A)に後続する箇所をまとめる。　(2)　下線部(B)に後続する箇所からまとめる。　(3)　①　フロリダ州では乱開発により湖の水域が劣化し，飲料水の供給が滞り，深刻な気候変動の影響を受けることになったことが述べられているので，空欄①には否定的な意のcontradictoryを入れ，「自然とは『相反する』関係」とするのが適切。②　“Save the Manatee”「マナティーを救え」というスローガンの下，マナティー像の郵便ボックスを製品化したり，マナティーフェスティバルを開催して多くの観光客を誘致したり，マナティーと泳げる海岸を設備したりするなど，マナティー保護に向けて積極的に活動を行っている点から，空欄②には肯定的な意のaffectionを入れ，「マナティーに対する『愛情』」とするのが適切。　(4)　海底砂漠については第7段落で言及している。解答には同段落2文目「数十年にわたって浄化槽から漏れた廃棄物や，農場や造成地から流出した肥料が藻の繁殖を促進し，藻がマナティーが食べる海草を枯らしてしまった」から適語を入れていく。

【中学校】

【1】(1)　①　キ　②　イ　③　オ　(2)　Ⅰ　ウ　Ⅱ　ア　Ⅲ　イ　(3)　explain　(4)　(解答例)　応募者は社内でも社外でも構わない。　(5)　(解答例)　最低5年の職務経験を有し，国際法規とM&Aの知識も豊富で，自分の財務スキルに自信があり最新のスキルを身に付けている即戦力となる人材。

〈解説〉会話文読解問題では登場人物，接続詞と話題の転換，隠れた疑問文と欲求，希望，提案の表現に注意しながら読み進めよう。

(1)　①　形容詞が入ることを念頭に置くと，候補はエ，カ，キ，ク。求人広告に向けて職務内容に求められている具体的な人物像について質問しているのでキを選ぶ。　②　空欄が形容詞と前置詞に挟まれて

いることから名詞が入るので，候補はア，イ，ウ，オ。採用したい人物像としてM&Aに関する豊富な知識を持った人物と言いたいのでイを選ぶ。　③　空欄が形容詞と前置詞に挟まれていることから名詞が入るので，候補はア，ウ，オ。「採用候補が社外か社内かということよりも大切なこと」と述べているのでオを選ぶ。　(2)　I　採用人物として職務経験が最低5年ある方が好ましいと言っているので，その対比として新卒者ではふさわしくないと考える。　II　職務内容に関する経験があまりないと問題が発生した際に対処するのに困ることになるのでアを選ぶ。　III　空欄の後に複数名詞を指す代名詞theyがあるので空欄には複数形の名詞が入ることを考えつつ，求人応募者からのレジュメが届いたらHisatoにすぐに送ると言っているのでイを選ぶ。(3)　説明文の文意は「何かを説明したり情報を与えたりすることで，何かを明確にしたり理解しやすくしたりすること」。Hisatoの第1発話冒頭にあるexplainという語が適切。　(4)　either A or B「AかBかどちらでも」，with「～に関して，～としては」。対象・関連を表す。

(5)　Hisatoの言葉から採用したい人物の条件として，第1発話2文目，4文目，第2発話2文目，3文目の4つの特徴が述べられている。ただし，質問文に必須条件とあるので，imperativeという語から第2発話3文目に焦点を当ててまとめる。

【2】(1)　(解答例)　学習者が正確に言語を発話・生成するように，学習段階ごとに細心の注意をはらう必要があるという考え。　(2)　ア，オ　(3)　ウ　　(4)　(解答例)　学習者が，与えられたコミュニケーションの状況に応じて自分の言いたいことを表現する最適な表現方法を決めていくために，言語全般について考え，自分の言語能力範囲から検索すること。

〈解説〉Focus on Form (FonF)の概念に関する英文。Task-based Language Teaching の教授法と合わせて，Focus on Forms (FonFs)とFocus on Meaning (FonM)の概念について調べておくとよい。　(1)　後続するthe beliefの内容をまとめる。　(2)　形式重視のアプローチとの相違点を確認しながら，意味重視のアプローチの特徴を選ぶ。　ア「教師は，コミュニケーション活動の最初の段階で正確さを強調しようとはしない」。不正確でもできるだけ言語を学習者に使わせることが効果的とあるので正しい。　イ「教師は学習者に対し，特定の単語やフレーズに注目して勉強するよう促す」。教師から与えられた語彙や語句の意味を学習してから使用するのは，リアルなコミュニケーションの状況下で言語を使わせていく意味重視のアプローチではない。　ウ「学習者は，教師から例示された形をどのように活用するのがベストなのかを考えるために間を置く」。意味重視のアプローチでは，言語全般から自分の使える言語範囲内で自分の伝えたいことをどのように表現したらベストかを考える。教師から示された表現を正しく使おうと考えるのは形式重視のアプローチなので，ウは正しくない。　エ「学習者はコミュニケーション活動に入る前に，新しい文章を理解することになっている」。コミュニケーション活動に入る前に文章を考えるのは形式重視のアプローチである。　オ「教師は，学習者が言いたいことを形にして明確にする手助けをする」。学習者に自分の言いたいことを中心に言語活動させるのを促すのは，意味重視のアプローチである。　(3)　挿入する英文の文意は「例えば，『次のアイデアをどう表現するのがベストか』，『Xを表す単語は何か』，『ここでは過去形を使うべきか』など，少し間をおいて考える」。ここで述べられている具体例は，学習者は言語全般に意識を向けて自分の言いたいことを自力で表現方法を探している内容なので，意味重視のアプローチの範疇である。よって，意味重視のアプローチについて述べている段落中の【ウ】に挿入するのが適切。　(4)　下線部(C)の直前の英文をまとめる。

【3】(1)　エ　　(2)　イ　　(3)　イ　　(4)　ウ

〈解説〉(1)　build up「築き上げる，鍛え上げる，宣伝する」，bounce up「跳ね上がる」，stand up「立たせる，すっぽかす」，wrap up「うまく成立させる，仕上げる，包み隠す」。「彼は午後，会議のために仕事を終わらせようと懸命に働いた」。　(2)　find oneself～ing「自分が～していることに気づく」。「いつもよりミスが多いと感じたら，休みを取るべきだ」。 (3) There is/are＋S＋～ing/p.p. 構文「Sが～している/～されている」，nothing of～「～の何も…ない」。「学校が再建された後，生徒たちは元の建物の面影がまったく残っていないことに驚いた」。 (4) come down with「(病気)で倒れる，～にかかる」，get on toward「～に向かって進む」，stand by for「～に備えて待機する」，cut down on「～を削減する」。「乗客は，機内放送でアナウンスされる最新情報を待つよう言われている」。

【4】(1) work hard to catch up on my (2) six teaspoons of sugar is an appropriate amount for (3) of introducing more lessons for learning about cultures in (4) When you finish filling out the sheet, please submit it to me.

〈解説〉(1) catch up on「～に遅れずについていく，(遅れなど)を取り戻す」。 (2) 時間・距離・金額・重量などを表す語の複数形を単数扱いとする場合があることに注意し，"six teaspoons of sugar" を単数扱いの主語としてよい。 (3) introduce＋O＋in～「Oを～に導入する」。 (4) finish～ing「～するのを終わらせる」，fill out (or fill in)「～に記入する」，submit＋O＋to「～にOを提出する」。 please submit it to meは，please give it to meとしてもよい。

【5】(解答例) I have a favor to ask: could you please send a congratulatory message to your graduating students by the end of February? It would be wonderful if you could include a memorable teaching moment. Your impactful words will undoubtedly inspire them to embrace international perspectives and excel in future global endeavors. (51 words)

〈解説〉相手に依頼したい場合には，Could you please～?，I kindly request you～，Would it possible for you to～，I would be most grateful if you could～なども使える。「～までに」は，by～，no later than～。「印象に残っている」は，「忘れることができない大切な」と言い換えて，your cherished teaching memory, an forgettable teaching episode などもよいだろう。必要な要件を手短にまとめつつ，相手に喜んで協力してもらえるように，依頼内容が生徒たちにとって有意義であるという雰囲気を伝えるとよい。

【6】(解答例)　When conducting a performance test, it's crucial for teachers to focus on students' comprehension of the testing process. For example, when we assess students using "be going to", students must understand that the ALT will pose questions, requiring them to respond smoothly using "be going to." Teachers should guide students in contemplating their summer plans, practicing how to express their own plans in pairs beforehand. Post-test, teachers should provide individual feedback, highlighting strengths and areas for improvement, fostering the development of their speaking skills. (84 words)

〈解説〉中学校学習指導要領において，「話すこと[やり取り]」の目標は「ア　関心のある事柄について，簡単な語句や文を用いて即興で伝え合うことができるようにする。　イ　日常的な話題について，事実や自分の考え，気持ちなどを整理し，簡単な語句や文を用いて伝えたり，相手からの質問に答えたりすることができるようにする。　ウ　社会的な話題に関して聞いたり読んだりしたことについて，考えたことや感じたこと，その理由などを，簡単な語句や文を用いて述べ合うことができるようにする」と示されている。これらを踏まえた上で，自分ならどのような教授法を取り入れて授業を作っていくか，その際にどのようなパフォーマンステストを実施するかというような問題意識を持っておくことが必要である。

【高等学校】

【1】(1)　(A)　イ　　(D)　エ　　(2)　(解答例)　・車を運転する人にとって，エンジン音による速度の感覚が分からない。　・歩行者にとって，近づいてくる車の存在が分からない。　(3)　(解答例)　EVの内

部および外部スピーカーから流れる新しい音を作り，EVの安全性と市場性を高めるため。　(4)　(解答例)　人々が電気自動車に乗り換えるのが遅れれば遅れるほど，内燃機関が地球に与えるダメージは大きくなるから。　(5)　(解答例)　バッテリーの生産と発電は，環境に大きな負荷を強いるから。

〈解説〉電気自動車とエンジン音に関するエッセイである。自動車好きには理解しやすいが，車に関心がないと理解しにくいかもしれない。(1)　(A)　dupeの意は「騙す」。　(D)　ethosの意は「精神」。　(2)　第2段落2文目のbut以降から運転者と歩行者に対する危険性をまとめる。質問文に「人に」とあるので，3文目の自動車会社にとってのデメリットは解答にあたらない。　(3)　下線部(C)に後続する箇所からまとめる。(4)　下線部(E)に後続する英文をまとめる。The比較級…，the比較級～の構文とdo damage to「～にダメージを与える，被害を及ぼす」のイディオムに注意。「内燃機関」はガソリン車に使われるエンジンのこと。　(5)　下線部(F)に後続する英文をまとめる。exactが述語動詞であることとtollの意味に注意。exact「～を強要する」，environmental toll「環境への悪影響」。

【2】(1)　①　(解答例)　授業者に知識の伝達しか期待せず，教材を表面的にのみ理解し，教材を暗記し，テストではそれを再生する。
②　(解答例)　書物，動画，ポッドキャスト，講義などから様々な視点を持った考えを取り込んでいく。　③　(解答例)　学生同士のやり取りを通じて，協働的に知見を高めていく。　(2)　⑤
(3)　(解答例)　・授業前の準備に今までよりも時間と労力がかかる。・授業全体と教材のすべてを事前に準備する必要がある。　・オンラインで使えるように授業者自らスクリプト作成や動画作成を行い，デジタルコンテンツを準備する必要がある。

〈解説〉反転学習をテーマにした英文である。knowledge transmissionとco-construction of knowledgeの概念について理解しよう。　(1)　①　第1段落3文目から反転学習導入前の特徴として，transmit～，grasp～， remember～，restate～の箇所をまとめる。　② 第1段落6文目から，導入した際に授業実施前の特徴として，take in～の箇所をまとめる。③ 第1段落6文目から，導入した際に授業実施後の特徴として，enhance～の箇所をまとめる。　(2) 反転学習を導入すると，授業で学習し自宅で復習するパターンが変わり，自宅で予習し授業で深めるパターンとなる。それに応じて，授業者の指導も，空欄(A)から空欄(B)に移り変わっていくと説明しているが，それは，知識伝達から知識の協働構築に重点を移していくことに他ならない。ウ「情報発信者としてだけの役割」は知識伝達を意味しているので空欄Aにはウが適切，反転学習を成功させるためには学習者に学習の流れを身につけさせる必要があるので空欄Bにはアが適切。空欄Cについて，反転学習を実施すると学習者による予習を前提とした授業作りになるので，授業時間中は予習済みの知識をさらに深め，発展的な課題に取り組ませることになるため，イが入る。　(3) 第4段落冒頭にchallengesとあるので，反転学習導入時における問題点が述べられていることが分かる。2文目の文末にmore time-consumingとあり，ここから後続する3文目，4文目をまとめていく。設問文に「授業者の視点から」とあるので，学習者の問題点には触れる必要はない。

【3】(解答例)　(1)　・生徒が心に思い描いたイメージを，自分の知っている表現を使い即興で言語化しやすくするために，アニメ，イラスト，写真などの視覚的素材を提示する。提示された素材の描写について一人が質問し相手が答えるという流れを作り出す。　・Yes, Noや短いフレーズだけで答えられてしまう質問は避けつつ，短い文で答えやすい質問を投げかけていく。　・対話と発話を繰り返していくには発話する人と聞く人の相互の協力が必要であることを理解させ，相手から考えを引き出すことに意識を持たせる。簡単な短いフレーズによる，そのための表現方法を学習させる。　(2)　・自分の考えを持たせるために，インターネット検索，書籍，資料からそのテーマについての知識や情報を深めさせ，自分の身近な事象で関連している点がないか

を考えてまとめる作業をさせる。　・自分の考えをまとめるにあたり，どうしてそのように考えたのか，何が原因なのか，どうすれば解決できるのかなど論理的に整理する視点を与えて，その視点に沿って自分の考えを理由とともに形成させる。教師側で，必要に応じて論理的に形成した考えをアウトライン化するテンプレートを作成しておく。　・自分の考えを表すのに必要な語彙や文を教材や翻訳アプリなどを利用して検索，作成させ，段落構成と自然な論理的展開について教師に確認してもらい，もっと分かりやすい英語で書き直させる。

〈解説〉(1)，(2)ともに高等学校学習指導要領解説外国語編・英語編に記載されている内容に着眼点が示されているので参考にするとよい。特に，「第2章　外国語科の各科目　第2節　英語コミュニケーションI(～第7節　論理・表現III)　2　内容　(3)　言語活動及び言語の働きに関する事項」に五つの領域ごとに言語活動のヒントが示されている。これらを基本に，五つの領域での言語活動内容を組み合わせたり自分の考えを加えたりしながら，具体的な方策をまとめてみよう。

【4】(1)　ウ　(2)　ウ　(3)　ウ　(4)　イ　(5)　ア

〈解説〉(1)　indict「告訴・告発する」，prosecute「起訴する」，defend「守る」，vote「投票する」。「被告人には法廷で弁護される基本的権利がある」。　(2)　contagion「伝染(病)，接触感染」，conglomerate「集塊，複合企業」，conclusion「結論，終局」，concession「譲歩，許可，利権」。「その科学的研究の結論は，この分野に革命をもたらすかもしれない画期的な発見を明らかにした」。　(3)　bite the bullet「歯を食いしばって頑張る，耐える」，break a leg「演技や舞台がうまくいくことを祈る，成功を祈る」，hold one's horses「はやる気持ちを抑える，あせらない」，cost an arm and a leg「大きな代償を払う，(出費など)高くつく」。「私は試合を始めたかったが，コーチは『慌てるな。次の指示を待て』と言った」。　(4)　clench「握りしめる，しっかりつかむ，食いしばる」，deduce「推測する」，thwart「妨害する」，apprehend「捕らえる，逮捕する，把握する，理解する」。「探偵は証拠を丹念に分析し，容疑者に尋問することでその謎を推理した」。　(5)　vibrant「震える，鮮やかな」，dull「鈍い，ぼんやりした，光沢のない」，ordinary「普通の，平凡な」，somber「薄暗い，くすんだ，陰鬱な」。「夕日が鮮やかな色彩で空を染め，風景に暖かく魅惑的な輝きを投げかけている」。

【5】a)　(1)　記号…B　　正しい英語…does he excel　　(2)　記号…B　　正しい英語…assigned them to　　(3)　記号…D　　正しい英語…grateful　　b)　(1)　下線を引く部分…my learning　　正しい英語…me learn　　(2)　下線を引く部分…appreciate if　　正しい英語…appreciate it if

〈解説〉a)　(1)　否定語が文頭に来ると倒置構文となり，疑問文の語順になることに注意。「優秀な成績だけでなく，彼は芸術にも強い情熱を持っている。学業だけでなく，複数の楽器の演奏にも長けている。教室の枠を超えたオールラウンドな才能の持ち主なのだ」。　(2)　assignは他動詞なので目的語が必要。assign＋O＋to do「Oに～するよう任命する，命じる」。「教師は生徒に明確な説明をし，参考になる例を示し，週末までに宿題を終わらせるように指示した。生徒たちは，教師からの指導内容をもとに自信を持って進んで課題に取り組んだ」。

(3)　be動詞の後のgrate「鉄格子」では意味が通らない。be grateful to(人) for「～に対し(人)に感謝の念を持つ」のイディオム表現に正す。「私たちが幼い頃から，両親は無条件の愛と支えの源だった。両親の指導と犠牲が私たちの人生を形作っており，その献身にどれだけ感謝しているかを表現するのは難しい」。　b)　(1)　helpの語法として，help＋O＋(to) do「Oが～するのに役立つ」の語順にする。「好きな科目は数学。問題を解くのが好きなんだ。数学は，数え方，足し算，引き算，掛け算，割り算を学ぶのに役立つ。パターンを考えたり，図形で遊んだりするのも楽しい。数学のパズルを解いて，物事がどのように組み合わされるかを見るのは楽しい」。　(2)　appreciate は他動詞なので目的語が必要。ここでは後続するif節を指す形式目的語のitが必要。簡単な例文として，I would appreciate it if you could help me.などで覚えておこう。「制服を廃止するのはいい考えだと思う。なぜなら，生徒たちは自分の服装で自分流を示すことができるからだ。校長先生には制服の廃止を検討していただけるとありがたい。みんながそれぞれお互いに違ったように見せる自由があれば，もっと楽しくなれると思う」。

【6】(解答例)　When I come across international students struggling with school challenges that affect their class involvement, it's crucial for me to understand their physical or mental well-being. If their problems are health-related and teamwork is needed, I'll collaborate with other teachers, doctors, and parents of the students. Yet, if their difficulties come from worries or stress they can't handle alone, I'll talk to them, figure out the reasons, and encourage self-reflection. This helps them identify issues and find solutions. Guiding students to see problems differently empowers them to overcome obstacles independently. (90 words)

〈解説〉質問に対する自分の考えをまとめられることと，それを正しい英語で表現することが問われている。書く内容については，非常勤講師，家庭教師，個人指導などで高校生に教えた経験がないとイメージするのが難しいかもしれない。自分が高校生だった頃に自分の周囲にクラスになじめない人がいなかったか思い返してみると，自分の考えをまとめるきっかけになる場合がある。普段から教育に関するニュースや記事などに接しておくことで教育に関する問題意識を持っておくことも必要であろう。自由英作文なので，自分の考えを英語にしやすいように整理して，文法上ミスがないように注意する。語数が少ないので，冗長になったり同じ単語を繰り返し使ったりすることは避け，簡潔にまとめることを意識する。そのためには，日頃から英文記事を読む練習を行い，使えそうな表現などはスマートフォンなどに整理保存して実際に自分で使ってみることをおすすめする。

2023年度　実施問題

【中高共通】

【１】リスニングテスト

Part A

(1) Write your answer on your answer sheet.

(2) Write your answer on your answer sheet.

(3) Write your answer on your answer sheet.

(4) Write your answer on your answer sheet.

(5) Write your answer on your answer sheet.

(6) Write your answer on your answer sheet.

Part B

(1) (A) 10:55.
(B) 11:00.
(C) 11:55.
(D) 2:25.

(2) (A) The man was out at that time.
(B) The delivery person thought nobody was at home.
(C) The man bought a battery.
(D) The woman asked them to bring it later.

(3) (A) Take Josh to the hospital.
(B) Attend the meeting from home.
(C) Call the company to take the day off.
(D) Ask her sister for a favor.

(4) (A) He's always too pessimistic.
(B) He often gets poor grades.
(C) She found the exams difficult.
(D) She would be happy if he taught her economics.

Part C

(1) Write your answer on your answer sheet.

(2) Write your answer on your answer sheet.

Part D

(1) オランダのリンゴ園で行われた実験の結果と，その結果をもたらした要因について，どのように述べているか。

(2) 環境保護のために何が必要で，またそれによってどのような効果があると述べているか。

(☆☆☆◎◎◎)

【2】次の英文を読んで，(1)～(4)の設問に答えよ。

WHEN HE WAS 2 YEARS OLD, BEN STOPPED SEEING OUT OF his left eye. His mother took him to the doctor and soon discovered he had retinal cancer in both eyes. After chemotherapy and radiation failed, surgeons removed both his eyes. For Ben, vision was gone forever.

But by the time he was 7 years old, he had devised a technique for decoding the world around him: he clicked with his mouth and listened for the returning echoes. This method enabled Ben to determine the locations of open doorways, people, parked cars, garbage cans and so on. (A)<u>He was echolocating</u>: bouncing his sound waves off objects in the environment and catching the reflections to build a mental model of his surroundings.

Echolocation may sound like an improbable feat for a human, but thousands of blind people have perfected this skill, just as Ben did. How could blindness give rise to the stunning ability to understand the surroundings with one's ears? The answer lies in a gift bestowed on the brain by evolution: tremendous adaptability.

Whenever we learn something, pick up a new skill or modify our habits, the physical structure of our brain changes. Neurons, the cells responsible for rapidly processing information in the brain, are interconnected by the thousands—but like friendships in a community, the connections between them constantly change: strengthening, weakening and finding new partners. Neuroscience calls this phenomenon (B)brain plasticity, referring to the ability of the brain, like plastic, to assume new shapes and hold them. More recent discoveries in neuroscience, though, suggest that the brain's brand of flexibility is far more nuanced than holding onto a shape. To capture this, we refer to the brain's plasticity as "livewiring" to spotlight how this vast system of 86 billion neurons and 0.2 quadrillion connections rewires itself every moment of your life. The brain's livewiring allows for learning, memory and the ability to develop new skills.

Recent decades have yielded several revelations about livewiring, but perhaps the biggest surprise is its (①). Brain circuits reorganize not only in the newly blind but also in the sighted who have temporary blindness. In (C)one study, sighted participants intensively learned how to read braille. Half the participants were blindfolded throughout the experience. At the end of five days, the participants who wore blindfolds could distinguish subtle differences between braille characters much better than the participants who didn't wear blindfolds. Even more remarkably, the blindfolded participants showed activation in visual brain regions in response to touch and sound. In other words, the blindfolded participants performed better on the touch-related task because their visual cortex had been recruited to help.

But such changes don't have to take five days; that just happened to be when the measurement took place. When blindfolded participants are continuously measured, touch-related activity shows up in the visual cortex in about an hour.

What do brain flexibility and rapid cortical takeover have to do with dreaming? Perhaps more than previously thought. Ben clearly benefited from the (②) of his visual cortex to other senses because he had permanently lost his eyes, but what about the participants in the blindfold experiments? If our loss of a sense is only temporary, then the rapid conquest of brain territory may not be so helpful. And this, we propose, is why we dream.

【出典　*TIME*, February 15/February 22, 2021】

(1)　下線部(A)について，彼は何をしていたのか具体的に日本語で書け。

(2)　下線部(B)のように呼ばれる理由を，30字程度の日本語で書け。

(3)　(　①　)，(　②　)に入る最も適切な語を，次のア～エからそれぞれ一つずつ選び，その記号を書け。

①　ア　sensibility　　イ　accountability　　ウ　rapidity
　　エ　availability

②　ア　redistribution　　イ　reconciliation　　ウ　reformation
　　エ　revitalization

(4)　下線部(C)の結果として，最も特筆すべき結果とその要因を，具体的に日本語で書け。

(☆☆☆☆☆◎◎◎◎)

【中学校】

【1】次の会話文を読んで，(1)～(5)の設問に答えよ。

TV Anchor : Millions of people need blood transfusions, but the number of blood donors has been decreasing. We're facing a looming blood shortage. The (　①　) number of donors in their teens and 20s is particularly worrying.

Diana : [　Ⅰ　]

John : Me? Yeah. Actually, I'm a regular blood donor. I'm making (A)<u>a contribution to society</u> through blood donation. Giving blood is a very simple thing to do, but not everybody wants to donate their blood.

Diana : I have never donated blood for two reasons. First, I don't like the pain of syringes.

John : [　Ⅱ　]

Diana : I have low blood pressure. Simply taking blood to do a blood test makes me (　②　). I am not opposed to the idea of blood donation. I just can't do it.

John : Yours is a rare case. According to the survey, one in four of those who haven't donated said they didn't know about the looming blood shortage. So, the Red Cross Society should make an effort to (　③　) people about the problem.

Diana : [　Ⅲ　] Donating blood is a volunteer activity. Therefore, once people are motivated to donate blood, won't the number of donors increase?

John : Yes. Moreover, (B)<u>donating blood has a big advantage</u>. It's like a free health screening. In 10 days, you will receive detailed information regarding your blood. It includes information about blood pressure, possible liver problems and so on. This way, blood donation not only saves lives, but also is a way for donors to get a medical check-up.

【出典　森秀夫，『50トピックでトレーニング　英語で意見を言ってみる』，ベレ出版】

(1) (　①　)～(　③　)に入る最も適切な語を，次のア～クから一つずつ選び，その記号を書け。

ア　astronomical　　イ　clumsy　　ウ　declining　　エ　dizzy
オ　inform　　カ　lessen　　キ　shame　　ク　tease

(2) [　Ⅰ　]～[　Ⅲ　]に入る最も適切なものを，次のア～ウから一つずつ選び，その記号を書け。

ア　I agree with you.　　イ　Have you donated blood?
ウ　What is the second reason?

(3) 下線部(A)について，あなた自身が普段取り組んでいることを一つ取り上げ，10語以上の英語で書け。ただし，blood donation以外の内容を書くこと。

(4) Johnが下線部(B)のように考える理由を，簡潔に日本語で書け。

(5) この会話文の概要を次のようにまとめるとき，空欄に当てはまる英語1語を，文中から抜き出して書け。

They are talking about how to (　　) the number of blood donors.

(☆☆☆◎◎◎◎)

【2】次の英文を読んで，(1)～(5)の設問に答えよ。

As an example, let us relate an anecdote about a teacher with whom Diane Larsen-Freeman was working some time ago. We will call her Heather, although that is not her real name. From her study of methods in Stevick (1980), Heather became interested in how to work with teacher control and student initiative in her teaching. Heather determined that during her student teaching internship, she would exercise less control of the lesson in order to (A)encourage her students to take more initiative. She decided to narrow the goal down to having the students take the initiative in posing the questions in the classroom, recognizing that so often it is the teacher who asks all the questions, not the students.

Diane was Heather's teaching supervisor. When Diane came to observe her, Heather was very discouraged. She felt that the students were not taking the initiative that she was trying to get them to take, but she could not see what was wrong.

When Diane visited her class, she observed the following：

HEATHER : Juan, ask Anna what she is wearing.
JUAN : What are you wearing?
ANNA : I am wearing a dress.
HEATHER : Anna, ask Muriel what she is writing.
ANNA : What are you writing?
MURIEL : I am writing a letter.

This pattern continued for some time. It was clear to see that Heather had successfully avoided the common problem of the teacher asking all the questions in the class. 【ア】 The teacher was not asking the questions—the students were. However, Heather had not achieved her goal of encouraging student initiative, since it was she who took the initiative by prompting the students to ask the questions. Heather and Diane discussed $_{(B)}$<u>the matter</u> in the post-observation conference.

Heather came to see that if she truly wanted students to take more initiative, then she would have to set up the situation in such a way that her participation in an activity was not essential. Diane talked about several ways Heather might do this. 【イ】 She realized that since she was a fairly inexperienced teacher, she felt insecure about having the students make the decisions about who says what to whom, and when. What if the students were to ask her questions that she was unable to answer? Having students take the initiative in the classroom was consonant with her values; however, Heather realized that she needed to think further about what level of student initiative would be comfortable for her at this stage in her career as a teacher. 【ウ】 The point was that it was not necessarily simply a matter of Heather improving her technique; she could see that that was one possibility. Another was to rethink the way in which she thought about her teaching (Larsen-Freeman 1993).

The links between thought and action were very important in Heather's teaching. She came to realize that when something was not going as she had intended, she could (　C　) her thought or she could (　C　) her action.

【出典　Diane Larsen-Freeman and Marti Anderson, *Techniques & Principles in Language Teaching*, OXFORD UNIVERSITY PRESS】

(1)　下線部(A)について，Heatherがその達成のために決意した内容を，日本語で書け。

(2)　次の英文が入る最も適切な箇所を本文中の【ア】～【ウ】から一つ選び，その記号を書け。

During this discussion, Heather came to another important awareness.

(3) 下線部(B)について，その内容を具体的に日本語で書け。

(4) (C)に入る最も適切な語を次のア～エから一つ選び，その記号を書け。なお，それぞれの空所には同じ語が入る。

ア connect　イ provide　ウ change　エ acquire

(5) 本県の最重点の教育課題の一つである“「問い」を発する子ども”の育成という観点から，英語の授業において，あなたはどのような指導の工夫をするか，日本語で書け。

(☆☆☆☆◎◎◎◎◎)

【3】次の(1)～(4)について，それぞれの英文の[　　]内に入る最も適切なものを，ア～エから一つずつ選び，その記号を書け。

(1) [　　] to think of it, I haven't visited foreign countries for many years.

ア Get　イ Go　ウ Come　エ Have

(2) The travel agent recommended us to reserve a hotel room that [　　] a fine view.

ア commands　イ reduces　ウ worsens　エ grows

(3) The language school is trying to [　　] it's range of class offering and schedules.

ア subsidize　イ diversify　ウ invest　エ implore

(4) Her idea was bright but she couldn't develop it into a [　　] theory.

ア coincident　イ messy　ウ wrong　エ coherent

(☆☆☆◎◎◎◎)

【4】次の(1)～(3)について，それぞれの日本語の内容を表すように，[　　]内の語句を並べかえよ。なお，文頭に来る語も小文字にしてある。(4)については，日本語の意味になるように英語で書け。

(1) 医者が冗談で緊張をほぐすと，その患者はよりリラックスした。

[with / the doctor / the ice / after / broke / a joke], his client became more relaxed.

(2) 大学生の中には，外食するより自炊する方が好きだという人もいる。

[college students / to / cooking at home / is / say / some / preferable] eating out.

(3) 他の生徒にとって悪い前例をつくることになるので，君に規則を破らせるわけにはいかない。

We cannot [the rule / break / would / you / because / to / it / permit] set a bad precedent for other students.

(4) 今まで発表していない人にチャンスを与えましょう。

(☆☆☆☆◎◎◎◎◎)

【5】あなたは，生徒が主体的に「読むこと」と「書くこと」に取り組めるように，校内に英語掲示板を設置することにした。次の趣旨を踏まえ，ALTに協力を依頼するメール文の内容を考えて，50語程度の英語で書け。挨拶などの英文は省略するものとする。※語数を数えて記入すること。(符号は語数に含めない)

〈英語掲示板を設置する趣旨〉 英語掲示板をとおして，生徒は社会的な事柄に関する英文を読んだり，自分の考えなどを書いてALTと交流したりすることができる。

(☆☆☆☆☆◎◎◎◎)

【6】中学校学習指導要領(平成29年3月告示)では，生徒が身に付けるべき資質・能力や生徒の実態，教材の内容などに応じて，視聴覚教材やコンピュータ，情報通信ネットワーク，教育機器などを有効活用することが求められている。授業において，1人1台端末を活用することのよさについて，活用例を二つ挙げ，70語程度の英語で書け。※語数を数えて記入すること。(符号は語数に含めない)

(☆☆☆☆☆◎◎◎)

【高等学校】

【1】次の英文を読んで，(1)～(5)の設問に答えよ。

Self-esteem is an important part of achieving *nagomi*. Self-confidence is a good thing so long as it does not go too far, as too much of it will result in an unbalanced life. If your ego is too big, you can lack the compassion and humility to be a good friend or partner. You can overlook the quieter people and arrogantly assume to know best, when you may benefit from listening to others, even if they are not as outwardly confident as you may be. The *nagomi* of self-esteem is knowing your true self, your good and your bad points, and accepting them. Embracing the things you cannot change is a fundamental aspect of the *nagomi* of the self. One way to apply this to your life is to forgive others, rather than hold on to anger or resentment or guilt. You have to forgive yourself for past transgressions and similarly forgive others for things they have done against you. You can't achieve *nagomi* if you don't have (A)<u>this balance</u>.

If you accept who you are, nobody can make you feel bad about yourself. What other people say or do cannot affect you, because self-esteem gives you the ultimate (　B　). An Australian friend of mine, who is now based in Tokyo, once quipped: 'There will always be people who are smarter than you, richer than you, and better looking than you. But remember, there is nobody better at being you than you!'

Another of the crucial ways to arrive at a *nagomi* of the self is *gaman*, which is a Japanese concept related to perseverance. It is one of the most important premises of Zen Buddhism and its principles have long been widely glorified and practised, especially among the samurai class in the Middle Ages. You may think that, since the samurai warriors were the ruling class, they would have had their own way in life, and that their values won't be particularly relevant to us in the modern day, but *gaman*, or self-restraint, could well be the ethics of the twenty-first century. For example, if you were on a spaceship, *gaman* could be one of the best virtues that you could have. A trip to Mars would take months. During that time, practising self-restraint, ***gaman***, especially in the context of not bothering other people and not requiring too much of the limited resources on board, would be essential. In fact, the selection process of astronauts already focuses on candidates' capacity for self-restraint.

However, no matter how we may work to improve the conditions around us, it is not possible to make a perfect world; indeed, the very premise of a perfect world has repeatedly led to earthly conditions of $_{(C)}$dystopia. With a bit of ***gaman***, we may be able instead to achieve a nagomi with the imperfect world we live in.

So, the ***nagomi*** of self is contingent upon attaining self-knowledge, acceptance, forgiveness and self-esteem. In its most extreme and simple form, the ***nagomi*** of self would lead to the erasing of all traces of $_{(D)}$ego-centered concerns.

【出典　Ken Mogi, *THE WAY OF NAGOMI*, QUERCUS】

(1)　下線部(A)とは何と何のバランスのことか，日本語で書け。

(2)　空所(　B　)に入る最も適切な語を次のア～エから一つ選び，その記号を書け。

ア　luxury　　イ　insult　　ウ　resilience　　エ　fragileness

(3)　宇宙飛行士に必要な "***gaman***" の具体例を2点日本語で書け。

(4)　下線部(C)の原因として述べられているのは何か，日本語で書け。

(5)　下線部(D)について，本文で示されている具体例を2点日本語で書け。

(☆☆☆☆◎◎◎◎)

【2】次の英文を読んで，(1)～(5)の設問に答えよ。

The interface between L2 motivation and metacognition has attracted some theoretical attention over the years, particularly among researchers interested in examining relationships between students' motivation and their use of language learning strategies. On the whole, however, this line of research has tended to adopt a quantitative analysis of associations between range or frequency of strategy use and degree or type of motivation (e,g, MacIntyre & Noels 1996; Schmidt, Boraie & Kassagby 1996; Schmidt & Watanabe 2001; Vandergrift 2005). While such studies can usefully uncover (A)general patterns in motivation and strategy use, this kind of research inquiry offers a limited analysis of how motivation may interact with metacognition in the L2 learning process, since it can shed little light on how motivation shapes the development of metacognitive thinking processes, or on what teachers can do to help learners in this regard.

To analyse the interface between motivation and metacognition, I will begin by discussing (B)two notions of autonomy, building on a useful conceptual distinction succinctly highlighted by Lamb (2007). In my earlier discussion of proximal self-motivators, I made the point that the process of setting and working towards optimal challenges not only promotes the development of metacognitive awareness and skills but can also cultivate feelings of competence and autonomy, thereby nurturing intrinsic motivation. This is because perceived competence and autonomy are theorised to be fundamental "nutriments" (Ryan & Deci 2002:7) or psychological needs underpinning the healthy growth and internalisation of motivation, particularly intrinsic motivation to engage in a skill-based activity where enjoyment and satisfaction derive from feeling effective and in control. Autonomy here is the sense that we are exercising personal control and agency in what we do, so that our actions and behaviours are freely chosen and self-determined rather than controlled by others —hence the motivational theory of self-determination (Ryan & Deci 2002) in which this concept of autonomy is grounded.

Yet, this psychological sense of autonomy shaping self-determined motivation and action does not necessarily lead to effective forms of learning. For example, learners might be freely and autonomously engaged in off-task behaviours during a language practice activity when unmonitored by the teacher. Or a learner may spend a great deal of time autonomously doing L2 activities she enjoys but pay scant attention to the less enjoyable aspects of learning or language use she needs to work on. In short, (C)autonomy in the sense of personal agency may underpin self-determined forms of motivation, but this may not necessarily be the motivation needed to engage with the increasing cognitive and linguistic challenges of learning.

However, as Lamb (2007) points out, there is also another concept of autonomy in the sense of taking responsibility for, managing and regulating one's learning — or what is more appropriately called *learner autonomy*, or even more specifically, as Little (2007) emphasises, *language learner autonomy.* Autonomy in this sense implies both (　D　) to take charge of one's language learning and a capacity for "detachment, critical reflection, decision-making, and independent action" (Little 1991:4). This capacity entails applying metacognitive skills and strategic thinking processes to overcome problems and difficulties in language learning and use, and to manage and regulate one's learning.

【出典　Edited by Lasagabaster, D., Doiz, A., & Sierra, J. M., *Motivation and Foreign Language Learning: From theory to practice*, John Benjamins Publishing Company】

(1)　下線部(A)を得るために一般的に行われている調査はどのようなものか，日本語で書け。

(2)　下線部(B)はそれぞれどのようなものであると第二段落，第四段落で説明されているか，日本語で書け。

(3)　最適な課題設定とそれに取り組む過程は2つのことに役立つと筆者は指摘している。その2点を日本語で書け。

(4)　下線部(C)を筆者はどのように説明しているか，日本語で書け。

(5)　空所(　D　)に入る最も適切な語句を，次のア～エから一つ選び，その記号を書け。

ア　a machinery　　イ　an obligation　　ウ　a willingness
エ　an evasion

(☆☆☆☆☆◎◎◎◎◎)

【3】次の(1)，(2)について，日本語で答えよ。

(1)　高等学校学習指導要領(平成30年3月告示)外国語において，「外国語による聞くこと，読むこと，話すこと，書くことの言語活動及びこれらを結び付けた統合的な言語活動を通して」，情報や考えなどを的確に理解したり適切に表現したり伝え合ったりするコミュニケーションを図る資質・能力の育成を目指すと述べられている。

これを踏まえ，①統合的な言語活動の例を一つ取り上げて具体的に書け。また，その際の②留意事項を箇条書きで2点答えよ。

(2)　高等学校学習指導要領解説外国語編英語編(平成30年7月文部科学省)には，「コミュニケーションを行う目的や場面，状況などを設定した上で，それぞれの言語活動に必要となる文法事項を提示して，実際のコミュニケーションにおけるその文法事項の活用の必然性に生徒が気付くような指導を行うことが重要である。」とある。

これを踏まえ，①具体的な文法事項を一つ取り上げ，目的や場面，状況などを設定した活動例を一つ書け。また，その際の②文法指導に関する留意事項を2点答えよ。

(☆☆☆☆☆◎◎◎)

【4】次の(1)～(5)の(　　)に当てはまる最も適切なものを，それぞれア～エから一つ選び，その 記号を書け。

(1)　He made a big mistake, but he is trying to (　　) his honor by giving his best presentation for our new product.

ア　recede　　イ　redeem　　ウ　retard　　エ　revoke

(2)　Our ALT is going back to his country in August. He is arranging his (　　) now.

ア　detour　　イ　drawback　　ウ　itinerary　　エ　swarm

(3)　I was very nervous when I heard I would be transferred to the US. But I was glad for a (　　) welcome from people there.

ア　coherent　　イ　contentious　　ウ　contradictory　　エ　cordial

(4)　Some schools have amended a rule of (　　) any cell phone when students are seen using one in school.

ア　confiscating　　イ　deceiving　　ウ　proclaiming

エ　teasing

(5) You have disobeyed his instructions many times. That makes him "(　　)."

ア　fall flat　　イ　hit the roof　　ウ　make ends meet

エ　turn over a new leaf

(☆☆☆☆☆◎◎◎◎◎)

【5】

a) 次の(1)～(3)の各英文には，それぞれ文法的な誤りが1か所ある。その部分の記号を書き，正しい英語に直せ。

(1) When you want to eat ${}_{A}$a toast with butter for breakfast, we recommend you ${}_{B}$use a frying pan. You can ${}_{C}$prepare for it in ${}_{D}$a short time! In addition, we can enjoy the same taste as when we use a toast oven.

(2) First of all, we ${}_{A}$highly appreciate ${}_{B}$your quick response about this difficult condition. We can never ${}_{C}$handle this condition without ${}_{D}$assisting from your company.

(3) Through "floating solar power generation" system, electricity is generated at a solar power plant ${}_{A}$floating on the water. The system ${}_{B}$is thought to be a good way to produce electricity because water keeps the solar panels ${}_{C}$cool enough to work most effectively even in the summer and ${}_{D}$enable the panel to gather a lot of sunlight with the help of the reflection.

b) 次の(1)，(2)は，次のタイトルで生徒が書いた英文であるが，それぞれ文法的な誤りが1か所ある。その部分に下線を引いて指摘し，下線の下に正しい英語を書け。ただし，タイトルは訂正しないこと。

(1) Title: An Email to the ABC Online Store

I regret to say that I am not happy with the coat which I bought online. This is not what I ordered. This is much smaller. I cannot put on this. I would like to exchange this for a larger one. Would you mind if you check my email and send me a new one? I am waiting for your reply.

(2) Title: A Trouble in a Foreign Country

This is what I experienced when I went abroad for the first time. I was stolen my bag at the station. My camera was in the bag. Soon I went to the police to ask for help. Luckily, my bag returned to me. You should watch all of your belongings wherever you go.

(☆☆☆☆◎◎◎)

【6】次の質問に，100語程度の英語で答えよ。

Suppose you are teaching in a high school. A new ALT has just arrived. She asked you a question, “I have heard that my job is to support Japanese teachers of English in classes. What should I do for that?” As a JTE, what would you say to her?

(☆☆☆☆☆◎◎◎)

解答・解説

【中高共通】

【1】Part A (1) C (2) A (3) B (4) C (5) A (6) A Part B (1) A (2) B (3) D (4) A

Part C (1) I should press nine. (2) I should buy a gift card.

Part D (1) 解答略 (2) 解答略

〈解説〉スクリプトは公開されていない。放送は繰り返されるのか，繰り返されるのであれば何回聴くチャンスがあるのかなど，指示もきちんと把握した上で取り組む必要がある。 Part A 選択肢が問題用紙に印刷されていないので，各選択肢の内容を聞き逃さないように注意したい。　Part B　選択肢は問題用紙に印刷されている。対話を聞いて選択肢で答える形式と思われる。対話を聞く前に印刷されている選択肢から内容を推測することができる。　Part C　英問英答形式であるが，解答が短文であることから，ポイントを聞き取れれば解答できると思われる。　Part D　英文を聞いて，印刷されている日本語の質問文に答える記述問題となっている。質問文に事前に目を通し，その答えを探すように英文を聞く。

【2】(1)　(解答例)　周囲の状況や物の位置を口から発した音の反響で把握すること。　(2)　(解答例)　プラスチックのように新しい形を取ることができ，その形を保持できるため。(35字)　(3)　①　ウ　②　ア　(4)　(解答例)　特筆すべき結果…目隠しをした被験者は，触覚や聴覚の刺激に対しても，脳の視覚領域が反応するようになったこと。　要因…目隠しをした被験者は，触覚の刺激に対する処理を，代わりに脳の視覚領域が助けるようになったため。

〈解説〉(1)　下線部の直後で述べられている内容をまとめればよい。

(2)　下線部の直後で述べられているlike以下の内容をまとめればよい。

(3)　①　空所の直後では，実験中に目隠しをした状態で点字を覚える被験者と，目が見える状態で点字を覚える被験者の実験が述べられている。5日という短い期間であったが，目が見えない状況を経験し点字を有意に学習することができたという結果や，視覚に関する脳の領域が活性化するという結果はlive wiringが急速に発達することを意味している。sensibility (感受性)，accountability (責任能力)，availability (可用性)。　②　空所の前の段落後半で述べられていた，脳のある領域が別の感覚の領域の働きを助けることから，視力を失ったBenの脳では視覚に関する領域が触覚や聴覚の処理を助けていると推測できる。この内容を適切に表したのはredistribution (再分配) である。reconciliation (和解)，reformation (改革)，revitalization (再活性化)。

(4)　Even more remarkablyで始まる文と，その言い換えであるIn other

wordsの文の内容をまとめればよい。結果と要因をそれぞれ記述することとなるが，因果関係をきちんと把握する必要がある。目隠しをして脳の視覚領域が使われないと，触覚や聴覚に関する領域が活性化し，脳は視覚を補おうとする。そして，視覚刺激を処理する領域も触覚や聴覚領域を処理するようになり，目隠しをした実験被験者たちは触覚に関するテストで成績がよかった。

【中学校】

【1】(1) ① ウ ② エ ③ オ (2) Ⅰ イ Ⅱ ウ Ⅲ ア (3) I sometimes pick up trash on the street as a volunteer. (11 words) (4) (解答例) 献血をすると，自分の血液の状態について詳細情報をもらえるため，無料で健康診断を受けるようなものであるから。 (5) increase

〈解説〉blood transfusion「輸血」に関する空所補充問題。 (1) ① 空所前の文にはdecreasingやshortageなどの語が使われており，10代から20代の献血者の数が減少していると推測できる。 ② low blood pressure「低血圧」であるDianaは採血するだけでdizzy「めまいがする」ようになってしまう。make O Cの形であり空所には形容詞が入ると推測できる。 ③ 過去に献血をしたことのない4人に1人が，献血をした後に貧血になることを知らなかった。この問題を赤十字社は人々に周知する努力をするべきであると推測できる。空所の後の直接目的語はpeopleであり，informする内容を表す際にはofもしくはaboutが後続する。 (2) 文レベルの空所補充問題は用いられている語彙のオーバーラップや上位語・下位語の言い換え，代名詞の結束性などを手がかりにして解答するとよい。 Ⅰ 空所の直前ではTV Anchorが献血する若者の数が減っていることを述べており，直後ではMe?と返答している。これらのことから，献血した経験を問うていると推測できる。Ⅱ 空所の直前では献血に伴う注射の痛み，直後では低血圧を，献血しない理由として述べている。2つの理由のうち片方を言い終えた後での疑問として，空所では2つめの理由は何かを問うていると推測できる。　Ⅲ　空所の直前では赤十字社が取り組むべき問題について述べていることから，その考えに賛成していると述べるのが適切。

(3)　社会貢献として，献血以外で普段取り組んでいることを英語でまとめる問題。解答例では道のゴミ拾いを挙げている。　(4)　下線部に続く文にa free health screeningとあるように，献血によって人を救うだけでなく自身の健康診断も無料できることをまとめればよい。

(5)　空所の直前にはto不定詞のtoが用いられていることから，空所は原形であることが推測できる。空所の後に献血者の数とあることから，数の増減を表す語が適切。また，Johnの主張は献血に対してポジティブなものであることから，increaseが適切。

【2】(1)　(解答例)　Heatherの教室では，生徒ではなく教師が質問する側であることを認識させ，生徒が自発的に問いを発するように目標を絞った。　(2)　イ　(3)　(解答例)　教室内で率先して問いを発するように，生徒に主導権を持たせる方法　(4)　ウ

(5)　(解答例)　「問い」を発する子どもを育成する方法の1つに，教科書で取り扱う内容の導入では生徒に身近な話題を用いることが挙げられる。生徒が主体的に英語を学習するためには，言語の形式だけでなくメッセージの内容にも着目するように，興味を引くようなオーラルイントロダクションを心がけたい。

〈解説〉(1)　下線部に続く文に，Heatherの決断がdecided to…と述べられている。この箇所をまとめればよい。　(2)　挿入される文にはthis discussionとあるため，直前に誰かが議論していることが推測できる。その議論は教育実習生のHeatherと指導教員のDianeの議論であり，Dianeと会話している様子が述べられているのは空所イの部分である。

(3)　下線部には定冠詞theが用いられており，直前の内容を指していると推測できる。直前では生徒が問いを発するように促して主導権を握っていたのがHeatherであり，生徒に主導権を取らせるような目的が達成できなかったことが述べられている。この内容をまとめればよい。

(4)　HeatherがDianeと議論する前は生徒が主体的に問いを発するわけ

ではなく，教師であるHeatherが主導権を握っていた。この現状は，教師としての経験の浅いHeatherが「生徒からの質問に答えられなかったらどうしよう」という不安を反映していたことが述べられており，この考えに気づいたことで自身の指導法について考え直すこととなった。このことから，意図していた指導がうまくいかなかった場合には自分の考えを変えることで，自身の指導を変える行動につながると推測できる。　(5)　Here and Now / There and Thereのように，子どもの発達段階は，自分のことや身近なことから，他人や社会的な話題へと発達していく。主体性を育む上では，自己表現が可能である身近な話題を取り上げることが方法の1つである。

【3】(1)　ウ　(2)　ア　(3)　イ　(4)　エ

〈解説〉(1)　come to think of it「(文頭・文末で) 今考えてみると，そういえば，今思い出したのだけれど」。when I come to think of itの省略表現。(2)　command A「A (景色など) を見渡せる」。主語には場所などが用いられ，人は使われない。進行形や受け身は不可。　(3)　diversify A「(企業・人が) A (製品・サービスなど)を多様化する，拡大する」。subsidize A「Aに補助金を与える(通例受動態)」，invest A「Aを投資する」，implore A to do「Aに～するよう懇願する」。　(4)　coherent「筋の通った」，coincident「一致して」，messy「散らかった」。

【4】(1)　After the doctor broke the ice with a joke　(2)　Some college students say cooking at home is preferable to　(3)　permit you to break the rule because it would　(4)　Let me give a chance to those who have not spoken yet.

〈解説〉(1)　時を表す副詞afterがあることから，副詞節が作れると判断する。過去時制を担うbrokeの主語となるのはthe doctorであり，break the iceは「話の口火を切る，場を和ませる」という意味を表す。with a jokeはa pen to write withの「～を使って」という意味のwithである。(2)「Aの中には～な人がいる」はSome Aを使って表す。主動詞は複数形と一致するsayを用い，isはthat節の動詞として使う。preferableは比較対象としてtoを用いる。　(3)　permit A to do「Aに～することを許可する」，break the rule「規則を破る」を組み合わせる。空所の直前には助動詞cannotが用いられているため最初は原形の動詞が用いられるが，日本語を参考にするとpermitであるとわかる。　(4)　和文英訳問題である。解答例では「与えましょう」を使役動詞letを用いてlet me give A to Bと表現している。「今まで発表していない人」は関係代名詞those whoを用いている。また「今まで」を表現するために現在完了形を用いている。

【5】(解答例)　I have set up an English bulletin board to encourage students' participation in English reading and writing activity. On the board, students can read about social problems in English and share their opinions. I would be grateful if you could encourage the students to use this platform to communicate with you, ALTs and participate in opinion exchange. (57 words)

〈解説〉ALTへの依頼のメール文ということを踏まえ，以下の3点を50語程度の英語でまとめる。「(1)　生徒が『読むこと』，『書くこと』の活動に取り組めるよう英語の掲示板を用意した」，「(2)　掲示板上では社会的な事柄に関する英文を読み，意見交換できる」，「(3)　ALTとのコミュニケーションや，意見交換に参加するよう生徒に促してほしい」の3点をまとめればよい。

【6】(解答例)　By owing his own computer in the class, each student can develop important digital literacy skills, such as Internet literacy. Teachers can encourage students to solve problems by searching the Internet for information, which requires students to have Internet literacy. Teachers can also assign online homework that utilizes audio-visual materials such as videos and animations. With access to computers, students can get valuable learning materials from anywhere and at any time. (71 words)

〈解説〉1人1台の端末を活用するという考えは，2019年文部科学省の

GIGAスクール構想を踏まえたもの。児童生徒が1人で端末を占有することで，教師側は「生徒1人ひとりの習熟度に合わせた授業を実現しやすい」，「課題などのプリントを用意する手間が不要となり効率的に授業を行える」，「教員間で容易に情報共有できる」，「生徒の答案や成績などのデータを活用できる」，生徒側には「周囲の目を気にしなくて済むので，間違いを恐れずに学習できる」，「動画や音声を使った教材を活用できる」，「視覚・聴覚を駆使して学べるためモチベーションが上がる」，「インターネットを活用して自分で調べることで主体的な学習ができる」，「コンピュータスキルを身に付けることができる」などの利点がある。これらの利点をふまえて考えられる活用方法を2つ例示すればよい。解答例では，生徒にインターネットの情報収集によって課題解決をすること，音声や画像を使った宿題を出すことを挙げている。

【高等学校】

【1】(1)　(解答例)　過去に自分が犯してしまった過ちを許すことと，他人が自分に対してしたことを許すことのバランス　(2)　ウ　(3)　(解答例)　・宇宙船の他の乗組員に対して迷惑をかけないこと　・限られた資源を求めすぎないこと　(4)　(解答例)「完全な世界」が存在するというまさにその前提　(5)　(解答例)　・友人やパートナーとしての思いやりや謙虚さに欠けてしまう　・自分よりもおとなしい人を見過ごし，自分が一番よく知っていることに傲慢になりがち

〈解説〉(1)　代名詞thisが用いられていること，直前の文にあるforgiveという動詞の重複，類似点を表すsimilarlyから，下線部のバランスとは直前の内容のことを指しているとわかる。　(2)　空所の前後の文では，ありのままの自分自身を受け入れれば，他人の言動から悪影響を受けることはないと述べられている。したがって，自尊心は最大のresilience「回復力，元気」を与えてくれると推測できる。luxury「贅沢さ」，insult「侮辱」，fragileness「壊れやすさ」。　(3)　宇宙飛行士と

我慢の実践についてはA trip to Mars以降の文に示されている。
(4)　dystopia「ディストピア」は理想郷(utopia)の反意語であり，この世の全ての不幸や罪悪で満ちているとされる仮想上の場所や社会のことを指す。dystopiaとの因果関係を表すのはlead toの主語であるthe very premise of a perfect worldである。　(5)　第1段落では，エゴが大きすぎる場合どのような人物になってしまうのかを示しており，ego-centeredの具体例が述べられている。compassion「思いやり」，humility「謙虚，謙遜」，arrogantly「傲慢に」。

【2】(1)　(解答例)　ストラテジーの使用範囲や頻度とモチベーションの程度や種類との関係性について定量的に分析する調査　(2)　(解答例)　1つ目は学習者が主体的に自分の行動や振る舞いを自由に管理し，自己決定をするものである。2つ目は学習者が自分の学習に対して責任を持ち，その学習を管理・統制しようとするものである。
(3)　(解答例)　・メタ認知の意識とそのスキルの発達を促進することができる。　・能力と自律性の感覚を高め，内発的動機を育むことができる。　(4)　(解答例)　個人の主体性としての自律性は心理的な自律性のことを指している。この自律性は自己決定的な動機づけや行動を形成するが，これは必ずしも効果的な学習行動につながるわけではない。　(5)　ウ
〈解説〉(1)　下線部の前のOn the wholeから始まる文で述べられている内容をまとめる。なお，quantitativelyとは量的研究(アンケートなどの数値に対して統計処理を行う研究手法)のことを指す。　(2)　2種類のautonomyについて，1つ目は第2段落，2つ目は第4段落でそれぞれまとめられている。1つ目のautonomyはAutonomy here is the sense that…の文で述べられている内容が該当し，2つ目のautonomyはthere is also another concept of autonomy…の内容が該当する。　(3)　第2段落のIn my earlier discussion of proximal self-motivators,で始まる文にnot only A but also Bの構文があり，この2つをまとめればよい。　(4)　下線部を含む文は，言い換え表現のマーカーとなるIn shortで始まっているため，

その前で述べた内容を言い換えていると推測できる。ここでは例が2つ示されており，その内容はトピックセンテンスとなる第3段落冒頭のYet, this psychological sense of autonomyを指す。下線部はthis psychological sense of autonomyのことであるため，トピックセンテンスの内容をまとめればよい。　(5)　空所の前の文にはtake responsibility for A「Aに責任を持つ」という表現が使われていることから，学習に対してポジティブな意味を持つan obligationもしくはa willingnessが候補となる。これまでの段落では，学習者が自らの学習を管理することを述べてきているため，内発的な責任であることが推測できることから，a willingness「自発的に～すること」が適切。a machinery「(可算名詞で)手続き，手順」，an obligation「義務，恩義」，an evasion「言い逃れ，ごまかし」。

【3】(1)　(解答例)　①　言語技能を統合的する活動の例として，再話が挙げられる。再話とは，読んだり聞いたりした英文の内容を，知らない人に伝える活動のことを指す。例えば，昨日見た映画の内容を友達に伝えるなど，再話は日常的に行われており，言語活動としての真正性も高い。教室内での再話活動としては，ペアで異なる観点から書かれた英文を読み，その内容を相手に伝え合い，それに基づいてペアでの意見を書いたり，発表したりする活動が考えられる。　②　・読解する英文の難易度を生徒に適切であるように調整する。　・ペアでやり取りの必要性を持たせるためにインフォメーションギャップを含む英文を用意する。　(2)　(解答例)　①　【文法事項】形容詞的用法のto不定詞「～するための」。　【活動例】目的：表現できない道具の名前を，上位語＋to不定詞で表現する。　場面・状況：ホームステイ先で，日本から持ってきたインスタントの味噌汁をホストファミリーに振る舞いたい。お湯を沸かすためのヤカンを借りたいが，ヤカンに相当する英単語を知らない。　活動：“I need a container to boil water.”のように，ヤカンの上位語とto不定詞を使ってパラフレーズする。　②　・to不定詞の意味的な違いを名詞的用法や副詞的用

法と比較しながら指導する。　・a house to live inやa pen to write withのような群前置詞を伴うto不定詞は，意味上の主語や動詞の自動詞・他動詞の区別を取り上げながら指導する。

〈解説〉(1)　①　解答例では読むことと話すことの統合である再話(retelling)を取り上げている。設問では言語活動の例を具体的に書くことが求められており，どのような言語活動であるかを簡潔にまとめ，そのメリットや教室現場を想定した活動を述べるとよい。他の技能統合型の言語活動の例としては，読んだ内容を書いてまとめる要約，聞いた内容に基づいて自分の意見を述べるディベートなどが挙げられる。　②　設問では留意点を箇条書きで2点書くことが求められている。解答例では再話における留意点として，用いる英文の観点から2点取り上げたが，他にも生徒への手助けや理解度の確認，活動の評価方法などの観点で留意点を書くことも可能である。　(2)　①　解答例ではto不定詞を定着させる活動を取り上げている。設問では具体的な文法事項を取り上げること，コミュニケーションの目的や場面，状況などを設定することが求められている。それぞれの観点ごとに簡潔にまとめるとよい。なお，コミュニケーションの目的は，自分・相手が知らない情報を交換する必然性を持たせることや，言語的なやり取りをする理由を明確にすることで明示できる。この目的のために，コミュニケーションの場面や状況(やり取りする相手は誰か，場所はどこか，時間は何時か)を具体的に設定するとよい。　②　解答例では，to不定詞にかかわる重要な指導事項をまとめている。文法事項の指導で留意する点を2点述べることが求められているため，設問①よりも，先にこちらの問題を軸に据えて解答するとよい。指導において留意するべきポイントの観点としては，既習事項との関係性や日本語を母語とする英語学習者が誤りやすい点などをまとめるとよい。

【4】(1)　イ　(2)　ウ　(3)　エ　(4)　ア　(5)　イ

〈解説〉選択肢の難易度が比較的高く，単語レベルでなくコロケーションレベルを心がけた語彙学習が重要となる。　(1)　recede from A to B

「AからBへと後退する」，redeem A「Aを補う，A (名誉など)を回復する」，retard A from B「AをBから遅らせる，妨げる」，revoke A「Aを無効にする，取り消す」。 (2) a detour「遠回り，寄り道」，a drawback「欠点，不利な点」，an itinerary「旅行計画」，a swarm「(昆虫や蜂などの)大群」。 (3) coherent「論理的な，結束した」，contentious「争い好きの，議論を呼び起こす」，contradictory「矛盾した，反対の」，cordial「心からの，友好的な」。 (4) confiscate A from B「AをBから没収する」，deceive A into doing「Aをだまして～させる」，proclaim A to be B「AがBであると宣言する」，tease A into doing「Aをからかって～させる」。 (5) fall flat「(冗談・話・演技が)相手にさっぱり通じない」，hit the roof「頭にくる，ひどく腹を立てる」，make ends meet「収支を合わせる」，turn over a new leaf「心機一転する」。

【5】(記号／正しい英語の順) a) (1) A／a piece of toast (2) D／assistance (3) D／enables

b) (1) 下線を引く部分…4文目のput on this 正しい英語…put this on (2) 下線を引く部分…2文目の I was stolen my bag 正しい英語…My bag was stolen／I had(got) my bag stolen

〈解説〉a) (1) toast「トースト」は不可算名詞であるため，「1枚のトースト」を表現する際にはa piece of toastもしくはa slice of toastを用いる。Bはrecommendが仮定法現在の用法であるため原形で適切。prepare A for B「AをBのめに準備する」，in a short time「短時間で」。 (2) 前置詞withoutの直後であるため，一見動名詞で適切なように思われるが，assistは他動詞であるため目的語が必要となる。この目的語は主語のweのことであるため，動名詞は不適切。名詞形のassistanceとすることでfrom your companyとつながる。 (3) 正答enablesの直前にあるandはenablesとkeepsをつないでいる。原形の場合，cool enough toのto不定詞と解釈されるが，夏に十分に涼しいためパネルが多くの日光を集めるという因果関係になってしまうため，不定詞としての解釈は不適切。b) (1) 句動詞put on A「Aを身につける」はAが一般名詞の場合には

put glasses on／put on glassesの両方が可能であるが，thoseやitのような代名詞の場合にはput A onの形に固定となる。　(2)　steal A「Aを盗む」の受動態は日本語と英語で異なる。類似のrob A of B「A(人)からB(もの)を奪う」の受動態はI was robbed of my bag by him.であるが，stealは目的語が「もの」であるため設問の形は不適切。解答例では目的語のmy bagを主語としたbe受動とIを主語としたhave受動の2種類が示されている。haveを使った受動態は日本語の間接受動態と似ており，被害を表すことが多い。日本語では「雨に降られる」,「深夜に隣人に騒がれる」のように，自動詞であっても被害の意味が含まれれば受動態となる。

【6】(解答例)　The key to success of an English language program in a Japanese school depends on effective communication and collaboration between you, the ALT, and me, the Japanese teacher. You can support me by leading small group activities, working with individual students, introducing your cultural backgrounds, and creating a supportive learning environment for our students. The goal is to help them improve their English skills and increase their confidence in using the language. Our collaboration and communication should be based on a shared commitment to the students' learning. I want you to share whatever in English classes with me. (98 words)

〈解説〉高校にやってきた当日のAssistant Language Teacher(ALT)に対して，Japanese Teacher of English(JTE)として何を伝えるかが問われている。解答例では，ALTとJTEのコミュニケーションや協力が重要であることを伝え，ALTが英語の授業中に担う役割の具体例を述べている。他に，JTEとのモデルコミュニケーションやリンキングをはじめとした発音の実践などについて言及してもよいだろう。

2022年度　実施問題

【中高共通】

【1】リスニングテスト

Part A

(1) Write your answer on your answer sheet.

(2) Write your answer on your answer sheet.

(3) Write your answer on your answer sheet.

(4) Write your answer on your answer sheet.

(5) Write your answer on your answer sheet.

(6) Write your answer on your answer sheet.

Part B

(1) (A) Hotel receptionist.
　(B) Construction worker.
　(C) Furniture sales staff.
　(D) Real estate agent.

(2) (A) He has a pain that won't go away.
　(B) He must carry a heavy bag.
　(C) He has troubles sending a message.
　(D) He has no time to take exercise.

(3) (A) The injection she's required to take.
　(B) The expense for the medical treatment.
　(C) The man's health condition.
　(D) The distance from home to the clinic.

(4) (A) Registering online on Monday.
　(B) Losing weight as a prerequisite.
　(C) Attending the orientation before registration.
　(D) Consulting the professor face to face.

Part C

(1)　Write your answer on your answer sheet.

(2)　Write your answer on your answer sheet.

Part D

(1)　うわべだけの自信や自分の優位性を動作で示そうとしても上手くいかない理由を書け。

(2)　否定的な仕草を相手に伝えないようにするために意識的に行うべきことを書け。

(☆☆☆◎◎◎)

【2】次の英文を読んで，(1)～(4)の設問に答えよ。

ILLNESS IS UNIVERSAL, HEALTH CARE IS NOT. OVER HALF OF the world's 7.3 billion people, including 1 billion in rural communities, lack access to health care. Approximately 13 million children still go without a single dose of any vaccine. Nearly 9 million newborns, children and mothers still die each year from preventable or treatable conditions.

Compounding (A)this crisis is a massive health-worker shortage, forecast to grow to 18 million by 2030. Training more doctors is necessary, but because doctors are concentrated in cities, they alone are insufficient to close (B)this gap. What if the residents of rural communities — even those without a high school degree — could become a vital part of our health care team?

I recently visited Ruth Tarr in an isolated community in Liberia, the country where I was born and have worked with my team at Last Mile Health for 12 years. In sixth grade, Ruth was forced to drop out of school because her parents could no longer (　C　) it. As an adult, she could not find work — until 2016, when she was hired as a community health worker. Over a few weeks, a nurse trained Ruth, equipped her with medicine and supplies — like a handheld test for malaria, antibiotics to treat pneumonia, and contraceptives — and gave her a smartphone with video lessons on topics like assessing a child for malnutrition. Ruth now serves the daily health needs of her neighbors. When a patient has a condition Ruth can't care for — like a patient we diagnosed with a damaged heart valve from rheumatic heart disease — she works with outreach nurses to refer her to a network of clinics and hospitals.

Community health workers save lives. A few years ago, when Ebola was spreading like wildfire across West Africa, community health workers teamed up with nurses to go door-to-door to bring patients into care. Later, Liberia's government created a national program to put a community health worker in every rural community. Those workers have now identified over 4,000 potential epidemic events, improved vaccination coverage and increased the rate of children receiving medical care by over 50%. Community health workers also (D) health care costs. One of every three children with malaria is now diagnosed and treated at home, avoiding expensive hospitalization. For every $1 a country invests in community health workers, $10 is returned to society.

LIBERIA IS NOT ALONE. In September, 15 countries made commitments to invest in community health workers. If this were scaled globally, 3 million deaths could be prevented each year. We've built an online academy through which anyone, anywhere, can learn to create similar programs in their own regions. Americans enrolled in the academy are sharing lessons from places like rural Alaska, where community health workers are caring for patients with diabetes, opioid addiction and dental cavities, who were previously out of reach.

But to realize this future of health for all, we must confront (E)<u>an injustice</u>. Though Ruth is an exception, most community health workers remain unpaid. A recent World Health Organization report found that the poorest women in the world subsidize health care with their unpaid work to the tune of $1 trillion — a figure that's larger than the economies of over 150 countries.

【出典　*TIME*, November 4, 2019】

(1)　下線部(A)の具体例を，3点日本語で書け。

(2)　下線部(B)を解消するために筆者が提案していることを，35字程度の日本語で書け。

(3)　空所(　C　)と(　D　)に入る最も適切な語を，次のア～オから一つずつ選んで，その記号を書け。

ア　afford　　イ　verify　　ウ　absorb　　エ　lower　　オ　boost

(4)　下線部(E)の具体的な内容を，20字程度の日本語で書け。

(☆☆☆☆◎◎◎◎◎)

【中学校】

【1】次の会話文を読んで，(1)～(5)の設問に答えよ。

英語圏のある国での予算会議の場面である。

A : 議長Ms. ホワイト　　B : 書記Mr. ターナー　　C : Ms. 井出

D : Mr. ニューマン

C : As for me, I believe the tourism budget should be diverted to education. As you know, I'm of Japanese descent. Last month I visited Japan for the first time in ten years. I was impressed with the (　①　) of Japan. I believe education made Japan a beautiful country.

D : [　Ⅰ　] The education budget should be increased from 15 to 30% and in turn the budget for tourism should be decreased by 15%. What I mean is that we should revise our budget plan. It's time we faced reality. Now, students take turns coming to school because there are not enough desks and chairs to go around.

A : <u>That</u>'s certainly a terrible situation. It's a disappointing reality that children are ordered to take turns going to school.

B : [　Ⅱ　]. There are too many roads which aren't paved. This is a problem, because after heavy rain puddles are left. This attracts mosquitoes which can be (　②　) to health.

A : [　Ⅲ　]. Please explain what you mean by that.

B : I mean, we should (　③　) more money to improving the present infrastructure which includes sewage and the roads, not only to attract more tourists but also to improve our life. We should increase our budget from 10 to 15%.

A : Oh, I see. That explains it well. Improving this infrastructure is related to the promotion of tourism.

D : I tend to agree with Mr. Turner's opinion. The key point is our budget is limited. The budget for education as well as infrastructure should be increased. My opinion is we shouldn't support (A) at the expense of (B).

【出典　柴山　かつの，『世界で戦う　伝わる英語ミーティング』，明日香出版社】

(1) (①)～(③)に入る最も適切な語を，次のア～カから一つずつ選び，その記号を書け。

ア beneficial　イ harmful　ウ instability　エ cleanliness
オ allocate　カ curtail

(2) [Ⅰ]～[Ⅲ]に入る最も適切なものを，次のア～エから一つずつ選び，その記号を書け。

ア I still think tourism is important
イ I agree with the first point Ms. Ide said
ウ I should take turns being the note taker
エ I'm sorry, but I can't understand that

(3) 下線部の内容を，具体的に日本語で書け。

(4) Ms. ホワイトはMr. ターナーの意見をどのようにまとめたか，簡潔に日本語で書け。

(5) 空所(A)と(B)に入る語句の最も適切な組み合わせを，次のア～ウから一つ選び，その記号を書け。

ア (A : the tourism industry　B : children's education)
イ (A : the infrastructure　B : the tourism industry)
ウ (A : children's education　B : the infrastructure)

(☆☆☆◎◎◎◎◎)

【２】次の英文を読んで，(1)～(5)の設問に答えよ。

Pragmatics is the study of how language is used in context to express such things as directness, politeness, and deference. Even if learners acquire a vocabulary of 5,000 words and a good knowledge of the syntax and morphology of the target language, they can still encounter (A)difficulty in using language. They also need to acquire skills for interpreting requests, responding politely to compliments or apologies, recognizing humour, and managing conversations. They need to learn to recognize the many meanings that the same sentence can have in different situations. Think of the many ways one might interpret an apparently simple question such as (B)'Is that your dog?' It might precede an expression of admiration for an attractive pet, or it might be an urgent request to get the dog out of the speaker's flowerbed. Similarly, the same basic meaning is (　C　) when it is expressed in different ways. For example, we would probably assume that the relationship between speaker and listener is very different if we hear 'Give me that book' or 'I wonder if you'd mind letting me have that book when you've finished with it'.

The study of how second language learners acquire this aspect of language is referred to as 'interlanguage pragmatics' (Bardovi-Harlig 1999). Some of this research has focused on the ways in which learners express speech acts such as inviting and apologizing in relation to differences in their proficiency level or their first language background. Other studies have examined learners' ability to perceive and comprehend pragmatic features in the second language and to judge whether a particular request is appropriate or inappropriate in a specific context.

Since the early 1990s more research has directly investigated the acquisition of second language pragmatic ability. This includes longitudinal and cross-sectional studies describing the acquisition of several different speech acts. One that has been the focus of considerable attention is 'requesting'. (D)Requests are an interesting pragmatic feature to examine because there are identifiable ways in which requests are made within particular languages as well as differences in how they are expressed across different languages and cultures.

In a review of longitudinal and cross-sectional studies on the acquisition of requests in English, Gabriele Kasper and Kenneth Rose (2002) outline a series of five stages of development. Stage 1 consists of minimal language that is often incomplete and highly context-dependent. Stage 2 includes primarily memorized routines and frequent use of imperatives. Stage 3 is marked by (E) use of formulas, (F) productive speech, and some mitigation of requests. Stage 4 involves more complex language and increased use of mitigation, especially supportive statements. Stage 5 is marked by more refinement of the force of requests.

【出典 Pasty M. Lightbown & Nina Spada, *How Languages are Learned*, OXFORD UNIVERSITY PRESS】

(1) 下線部(A)の克服のために，学習者に求められることを，2点日本語で書け。

(2) 下線部(B)について，例示されている二つの解釈を，日本語で書け。

(3) 空所(C)に入る最も適切な語を，次のア～エから一つ選び，その記号を書け。

ア altered　イ prohibited　ウ obtained　エ standardized

(4) 下線部(D)が，調査すべき興味深い語用論上の特性であると筆者が述べている理由を，60字程度の日本語で書け。

(5) 空所(E)と(F)に入る語の最も適切な組み合わせを，次のア～エから一つ選び，その記号を書け。

ア (E : less　F : less)　イ (E : less　F : more)

ウ (E : more　F : less)　エ (E : more　F : more)

(☆☆☆☆◎◎◎◎◎)

【3】(1)～(4)について，それぞれの英文の[　　]内に入る最も適切なものを，ア～エから一つずつ選び，その記号を書け。

(1)　In case of [　　] identity, security guard at the hotel detained the man for an hour.

ア　confused　　イ　invaded　　ウ　interrupted　　エ　mistaken

(2)　Your computer is broken. You must [　　].

ア　have it repair　　イ　have it to repair　　ウ　have it repaired

エ　have repaired it

(3)　These new hybrid vehicles [　　] 10% less energy than the old models.

ア　deliver　　イ　consume　　ウ　dissolve　　エ　induce

(4)　It's almost impossible to tell a man from a robot except [　　] several minutes' conversation.

ア　before　　イ　after　　ウ　for　　エ　but

(☆☆☆◎◎◎◎◎)

【4】(1)～(3)について，それぞれの日本語の内容を表すように，[　　]内の語句を並べかえよ。なお，文頭に来る語も小文字にしてある。(4)については，日本語の意味になるように英語で書け。

(1)　その家具の組み立てができないという方には，いつでも当社の専門家がお教えします。

[in / having / the furniture / anyone / difficulty / assembling] may have the advice of our experts.

(2)　警官たちは，窓が全て閉まっていることを確認した。

Police officers [were / themselves / that / all / the / satisfied / windows] secure.

(3)　その生徒たちは，先生が見たら驚くようなよい振る舞いを見せた。

The students showed [it / which / behavior / have / good / surprised / would] their teachers to see.

(4)　5年経てば，この町はもっと住みよい場所になるだろう。

(☆☆☆◎◎◎◎)

【5】授業において，昨夏に任期を終えて帰国したALTとオンラインで英語によるやり取りを行うことにした。次の状況を踏まえ，ALTに事前に伝えるメール文の内容を考えて，60語程度の英語で書け。ALTへの挨拶などの英文は省略するものとする。※語数を数えて記入すること。(符号は語数に含めない)

・教室とALTの自宅との間でオンラインで行う。 ・生徒は，最近の学校での出来事を伝えたり，ALTが帰国後にどのように過ごしているかなどについて質問したりしたいと考えている。

(☆☆☆☆◎◎◎◎)

【6】授業において，伝える内容及び必要な表現を生徒が主体的に考えてコミュニケーションに取り組めるようにするために，あなたはどのような工夫をするか。有効と思われる手立てを二つ挙げ，80語程度の英語で書け。※語数を数えて記入すること。(符号は語数に含めない)

(☆☆☆☆☆◎◎◎)

【高等学校】

【1】次の英文を読んで，(1)～(4)の設問に答えよ。

Learning to speak a second language may be similar to history since it certainly requires the memorization of lots of vocabulary. However, I think it may be more instructive to look at research on the learning of physics as a subject area more parallel to language learning. This is because researchers have found that students learning physics are often hampered by their previous knowledge, which is basically folk knowledge or naive preconceptions about the way forces in the world work. In the same way, students of language may be hampered (or helped) by their knowledge of how their own native language works, although in large part this will be knowledge that is procedural (done unconsciously). In other words, students of language already know how to speak their own native language — they know how to *do* their language, even if they are probably not able to describe grammar rules for their native language. Another parallel from language learning to physics is that students may perceive learning as memorizing a number of unrelated facts or formulas (like vocabulary and grammar rules) and not really put the whole thing together to understand how things around them work (or, in the case of a language, never really be able to speak to a speaker of that language).

Researchers studying how well students learn physics in high school and college courses have found that students' folk knowledge is quite resistant to change, and that often students do not seem to be able to apply physics laws and formulas to real-life examples. Here's an example from a case study by Chu, Treagust, and Chandrasegaran (2008). This study examined 10 students who were taking an introductory physics course. The researchers asked the students to answer questions about different physics applications of sound and wave motion to real-life situations before the semester-long course and after it. The participants had weekly interviews to determine what they were learning. The researchers found that only 2 out of the 10 students developed appropriate physics conceptions after the course. Here is an example of a student who continued to use $_{\text{(A)}}$<u>prior beliefs</u> even after the semester was over. The question posed was, "Is the time required to swing to and fro on a playground swing longer or shorter when you stand rather than sit?" (Chu, Treagust, & Chandrasegaran, 2008, 118). One participant's answer before instruction was, "If we stand up and are moving against air resistance, it will take longer" (p.119). Here is her answer after the end of the semester: "When I was a child, if I was standing on the swing it went faster, as I remember" (p.120).

Why explore how well students learn history and physics? This is because of the suspicion that many students feel they have learned a lot in most of their content courses but very (　B　) in their language courses. Because they cannot speak a foreign language, even one that they have studied for years in high school or college, students may think that language learning is much (C) difficult (or poorly taught) than other subjects. But when we look at actual learning outcomes in subjects like physics, which require students to overcome their tendency to transfer their previous knowledge and learn things that may go counter to what they think they know and also to bring together seemingly disparate formulas and apply them to real-world events, students have not been found to be very successful at this after one college course. Similarily, in learning a language, students must overcome their unconscious tendency to transfer their knowledge of how their native language works and also bring together a number of disparate areas such as vocabulary, grammar rules, pronunciation, and pragmatics in order to successfully speak a language. It may be no wonder that (D)<u>so few students feel they succeed at this task.</u>

【出典　Steven Brown, Jenifer Larson-Hall, Second Language Acquisition Myths】

(1) 物理学の学習と言語の学習が類似している理由について，筆者はどう述べているか。第一段落から2点日本語で書け。

(2) 下線部(A)について，高校や大学で学生が物理学をどの程度習得しているかを調査している研究者はどのようなものであると捉えているか。日本語で書け。

(3) 空所(B)と(C)に入る最も適切な語を，次のア～エから一つずつ選び，その記号を書け。

ア less　イ more　ウ many　エ little

(4) 下線部(D)について，言語を学ぶ際には具体的にどのようなことをする必要があると筆者は述べているか。日本語で書け。

(☆☆☆☆◎◎◎◎◎)

【2】次の英文を読んで，(1)～(5)の設問に答えよ。

Coaching conversations

Coaching takes place primarily through the medium of conversation. In essence, the role of a coach is to create a conversational space in which the coachee can reflect on aspects of their professional and/or personal life or situation with a view to solve problems, explore and resolve dilemmas, attain greater clarity, develop insights, achieve greater emotional wellbeing, and/or move towards desired goals. Sir John Whitmore, one of the worldwide leaders in the emergence and development of workplace coaching, suggests that two of the primary aims of coaching conversations are to raise awareness and to develop responsibility (Whitmore, [1992] 2002).

Raising awareness

Awareness has two components: the coachee's awareness of what is happening in their surrounding context, and their self-awareness of what they are experiencing internally. A key function of the coach is to facilitate the coachee's exploration of their situation so that it enhances the clarity of their perception, enables them to determine what is relevant, and increases their degree of self-awareness with regard to their own emotions, desires and interpretations.

Developing responsibility

Similarly, there are a number of components to responsibility. First, the coach is careful to ensure that $_{(A)}$<u>the coachee retains ownership of the problem or situation</u> — that is, the coach does not take the monkey from the person's back by assuming responsibility, taking the load, and trying to solve the problem for them. Instead, the emphasis is on creating a space in which the person can talk through their situation with the coach acting as a sounding board rather than an expert fixer. Throughout the conversation, the coach works with the coachee in such a way so as to support the person in maintaining focus on those aspects of their internal or external situation that they can control or influence. Finally, the coach works to ensure that the coachee retains ownership of any actions they do or do not decide to take as a result of the conversation. *Choice* is paramount, and the coach respects the person's right to determine the path they would like to take. This is important for strengthening commitment to any actions undertaken, while also recognizing that the coachee retains responsibility for any consequences — positive or otherwise — which occur as a result of their actions. It is the person who must continue to live with their situation once the coaching conversation or engagement has ended, and we must never $_{(B)}$(l　　) sight of that.

If these are the aims of a coaching conversation, the question then becomes: how are those aims achieved? What (　C　) can a coach use to facilitate the coaching conversation towards those outcomes? There are a number of core tools that the coach can draw upon, but before exploring the detail of those, it is first important to capture something of the broader essence and (　D　) of coaching. These crucial principles are more about the manner in which the coach approaches the engagement and the beliefs they have about people than they are about the exercise of any specific technique.

【出典　Mark Adams, *COACHING PHYCHOLOGY in SCHOOLS,* Routledge】

(1) コーチングする人の重要な役割として，コーチングを受ける人の状況を自らが振り返るように促すことが挙げられている。その効果として本文に挙げられていることを日本語で書け。

(2) 下線部(A)について，コーチングする人がしないこととして筆者が述べていることを，具体的に日本語で書け。

(3) コーチングを受ける人が行動に対する関わりを強めるために，コーチングする人が尊重するべきものは何か。日本語で書け。

(4) 空所(　B　)に入る英単語一語を書け。ただし解答は(　　)内で示されている文字で書き始めること。

(5) 空所(　C　)，(　D　)に入る英単語の組み合わせとして正しいものを，次のア～カから一つ選び，その記号を書け。

ア　C: aims　D: skills　　イ　C: aims　D: spirit
ウ　C: skills　D: aims　　エ　C: skills　D: spirit
オ　C: spirit　D: aims　　カ　C: spirit　D: skills

(☆☆☆☆◎◎◎◎◎)

【３】次の(1)，(2)について，日本語で答えよ。

(1)　高等学校学習指導要領外国語編には，「授業は英語で行うことを基本とする」とある。この観点において，①授業で教師が用いる英語について留意すべき点を説明せよ。また，授業において②録音された音声や録画された映像を使用してまとまりのある内容を聞き，必要な情報や話し手の意図を把握する活動を行う場合に教師が配慮すべき点について具体的に箇条書きで答えよ。

(2)「生徒の豊富な英語使用を促し，英語による言語活動を行うことを授業の中心とする」ことを踏まえ，英語の授業において，あるテーマについてグループで意見をまとめ，英語で発表する活動を取り入れる際に留意すべき点について具体的に箇条書きで答えよ。

(☆☆☆☆☆◎◎◎◎)

【４】次の(1)～(5)の(　　)に当てはまる最も適切なものを，それぞれア～エから一つ選び，その記号を書け。

(1)　His house was built on a weak ground, making it (　　) to earthquakes.

ア　tangible　　イ　negligible　　ウ　vulnerable　　エ　plausible

(2)　Seeing a cat pop out of the bush, the driver hit the brakes and brought his car to a screeching (　　).

ア　jerk　　イ　jolt　　ウ　tilt　　エ　halt

(3)　Following the president's death, some executives began (　　) for the vacant post.

ア　atoning　　イ　rooting　　ウ　surging　　エ　vying

(4)　Something unexpected could upset our plans at any time. So we must be ready to (　　).

ア hit the spot　イ play it by ear　ウ do the trick

エ take it for granted

(5) On the morning of the first day, his car had an electrical problem. But during the rest of the day, there were no other happenings to (　　) the peace of his journey.

ア mar　イ extol　ウ rig　エ begrudge

(☆☆☆☆◎◎◎◎◎)

【5】a) 次の(1)～(3)の各英文には，それぞれ文法的な誤りが1か所ある。その部分の記号を書き，正しい英語に直せ。

(1) The expense deterred him $_{A}$to fly to Australia during the winter vacation. Not only were the flights $_{B}$expensive, but when $_{C}$accommodation costs and food were added, the whole thing $_{D}$was simply out of the question.

(2) $_{A}$Despite the bad weather, the festival, which $_{B}$concluding with remarks by the mayor, $_{C}$has been deemed a great $_{D}$success by the executive committee.

(3) The meeting scheduled $_{A}$on May 27 $_{B}$has been rescheduled to May 25. Remember $_{C}$to email meeting documents to the general affairs section at least three days $_{D}$in advance.

b) 次の(1)，(2)は，以下のタイトルで生徒が書いた英文であるが，それぞれ文法的な誤りが1か所ある。その部分に下線を引いて指摘し，下線の下に正しい英語を書け。ただし，タイトルは訂正しないこと。

(1) Title: My dog

I have a dog. She is so lovely and I sleep with her every night. One day, she ran away from my house. I searched her for three hours in my town but I couldn't find her. Next morning, I woke up with the barking of a dog. She came back home. I was relieved to see her.

(2) Title: Homestay

I had a homestay in Australia for two weeks during the summer vacation. I was worried at first, but everyone in my host family was kind and I had a great time. The next time I will go abroad, I will be a good speaker of English.

(☆☆☆◎◎◎◎)

【6】次の質問に，100語程度の英語で答えよ。

Suppose you are teaching in a high school. One day one of your students came to you and said, "I don't understand why I have to study English in high school. I don't think I'm going abroad in the future. I will not go to university or college. I don't need to study English." How do you encourage this student to study English?

(☆☆☆☆☆◎◎◎)

解答・解説

【中高共通】

【1】Part A　(1)　B　(2)　A　(3)　B　(4)　C　(5)　A　(6)　B　Part B　(1)　D　(2)　A　(3)　C　(4)　D

Part C　(1)　(I should) show my room key to the restaurant staff.

(2)　(I should) cooperate in conserving water.　Part D　(1)　解答略

(2)　解答略

〈解説〉スクリプトは非公開である。　Part A　英文も質問文も選択肢も文字情報はなく，すべて聞き取らなければならないので，集中力を要する。質問文が5W1Hで始まる疑問文なのか，Yes-Noで答える疑問文なのか，orを用いた選択疑問文なのか，Would you…?やMay I…?などの助動詞を用いた，依頼や許可などの疑問文なのかをしっかり捉えることが大切である。　Part B　選択肢は問題用紙に印刷されている。放送前に目を通しておくと，どんなことを問われるのか想像がつく。

その際，選択肢の主語はだれ(なに)と，動詞の時制をしっかり把握しておこう。 Part C Part Aと同様に，文字情報はない。質問文の形式をしっかりとらえ，それに応じた答えを書く。その際，主語を代名詞で置き換え，また，動詞の時制や主語と動詞の一致に気をつけよう。Part D 質問文に事前に目を通し，その答えを探すように英文を聞く。一語一語をすべて聞き取ろうとせず，どんな内容なのか大まかにとらえ，聞き取れないところは推測しながら，自分で大筋を組み立てる。採点の主な観点として，(1)では「全てを抑制できるとは限らない」等，(2)では「受容的姿勢を保つ」,「理解しようとする」等のキーフレーズが挙げられている。キーフレーズを踏まえた解答を心掛けたい。

【2】(1) (解答例) ・農村部の10億人を含む，世界の人口73億人のうち半数以上が，医療を受けられない。 ・約1,300万人の子どもたちが，いまだに1度もワクチンを接種していない。 ・毎年900万人近くの新生児や子どもや母親が，予防や治療可能な疾患で亡くなっている。
(2) (解答例) 農村地域の住民，それも高卒でない人たちが，医療チームの重要な一員になること。(38字) (3) C ア D エ
(4) (解答例) ほとんどの地域医療従事者は無給のままであること。(24字)

〈解説〉(1) 下線部のthisは，すぐ前に出てきた事柄を受けている。医療を受けられないこと，ワクチンを接種していないこと，予防可能な疾患で亡くなる人がいることが危機の内容なので，数字などを挙げて具体的に書く。 (2) 直後に，What if…「もし…としたらどうなるだろうか」と仮定の話をしながら提案をしている。 (3) C 空所を含む文は「ルースは第6学年のとき，学校を退学させられた。なぜなら両親はもはや(　　　)できなかったから」という意味なので，(学費を)支払う余裕がなかったと考える。can no longer afford…は「もはや…の余裕がない」。 D 空所を含む文の後に「マラリアにかかっている子どもの3人に1人は，自宅で診断・治療を受けており，高額な入院を回避している。国が地域医療従事者に1ドル投資するごとに，10ドルが社

会に還元される」と，地域医療従事者がいると費用が少なくて済むとあることから判断する。　(4)　injusticeは「不当な行為」という意味。下線部(E)以下にルースは例外だが，ほかの地域医療従事者はunpaidだとある。

【中学校】

【1】(1)　①　エ　②　イ　③　オ　(2)　Ⅰ　イ　Ⅱ　ア　Ⅲ　エ　(3)　(解答例)　机と椅子が足りないので，生徒が交替で登校していること　(4)　(解答例)　インフラを整備することが，観光事業の促進につながる。

(5)　ア

〈解説〉(1)　①　空所を含む文は，「日本の(　　)に感心しました」となる。直後に感心した理由として「教育が日本を美しい国にしたのだと思います」と続くので，美しい国のもととなる「清潔さ」に感心したと考える。　(2)　Ⅰ　空所の後に，「教育予算を15%から30%に増やし，その分，観光予算を15%減らせばいい」とあり，Ms. 井出が最初に言った「観光予算を教育に回すべきだと思っています」を，数字を挙げて詳しく述べていることから判断できる。　Ⅱ　空所の直後に「舗装されていない道路が多すぎる」とあり，Mr. ターナーの2つ目の発言で，その理由として「下水道や道路など，現在のインフラを改善するためにもっとお金を割くべきで，観光客を増やすだけでなく，私たちの生活を向上させるためにも必要だということです。」と，観光客を増やすことを述べていて，観光業が大切だと考えている。　Ⅲ　空所の直前にあるMr. ターナーの「大雨が降ると水たまりができて，蚊が寄ってきて，健康に害を及ぼします」という発言を受けて，Ms. ホワイトは「(　　)。どういう意味か説明してください」とあるので，理解できないので説明してくださいという流れだと判断する。

(3)　ひどい状況とはMr. ニューマンの発言にある「今は机と椅子が足りないので，生徒が交替で登校しています」を指している。go around「(量が)みなに行き渡る」。　(4)　Mr. ターナーの意見とはMr. ターナーの2つ目の発言の「つまり，下水道や道路など，現在のインフラを改善するためにもっとお金を割くべきで，観光客を増やすだけでなく，私たちの生活を向上させるためにも必要だということです」にあたるので，これを簡潔に書く。　(5)　最初にMs. 井出が,「観光予算を教育に回すべきだと思っています」と提案し，それに対し，Mr. ターナーは「観光事業は大切だ」と反対している。Mr. ニューマンの最後の発言で「どちらかと言えばMr. ターナーの(観光事業の予算を増やす)意見に同意します」としているが，予算に限りがあり，インフラだけでなく教育の予算も増やすべきだと述べている。最後に「私の意見は，(　　)を犠牲にしてまで，(　　)を支援すべきではないということです」と，まとめていることから判断する。

【2】(1)　(解答例)　依頼の解釈，褒め言葉や謝罪への丁寧な応答，ユーモアの認識，会話の管理などのスキルも身につけることと，同じ文章でも状況によって様々な意味があることを認識すること。

(2)　(解答例)　魅力的なペットに対する褒め言葉の前置きと，話し手の花壇から犬を追い出すようにという緊急の要求。　(3)　ア

(4)　(解答例)　特定の言語の中で依頼をするには特定の方法があり，異なる言語や文化間では表現方法が異なるため。(46字)　(5)　イ

〈解説〉(1)　下線部(A)の後に，言葉を使うことの難しさに直面する学習者に必要なことが，They also need to acquire…とThey need to learn to recognize…の文で2点述べられている。　(2)「あれはあなたの犬ですか」と簡単な質問をされたときに，状況次第で称賛なのか非難なのか解釈が分かれると考える。　(3)　空所を含む文は「同じように，同じ基本的な意味でも，表現方法が異なれば，その意味は(　　)」という意味。その後に例えとして「『その本をちょうだい』と言う場合と，『その本を読み終えたら，私に譲っていただけませんでしょうか』と言う場合では，話し手と聞き手の関係が大きく異なると考えることができるだろう」とあるので,「その意味は変わる」と考える。

(4)　下線部を含む文の後半のbecause以降に，調査すべき興味深い語用

論上の特性である理由が述べられている。　(5)　最後の段落は依頼表現の習得に関する発達段階を示している。「第2段階は，主に暗記された決まり切った表現と，頻繁に使われる命令形が含まれる。第3段階は，その定型文(＝決まり切った表現)の使用が(減り)，実りのある発話が(増え)，依頼表現がある程度和らげられることが特徴である」と考える。mitigation of requests「依頼の緩和」とは，依頼の表現がぶしつけではなく，洗練されてくることを指す。

【3】(1)　エ　　(2)　ウ　　(3)　イ　　(4)　イ

〈解説〉(1)　問題文は「(　　)ということで，ホテルの警備員が1時間ほど男性を拘束した」という意味。「誤った身元＝人違い」だと考える。(2)　問題文は「あなたのパソコンが故障している。修理してもらわなければならない」という意味の文を作る。故障したパソコンは修理屋で修理してもらうと考え，使役動詞のhaveを使い，you must have the repairperson repair it.を受け身にして，You must have it repaired (by the repairperson).とする。　(3)　問題文は「この新しいハイブリッド車は，旧モデルに比べて電力を10%少なく(　　)」という意味なので，10%少なく「消費する」と考える。　(4)　問題文は「数分間会話(　　)以外に，人間とロボットを見分けるのはほとんど不可能である」となる。数分間会話したあとに，人間かロボットかを見分けると考える。

【4】(1)　Anyone having difficulty in assembling the furniture
(2)　satisfied themselves that all the windows were　(3)　good behavior which it would have surprised　(4)　This town will be a better place to live in in five years.

〈解説〉(1)「その家具を組み立てることが困難な人は誰でも～」と考える。having difficulty in assembling…は「…を組み立てることが困難である」がanyoneを後ろから修飾して，問題文の主語を構成している。
(2)　satisfy oneself that「～を確かめる，見極める」という意味。secureは「しっかり固定した，動かない」という意味の形容詞。　(3)　問題文は，The students showed good behavior.とIt would have surprised their teachers to see good behavior.のgood behaviorをwhichの先行詞にした文。2つ目の文は，itが形式主語で，to see good behaviorが真主語になる「よい振る舞いを見ることは先生たちを驚かせただろう」という意味。(4)「5年後には，この町は今よりももっと住みよい場所になるだろう」と考え，a better placeやa more comfortable placeなどにする。現在を起点にして「～後に」はinで表す。a better place to live inとin five yearsとなるので，inは2つ必要。

【5】(解答例)　We would like you to conduct a class in English online, between you at home and our students in the classroom. The class should be as interactive as possible. Students will tell you about their recent school life. Then, you can ask them any questions you have about them. They will also ask you questions how you are spending your time back home, etc. Please tell them how your life is. (71 words)

〈解説〉まず，「だれ」が「だれ」に「どこ」で「どんな授業」をしてほしいのかを述べ，そのあとで，その授業で何を行うのか2点述べる。「やり取り」の授業であるので，解答例では，なるべく双方向性を目指し，生徒からの近況報告を聞いて質問したり，生徒からALTについての質問に答えたりすることを挙げている。

【6】(解答例)　I think we teachers should give students practical and useful class activities referring to their daily life. Therefore, we will set up situations that can be found in real life and society, such as giving directions role play activity, so that students can imagine specific situations and feel the need to speak in English. In addition, we will create situations where students can improvise and convey their opinions, thoughts, and information to others by introducing debate and discussion on students' favorite topics. (82 words)

〈解説〉解答例では，生徒の日常生活に即した実践的な教室活動を行うことを挙げている。例えば，道案内のロールプレイのように，英語を話さなければならない実際的な場面を設定したり，生徒の好きなトピックでディベートやディスカッションを行うことで自分の意見や考え，情報を即興で相手に伝えられるような状況を作ったりすることが考えられる。

【高等学校】

【1】(1)　(解答例)・ともに既存の知識が学びの妨げになるから。・ともに大量の公式や規則の暗記が学習だと思い込み，全体をまとめて理解しないから。　(2)　(解答例)　学生の既存の知識は根強く，変化させることが困難で，物理の法則や公式を実例に適用することができないように見える。　(3)　B　エ　C　イ　(4)　(解答例)　学生は，無意識のうちに母国語の仕組みを知識として転移する傾向を克服しなければならないし，語彙，文法規則，発音，語用論など多くの異なる分野をつなぎ合わせて，うまく言語を話せるようにしなければならない。

〈解説〉(1)　第1段落3文目に「これ(＝より言語の学習に類似している分野として，物理学の学習に関する研究を見てみること)はなぜなら～」とあり，because以降に1つ目の類似している理由が述べられている。また，6文目に「もう1つの言語の学習の物理学との類似点は～」とあり，that以降に2つ目の類似している理由が述べられている。　(2)　第2段落の1文目に「高校や大学の授業で学生がどの程度物理を学んでいるかを研究している研究者は～」とあり，that以下にprior beliefsの説明が述べられている。　(3)　(B)と(C)を含む文章は，多くの学生が歴史や物理などのcontent courseで多くを学んだと感じているのに，language courseではほとんど学んでいないという疑念を抱いていること，そして高校や大学で何年も勉強した外国語であっても話すことができないため，学生は言語の学習がほかの科目よりもずっと難しいと思っているかもしれない，と述べられている。　(4)　(D)を含む文の直前の文のstudents must…以下に，学生がしなければならない数多くのことが述べられている。

【2】(1)　(解答例)　コーチングを受ける人の意識を高めることと，責任感を育むこと。　(2)　(解答例)　責任を負ったり，負担を負ったり，問題を解決しようとしたりしない。　(3)　(解答例)　コーチングを受ける人が進みたい道を決める権利を尊重する。　(4)　lose
(5)　エ

〈解説〉(1)　第1段落の3文目の後半に，「コーチングの会話の主要な目的の2つは意識を高めること，および責任感を育むことである」とある。コーチングを受ければ，目的としているこの2つの効果があると考える。　(2)　下線部は「コーチングする人は，コーチングを受ける人が問題や状況のオーナーシップを保てる(＝問題や状況を我が事として引き受ける)ように注意する」という意味。直後に「コーチングする人は，責任を負ったり負担を負ったり問題を解決したりすることで，その人の困りごとを取り除いたりはしない」と，コーチングする人が「しないこと」が述べられている。monkeyは「解決が難しい，厄介な問題」のこと。　(3)　第3段落の7文目に，「これは，実行する行動に対する関わりを強めるために重要であり，～」とあり，「これ」とは直前のコーチングをする人に関する記述を指す。　(4)　空所を含む文は「コーチングの会話や関わりが終わった後も，自分の状況と共に生き続けなければならないのはその人自身(＝コーチングを受ける人)であり，私たち(＝コーチングをする人)はそのことを決して(　　)ならない」という意味。コーチングを受ける人は自分の問題や状況を認識し，それと共に責任をもって生きていき，コーチングをする人は，その人を最後まで見失わずに見守ると考える。lose sight of…で「…を見失う」という意味。　(5)　空所を含む文章は「もし，これがコーチングの会話の目的であるならば，問題はどのようにしてその目的を達成するかということになる。コーチングをする人はどのような(　　)を駆使して，そのような成果に向けてコーチングの会話を促進できるのだろうか？コーチングをする人が活用できる核となるツールがいくつかあるが，それらのツールの詳細を探る前に，まず，コーチングの広範な本質と(　　)について何か捉えることが重要である」という意味。Cはコーチングの会話を促進して，成果を上げるためにコーチングをする人が使うものは何かを考える。Dは，ツールの詳細を探る前に，コーチングの「本質」といっしょに何を捉えることが重要なのかを考える。

【3】(1)　(解答例)　①　生徒の理解の程度に応じて発話の速度や明瞭さを調整したり，使う語句や文を平易に言い換えたり，繰り返したり，具体例を提示したりする。また，一度にたくさんの情報を伝えるのではなく分けて伝えたりする。　②　・写真や実物を活用して，生徒が聞く内容を推測できるようにする。　・聞き取る内容と関連のある話をする。　・聞き取る上でのキーワードや表現を生徒に提示する。　(2)　(解答例)・実際の発表などの豊富な例を生徒に示す。・使用する表現や話の構成，論理の展開などを学ばせる。　・生徒が考えを整理するための時間を設定する。　・発表する内容をまとめたメモなどを活用する。　・発表の際に写真や映像，実物などの視覚的補助を活用する。

〈解説〉(1)　①　高等学校学習指導要領(平成30年3月告示)の第3款「英語に関する各科目にわたる指導計画の作成と内容の取り扱い」の項に，「生徒が英語に触れる機会を充実させるとともに，授業を実際のコミュニケーションの場面とするため，授業は英語で行うことを基本とする。その際，生徒の理解の程度に応じた英語を用いるようにすること」と示されている。これを受けて，同解説外国語編・英語編では「生徒が積極的に英語を使って取り組めるよう，まず教師自身がコミュニケーションの手段として英語を使う姿勢と態度を行動で示していくことが重要である」こと，また「教師の英語使用に当たり，挨拶や指示を英語で伝える教室英語を使用するだけではなく，説明や発問，課題の提示などを生徒の分かる英語で話し掛けることから始め，徐々に新出の語彙なども入れていくような段階を踏みながら，授業全体が実際のコミュニケーションの場となるようにすることが必要である」と説明している。　②「必要な情報を聞き取り，話し手の意図を把握する」とは，「英語コミュニケーション」における「聞くこと」の目標の一部である。高等学校学習指導要領解説外国語編・英語編では，本項について「必要な情報とは，話し手の意図を把握するために必要となる情報を意味している。したがって，本科目では全てを網羅的に聞き取ろうとするのではなく，必要な情報に焦点を絞って理解した上で，そこから話し手が全体として何を伝えようとしているのかを把握することができるようにすることが求められる」と説明しており，「事実と意見などを区別し，整理しながら聞くようにあらかじめ生徒に伝えたり，聞き取るべきポイントを事前に明示しておいたりすることが考えられる」としている。 (2) 課題文中の「グループで意見をまとめ，英語で発表する」から，「話すこと[やり取り]」と「話すこと[発表]」を組み合わせた言語活動であると考えられる。「話すこと[やり取り]」などの活動においては，扱う話題によっては事前に関連する情報を十分に与えたり，必要となる表現や文などを提示したりすることが必要であるが，できるだけメモなどによって話すことに慣れ，事前に書いた原稿を読むことに終始するやり取りにならないようにすることが重要である。また「話すこと[発表]」では，生徒が実際に発表する前に，教師やALTによる実際の発表や，録音及び録画された発表などの豊富なモデルを示しながら，使用する表現や話の構成，論理の展開などを学ぶことができるようにすることが大切である。

【4】(1) ウ　(2) エ　(3) エ　(4) イ　(5) ア

〈解説〉(1) 問題文は「彼の家は地盤が弱い場所に立っていて，地震に対して(　　)」という意味。地盤が弱いので，地震に弱いと考え，vulnerable「脆弱な」となる。 (2) 問題文は「茂みから猫が飛び出してきたのを見て，運転手はブレーキを踏み，車を(　　)」という意味。bring…to a screeching haltで「…を急停止させる」という意味。
(3) 問題文は「社長の死後，何人かの幹部が空席のポストを(　　)始めた」という意味。社長のポストを巡って幹部が争ったと考える。
(4) 問題文は「いつ予期せぬ事態が起こるかわからない。だから，(　　)対応できるようにしておかなければならない」という意味。予期せぬことに対して，その場で対応する準備をしておくと考える。play it by earは「臨機応変に対応する」という意味。　(5)　問題文は「初日の朝，彼の車に電気系統のトラブルが発生した。しかし，それ以外の時間は，彼の旅の平穏を(　　)出来事はなかった」という意味。朝のトラブル以外は平穏を妨げる出来事はなかったと考える。

【5】a)　(1)　記号…A　　正しい英語…from flying　　(2)　記号…B　正しい英語…concluded　　(3)　記号…A　正しい英語…for

b)　(1)　searched→searched for　　(2)　will go→go

〈解説〉a)　(1)　deter…from doingで，「…が～するのを妨げる」という意味になる。　(2)　the festival has been deemed…committeeとthe festival concluded with remarks by the mayorの2つの文が，the festivalを先行詞として関係代名詞のwhichを用いて1つになった文。

(3)　scheduled for…で「…に予定されて」という意味になる。

b)　(1)　4文目にあるsearchは，search…(場所) for～(物)で「～(物)を求めて…(場所)を探す」という意味になる。　(2)　3文目にあるwill goは，the next timeを接続詞とする時を表す副詞節の中にあるので，未来のことは現在時制で表す。

【6】(解答例)　I would like to motivate the student to communicate with non-Japanese people by arranging cultural exchange classes. If he becomes to be interested in different people, cultures and countries, we will be able to foster his eagerness for global communication. Although he may think that he is not going abroad, nor does he go to university, he lives in a global society in which English is spoken as the common language. Even if English learning seems disconnected to his life at this stage, I will show him that English can be one of the most powerful tools to open up his future possibility. (103 words)

〈解説〉将来海外にも行かないし大学にも進学しないから英語を学ぶ必要がない，と言う生徒に対し，どのように英語学習を促すかが問われている。解答例では，外国人との文化交流授業を設定して，その生徒に国際コミュニケーションに対する興味を起こさせることを挙げ，現段階で英語は必要ないと感じていても，英語は自分の将来を拓く強力なツールであることを教えたいと述べている。ほかに，バイリンガルのほうが問題解決能力，創造力，記憶力などが優れていると言われていることを取り上げ，英語学習によって多角的な視野が身に付くことなどに言及するのもよいだろう。

2021年度　実施問題

【中高共通】

【１】リスニングテスト

Part A

(1) Write your answer on your answer sheet.

(2) Write your answer on your answer sheet.

(3) Write your answer on your answer sheet.

(4) Write your answer on your answer sheet.

(5) Write your answer on your answer sheet.

(6) Write your answer on your answer sheet.

Part B

(1) (A) He'd like full board.
(B) He'd like lunch served.
(C) He'd like half board.
(D) He'd like to play a board game.

(2) (A) Pay with a credit card.
(B) Review a list of available products.
(C) Find a receipt that was misplaced.
(D) Offer a 15% discount.

(3) (A) She encourages Professor Brown to talk with the man.
(B) She is convinced that Professor Brown will give the man a good suggestion.
(C) She wants the man to help her a lot.
(D) She needs to deliver a presentation today.

(4) (A) The booking system doesn't work.
(B) The cost of rooms remains consistent.
(C) Many people have canceled in recent days.

(D) The hotel is very popular in July.

Part C

(1) Write your answer on your answer sheet.

I should (　　).

(2) Write your answer on your answer sheet.

I should (　　).

Part D

(1) コンビニエンスストアのオーナーが，最近直面している二つの主な仕事上の問題は何か。

(2) 新たなポイントカードシステムを進める上で，オーナーの負担がないのはなぜか。

(☆☆☆◎◎◎)

【2】次の文章を読んで，(1)～(5)の設問に答えよ。

If an effective international agreement to curb climate change were not a tough enough nut to crack, consider the scale of (A)the challenge facing the United Nations Convention on Biological Diversity (CBD): to protect the biological, ecological and genetic diversity that sustains all life on Earth. Progress has been slow to non-existent. Governments are meant to turn this around at a summit in Kunming, China, in October 2020.

The CBD was one of a trio of conventions to come out of the Rio Earth Summit in 1992, along with the UN Framework Convention on Climate Change and the UN Convention to Combat Desertification. Together, these were intended to support a comprehensive strategy for sustainable development.

The climate element has taken centre stage in recent years, but to ecologists biodiversity is no less critical. Humans rely on there being a diversity of plants and animals in order to feed themselves. Indirectly, this biodiversity is also a key contributor to health, through medicines which are often inspired by molecules found in nature, and other basic needs such as clean water.

Ocean bivalves, for instance, help clean up toxic spills, and even tiny ocean plankton help form rain-bearing clouds. Yet modern civilisation is impinging on virtually every ecosystem.

In 2010, after nearly two decades of discussions among the 196 countries that are party to the CBD, 20 conservation targets were adopted: the Aichi targets, named after the Japanese prefecture where they were finalised. They were ambitious, to put it mildly. The text reads like a wish-list for a perfect future in which every human is aware of the value of biodiversity, every government has integrated this into its policies, nefarious subsidies are eliminated, all fishing is sustainable and pollution is under control. The delivery date for (B)this Utopia was 2020.

Unsurprisingly, an intergovernmental report on biodiversity published early in 2019 found that progress on the Aichi targets was poor. Indeed, overall, species are accelerating towards extinction.

Despite the bleak landscape, conservationists are (　C　) that 2020 could mark a new beginning. They are calling for a "Paris-like moment for biodiversity", in reference to the Paris agreement in 2015 on climate change. In Kunming, they hope, all 196 parties will adopt a new and more realistic framework to protect biodiversity.

Already, there is an awareness that any new targets must be more quantitative and preferably achievable. They may include a key number, which would through its symbolism and simplicity mimic the 1.5°−2℃ target for limiting the impacts of climate change and would, with luck, result in a similar (D)worldwide buy-in. The concept of "bending the curve" may help frame such a number: there are calls to halt the loss of biodiversity by 2030 in order to shift the focus towards restoration by 2050. How exactly to define and quantify that loss under the new framework — whether as a number of species, or some measure of ecosystem or genetic health — is still an open question.

The bigger issue is how to integrate the talks about biodiversity with those on climate, desertification, forests, wetlands and trade in endangered species. A month after governments meet in Kunming to discuss biodiversity they will reassemble in Glasgow for the next round of UN climate talks. That the degradation of ecosystems is responsible for 23% of global emissions suggests it would be more productive to bring (E)<u>these two sets of discussions</u>, at a minimum, under one roof.

【出典　*The Economist, The World in 2020*, December 30 2019 https://www.economist.com】

(1)　下線部(A)の具体的な内容を，40字程度の日本語で書け。

(2)　下線部(B)の具体的な内容を，75字程度の日本語で書け。

(3)　空所(　C　)に入る最も適切な語句を，次のア～エから一つ選び，その記号を書け。

ア　optimistic　　イ　pessimistic　　ウ　altruistic　　エ　egoistic

(4)　下線部(D)と同じ内容を表す語句を，本文から抜き出して書け。

(5)　下線部(E)の具体的内容を，75字程度の日本語で書け。

(☆☆☆☆◎◎◎◎◎)

【中学校】

【1】次のBarbara Vincent (BV)とFumio Toyama (FT)の会話文を読んで，(1)～(5)の設問に答えよ。

Barbara Vincent is discussing job evaluations with Fumio Toyama, the head of the company's *HR department.

BV : I've just been going through the company documentation on the procedures for job evaluations. I think I'd like to (　①　) some changes.

FT : Sure. Did you have anything specific in mind?

BV : Well, I agree with most of the categories here. For example, effective and continually improving communication skills are vital, especially in an international company like ours.

FT : Yes, I totally agree that this category should carry a lot of weight. That's one of the reasons that we provide free in-house English classes and also subsidize employees to take outside classes.

BV : Yes, that makes a lot of sense. Also, time management is an important category. However, I'd like to see less emphasis on spending long hours in the office. I think it's the mark of an efficient worker to get his or her work done in good time. I think we should maybe try using the job evaluation to encourage a better work-life balance.

FT : OK, but I think that may be a hard habit to (②), especially among the older workers.

BV : I'm also of the opinion that we should encourage employees to be good team players. But I would really like to see assertiveness and personal initiative play a part in the overall evaluation. It's only fair that people who put forward new ideas should be rewarded.

FT : Yes, I see your point, but in Japanese companies, a lot of employees believe that people should be treated equally.

BV : What do you mean exactly?

FT : Well, if the company is successful, that's not the result of the efforts of a few individuals, but of the company as a whole. Therefore, everyone should benefit equally.

BV : OK, I can (③) that, but it looks like we have a lot of hard discussions ahead of us!

(注)　*HR：Human Resources

【出典　竹村　和浩，ビル・ペンフィールド，『世界基準のビジネス英会話』，三修社】

(1) (①)～(③)に入る最も適切な語を，次のア～カから一つずつ選び，その記号を書け。

ア　benefit　　イ　discuss　　ウ　break　　エ　interrupt
オ　acquire　　カ　appreciate

(2)　Fumio Toyamaの会社が，社員の「コミュニケーション能力の向上」のために取り組んでいることを，日本語で書け。

(3)　Barbara Vincentが，「コミュニケーション能力の向上」に加えて，職務評価において重視したいと考えている二つの視点を，日本語で書け。

(4)　次の説明に該当する1語を，会話文中から抜き出して書け。

material that provides official information or evidence or that serves as a record

(5)　Fumio Toyamaは，日本の企業では職務評価に対して，従業員がどのような考えをもっていると述べているか。「個人」，「平等」という言葉を用いて，70字程度の日本語で書け。

(☆☆☆◎◎◎◎◎)

【2】次の英文を読んで，(1)～(4)の設問に答えよ。

How then can teachers achieve the most useful balance of demands and support when they plan lessons and adapt tasks from course books? If *language learning* is made the focus of this issue, the question then becomes, 'How can teachers ensure that the balance of demands and support produces language learning?" The answer we will pursue is that the teacher, in planning, must set clear and appropriate *language learning goals.*

As a bald statement, this may sound rather obvious. After all, surely language learning is a goal for all language teaching? At a general level, this may be so, but it does not always seem to be the case for individual lessons and tasks. Moreover, (A)goals that result in learning need to be tailored to particular learners. The course book or syllabus may dictate what is to be *taught*, but what is to be *learnt* can only be planned by a teacher who knows the pupils, and can make the book or syllabus work for them. Learning goals are objectives or intended learning for particular learners working on particular tasks, made specific from the general learning aims of book or syllabus.

In setting clear and specific language learning goals, teachers are *scaffolding* the task for children. Further scaffolding can involve breaking down tasks into manageable steps, each with its own sub-goals. The teacher takes responsibility for the whole task while learners work on each step at a time. Careful design of sub-goals should help ensure success and achievement at each step, and of the task as a whole. Young learners face many years of classroom lessons and it is important that they feel, and are, successful from the start. Too many demands early on will make them anxious and fearful of the foreign language; too few demands will make language learning seem boring. (B)<u>Careful selection and grading of goals</u> is one of the key tools available to teachers to build success into learning.

In primary language classrooms there is a further force that may shift teaching away from learning, and that is the borrowing of materials and activities from general primary practice. This transfer of methodology happens rather often at primary level, partly because of the methodological vacuum in teaching young learners, and partly because primary practice has some genuinely good techniques and ideas that clearly work well with children. My point is not that such transfer is wrong, but that, when ideas are transferred, (C)<u>they</u> need to be adapted for the new aim of language learning. Thinking through the demands, support and learning opportunities of activities may help in this adaptation. Prime examples of techniques transferred from primary education would be theme-based learning and the use of songs and rhymes.

【出典　Lynne Cameron, *Teaching Languages to Young Learners*, CAMBRIDGE Language Teaching Library】

(1)　教師が下線部(A)を行わなければならないと筆者は述べているが，その理由を，50字程度の日本語で書け。

(2)　言語学習の初期段階において，下線部(B)が行われない場合，どのようなことが懸念されると筆者は述べているか。70字程度の日本語で書け。

(3) 下線部(C)が具体的に指している内容を，本文から抜き出して書け。

(4) この論旨を踏まえ，中学校において，単元の指導計画を立てるとき，あなたはどのような工夫をするか。単元を一つ想定し，指導計画の工夫に関する具体例を日本語で書け。

(☆☆☆☆◎◎◎◎◎)

【3】(1)～(4)について，それぞれの英文の[　　]内に入る最も適切なものを，ア～エから一つずつ選び，その記号を書け。

(1) Ken overcame many [　　] circumstances on his way to becoming a doctor.

ア beneficial　イ affirmative　ウ adverse　エ constructive

(2) The audience was [　　] by the dancers' wonderful performance.

ア retained　イ enchanted　ウ endorsed　エ disappointed

(3) Thank you so much for your help, Tom. I promise I'll [　　] to you some day.

ア leave it off　イ give it in　ウ make it up　エ see it out

(4) In order to make it to the town before sundown, they knew they had to [　　], even though their legs were tired from all the hiking.

ア puff up　イ put off　ウ bow out　エ press on

(☆☆☆◎◎◎◎)

【4】(1)～(3)について，それぞれの日本語の内容を表すように，[　　]内の語句を並べかえよ。なお，文頭に来る語も小文字にしてある。(4)については，日本語の意味になるように英語で書け。

(1) ボブがあんなふうに激しく非難してきたので驚いた。

I was surprised [like / lashed / Bob / that / me / that / at / out].

(2) あなたが幸せでいることほど私の望むことはない。

[I / is / than / nothing / that / there / want / more] you should be happy.

(3)　既に始めたことは，続けていく覚悟がある。

I am prepared [go / have / with / what / begun / on / I / to].

(4)　もし10年前にこの本を読んでいたら，今の私の人生は違っているだろう。

(☆☆☆◎◎◎◎)

【5】新しく来日する予定の外国語指導助手(ALT)から，勤務する中学校のことについて教えてほしいという依頼の電子メールが届いた。その電子メールへの返信として，下の＜伝える内容＞を含んだ60語程度の英語を，指示された書き出しに続けて書け。ただし，あなたはALTの勤務校の英語担当教員であるとする。また，ALTへの挨拶やあなたの自己紹介などの英文は省略するものとする。

【書き出し】I will tell you about our school.

＜伝える内容＞

・生徒数は200人で，各学年とも2学級ある。
・英語教育に力を入れている。
・生徒は，学習に一生懸命に取り組み，英語の授業でALTと英語で話すことが好きである。
・生徒は，あなたのことやあなたの出身国について知りたいと思っているので，最初の英語の授業で紹介してほしい。
・あなたにもうすぐお会いできることを私たちは楽しみにしている。

(☆☆☆☆◎◎◎◎)

【6】「中学校学習指導要領(平成29年告示)解説　外国語編」には，「話すこと[やり取り]」の目標　アとして，「関心のある事柄について，簡単な語句や文を用いて即興で伝え合うことができるようにする。」という記載がある。言語活動を通してこの目標を達成させるために，有効

と思われる手立てについて，例を二つ挙げ，100語程度の英語で書け。
(☆☆☆☆☆◎◎◎)

【高等学校】

【1】次の英文を読んで，(1)～(4)の設問に答えよ。

This final chapter deals with assessment, although I also touch on evaluation because it is a closely related aspect of the curriculum. I also need to discuss it briefly because in some (mainly North American) contexts, evaluation is sometimes used as a blanket term to cover both assessment and evaluation. I have privileged assessment because the main focus of what teachers do in their day-to-day work is assessment rather than evaluation.

Books on curriculum and methodology conventionally deal with assessment and evaluation in the final chapter. I have followed this convention, although (A)I had some hesitation in doing so as, symbolically at least, it gives the impression that assessment and evaluation are the last activities to be carried out in the teaching/learning process. While it is true that we assess our students and evaluate our programs at the end of the course (this is known as summative assessment and evaluation), we also carry out assessment and evaluation tasks during a course. This is known as formative assessment and evaluation.

So, what do these two terms mean? (B)How are they similar, and how do they differ? Evaluation is the 'bigger' concept. It consists of a set of procedures aimed at helping us answer the question "How well did the course (and how well did the teacher) do in meeting the needs of the students?" The focus of assessment is directly on the students and deals with the question "How well did the students do?" As I have said, both assessment and evaluation can take place at any time, and can be ranged on a continuum from formal to informal. When preparing a course, we may need to select a new course book. We obtain inspection copies of several potential books from the publishers and review them to identify the most suitable one. This is a form of

(C). We might design a needs assessment survey and get colleagues to review it and provide feedback. This is also a form of (C). It's the same with (D). From the first day of class, we will be assessing our students. We might set them a small group task, and make a note of any errors they make as they complete the task. This is an informal type of (D).

At various points in the course, and again at the end, you might administer more formal assessments, either in the form of a test or through some other means. Students will do well on some of the items, indicating that they have achieved certain course goals, but not so well on others. In order to improve their performance, you need to know why they did well on some items but not so well on others. To find out why, (E)<u>you need to collect information other than the students' scores</u>. Was it that the textbook was inappropriate? Was there something wrong with the teaching? Were there problems with the online component of the course? Was student motivation a factor? What kind of data will enable you to answer these questions? Where, how, and when will you collect these data? These are all evaluation questions, and they reveal the relationship between assessment and evaluation.

An important distinction to bear in mind is between assessment *of* learning and assessment *for* learning (Charless *et al*., 2006). Assessment of learning provides information for external parties: the parents, the teachers, the institution, external funding authorities, and so on. Assessment for learning provides information for learners and teachers who can use the information to improve student performance. In other words, the assessment becomes a learning tool rather than a tool for judging the students.

【出典　David Nunan, *TEACHING ENGLISH TO SPEAKERS OF OTHER LANGUAGES An Introduction*, Routledge】

(1)　下線部(A)の理由を，in doing soを明らかにした上で，具体的に日本語で書け。ただし，次の語は英単語のまま使用すること。【assessment, evaluation】

(2)　下線部(B)について，assessmentとevaluationの類似点と相違点をそ

れぞれ具体的に日本語で書け。ただし，次の語は英単語のまま使用すること。【assessment, evaluation】

(3) (C), (D)それぞれに，適切な内容になるよう，assessmentまたはevaluationを書け。

(4) 下線部(E)について，① 何のために，② どのような情報を集めるのか，具体的に日本語で書け。

(☆☆☆☆◎◎◎◎◎)

【2】次の英文を読んで，(1)～(4)の設問に答えよ。

In 1973, the publication of *The Secret Life of Plants*, by Peter Tompkins and Christopher Bird, which portrayed vegetal life as exquisitely sensitive, responsive and in some respects comparable to human life, was generally regarded as pseudoscience. The authors were not scientists, and clearly the results reported in that book, many of them outlandish, could not be reproduced. But today, new, hard scientific data appears to be buttressing the book's fundamental idea that plants are more complex organisms than previously thought.

The research findings of the team at the Blaustein Institutes form yet another building block in (A)the growing fields of plant intelligence studies and neurobotany that, at the very least, ought to prompt us to rethink our relation to plants. Is it morally permissible to submit to total instrumentalization living beings that, though they do not have a central nervous system, are capable of basic learning and communication? Should their swift response to stress leave us coldly indifferent, while animal suffering provokes intense feelings of pity and compassion?

Evidently, empathy might not be the most appropriate ground for an ethics of vegetal life. But the novel indications concerning the responsiveness of plants, their interactions with the environment and with one another, are sufficient to undermine all simple, axiomatic solutions to eating in good conscience. When it comes to a plant, it turns out to be not only a what but also a who — an agent in its milieu, with its own intrinsic value or version of the good. Inquiring into justifications for consuming vegetal beings thus reconceived, we reach one of the final frontiers of dietary ethics.

Recent findings in cellular and molecular botany mean that eating preferences, too, must practically differentiate between (B)<u>vegetal what-ness</u> and who-ness, while striving to keep the latter intact. The work of such differentiation is incredibly difficult because the subjectivity of plants is not centered in a single organ or function but is dispersed throughout their bodies, from the roots to the leaves and shoots. Nevertheless, this dispersion of vitality holds out a promise of its own: the plasticity of plants and their wondrous capacity for regeneration, their growth by increments, quantitative additions or reiterations of already-existing parts do little to change the form of living beings that are neither parts nor wholes because they are not hierarchically structured organisms. The "renewable" aspects of perennial plants may be accepted by humans as a gift of vegetal being and integrated into their diets.

But it would be harder to justify the cultivation of peas and other (　C　) plants, the entire being of which humans devote to externally imposed ends. In other words, ethically inspired decisions cannot postulate the abstract conceptual unity of all plants; they must, rather, take into account the singularity of each species.

The emphasis on the unique qualities of each species means that (D)<u>ethical worries</u> will not go away after normative philosophers and bioethicists have delineated their sets of definitive guidelines for human conduct. More specifically, concerns regarding the treatment of plants will come up again and again, every time we deal with a distinct species or communities of plants.

【出典　Edited by Peter Catapano and Simon Critchley, *MODERN ETHICS*, The New York Times Company】

(1)　下線部(A)において，植物はどういう特性を持つと考えられているか。具体例として筆者が挙げていることを日本語で書け。

(2) 下線部(B)の区別が困難な理由を，具体的に日本語で書け。

(3) 空所(C)に入る最も適切な語を，次のア～エから選び，その記号を書け。

ア annual イ petrified ウ carnivorous エ barren

(4) 下線部(D)がなくならない理由を，具体的に日本語で書け。

(☆☆☆☆◎◎◎◎◎)

【3】次の(1)，(2)について，日本語で答えよ。

(1) 高等学校学習指導要領(平成30年7月 文部科学省)外国語において，「実際のコミュニケーションの過程で考えられる様々な配慮など」を「支援」と総称しているが，授業で読んだ内容について，自分の意見を理由や根拠とともに書く活動を行う際の支援について具体的に箇条書きで答えよ。

(2) 英語の授業において，あるテーマについて互いの考えを即興で述べ合う活動をグループで行ったところ，英語ではなく日本語を使っているグループが出てきた。①このような状況が起こる原因として考えられることを具体的に箇条書きで答えよ。また，このような状況を避けるために，②英語を使うように指示するほかに，事前準備及び授業中においてどのように対応したらよいか具体的に説明せよ。

(☆☆☆☆☆◎◎◎◎)

【4】次の(1)～(5)の( )に当てはまる最も適切な語を，それぞれア～エから一つ選び，その記号を書け。

(1) The local government's plan to ban smoking in public places has ( ) restaurant managers. Some support it, but others think it will damage business because smokers will not come.

ア polarized イ demolished ウ confederated

エ extricated

(2) When Makoto started his career as a correspondent, he was told which stories to write about. After accumulating considerable experience, however, he was given more (　　) in choosing what to report on.

ア rancor　イ retaliation　ウ reprisal　エ latitude

(3) Mr. Baker had hoped his speech would motivate his students, but the (　　) expression on their faces after his speech told him otherwise.

ア gallant　イ quizzical　ウ blissful　エ fervent

(4) The three executives have (　　) opinions about how the company should be managed. So their meetings often take long.

ア lenient　イ obsequious　ウ disparate　エ coherent

(5) Despite fears that the president's retirement would (　　) impact the sales of the company, they had one of their most successful years.

ア grudgingly　イ strenuously　ウ expediently

エ adversely

(☆☆☆☆◎◎◎◎◎)

【５】a) 次の(1)～(3)の各英文には，それぞれ文法的な誤りが1か所ある。その部分の記号を書き，正しい英語に直せ。

(1) Our section chief seldom suggested $_{A}$to us that we $_{B}$took a break but $_{C}$decided to do so only when some of us $_{D}$complained of tiredness.

(2) If $_{A}$the number of Japanese $_{B}$who have a good command of English language $_{C}$was to increase, the globalization of Jananese soociety would probably progress, $_{D}$that would be a good thing.

(3) A lot of scientists $_{A}$believe that, were they $_{B}$to explode, the volcanoes $_{C}$would set off devastating earthquakes and $_{D}$have put a large part of Japan under the ash.

b) 次の(1)，(2)は，以下のタイトルで生徒が書いた英文であるが，それぞれ文法的な誤りが1か所ある。その部分に下線を引いて指摘し，下線の下に正しい英語を書け。ただし，タイトルは訂正しないこと。

(1) Title: Club Activity

I am a member of the brass band club in my school. Every day after school, I practice the trumpet very hard. I am looking forward to performing in front of many audience in the next concert.

(2) Title: The place I want to live in

I want to live in Akita after I graduate from college. Some of my friends hope to live in urban areas but I prefer to Akita because it has fresh air and beautiful scenery and above all, people are kind. I want to contribute to my hometown throughout my life.

(☆☆☆◎◎◎◎)

【6】次の質問に，100語程度の英語で答えよ。

One day, some of your students came to you and said that their ALT speaks too fast for them to understand in your English class. Most of the students said they had no problems in understanding what the ALT says in English. As a JTE, what do you do for your students?

(☆☆☆☆☆◎◎◎)

解答・解説

【中高共通】

【1】Part A (1) (C) (2) (B) (3) (B) (4) (C) (5) (A) (6) (A) Part B (1) (C) (2) (A) (3) (B) (4) (D) Part C (1) (I should) enter when and where I want the walk. (2) (I should) show the man my student ID. Part D (1) 解答略 (2) 解答略

〈解説〉スクリプトは公開されていない。 Part A 英文，質問文，選択肢とも問題用紙には印刷されておらず，音声のみで解答しなければならない。読み上げられる選択肢から正しいものを選び記号で答える。

Part B　対話とその内容についての質問文を聞き，問題用紙に印刷された選択肢から正答を選ぶ問題と思われる。　(1)　選択肢はすべてHe'd likeで始まっているので，それ以降の英語に注目する。ほとんどの場合，本文で言われている英語と同じ内容で異なる表現のものが正解になる。　(2)　選択肢に事前に目を通し，支払い方法か，商品リストのことか，なくしたレシートのことか，ディスカウントのことか大まかに把握しておく。　(3)　Professor Brownに関連した話題かもしれないと見当をつけ，その名前が出てくる前後に注目して聞くようにする。　(4)　4つの選択肢からホテルに関する話題だと判断し，予約に関することか，部屋の料金なのか，キャンセルのことか，ホテルの人気に関することか大まかに把握しておいてから聞くと，答えを選びやすくなる。　Part C　英問英答形式の問題。音声のみで解答しなければならないが，解答が短文であることから，パッセージの登場人物が「何をすべきか」などを重点的に聞き取ればよいと思われる。

Part D　英文を聞き，問題用紙に印刷された日本語の質問2問に答える形式。あらかじめ質問に目を通しポイントを絞って聞き取ること。採点の主な観点として，(1)では「労働力不足」,「食品廃棄による損失」等，(2)では「ポイント分の支払い」,「会社が負担する」等のキーフレーズが挙げられている。キーフレーズを踏まえた解答を心掛けたい。

【２】(1)　(解答例)　地球上のすべての生命を持続させる生物学的，生態学的，遺伝学的多様性を保護すること。(41字)　(2)　(解答例)　人類が生物多様性の価値を認識し，すべての政府がこれを自らの政策に組み込み，不正な補助金は撤廃され，漁業は持続可能な産業になり，公害が抑制された完璧な未来。(77字)　(3)　ア　(4)　international agreement　(5)　(解答例)　新たな枠組みの中で生物多様性の喪失を定義・定量化する方法と，気候，砂漠化，森林，湿地帯による生物多様性の喪失と，絶滅危惧種の売買に関する対話を統合する方法。(78字)

〈解説〉(1)　下線部と同じ文の後半にあるコロン(：)から後にthe

challengeの内容が具体的に述べられている。 (2) この英文ではa perfect futureとUtopiaを同じ意味で使っている。つまりa perfect futureに続くin which以降にUtopiaの具体的な内容が述べられている。
(3) 空所を含む文の直前の2文に,「愛知目標の進捗状況は悪く,実際,全体的に見て,生物種は加速して絶滅に向かっている」とあり,続いて「その殺伐とした状況にも関わらず,自然保護活動家たちは,2020年は新しい始まりとなるかもしれないと～だ」と述べているので,「楽観的」だと判断する。 (4) buy-inは「同意」という意味。worldwide→international, buy-in→agreementと考える。 (5) 第7段落の最終文に,定義・数量化する方法はan open question「未解決の問題」であり,第8段落冒頭の文では,生態系の破壊と気候～の対話を統合することはthe bigger issueだと述べられている。これら2つをthese two sets of discussionsだと考える。

【中学校】

【1】(1) ① イ ② ウ ③ カ (2) (解答例) 社内の無料英会話教室を提供し,社外の授業を受ける従業員には補助金を出す。
(3) (解答例) ・長時間仕事に携わることではなく,効率よく仕事を終え,仕事と生活のバランスをとるタイムマネジメントができること。
・よい会社型人間であると同時に,自己主張ができ,個人の自主性を発揮し,新しい考えを提案できること。 (4) documentation
(5) (解答例) 会社の成功は少数の個人が努力した結果ではなく,会社全体の努力の結果であり,従業員はみな平等に扱われ,平等な報酬を受けるべきだと考えている。(69字)

〈解説〉(1) ① Barbara Vincent(BV)の1つ目の発言で,「職務評価の方法に関する社内文書をちょうど精査したところです。いくつかの変更点を～したいと思っています」とある。それを受けてFTは「もちろん。何か具体的なことを考えていますか」とあるので,変更点について話し合うが,それについて具体的なことがあるかという流れになる。
② 空所を含む文のthatは会社で長時間過ごすこと。それは特に年配

の社員には捨てるのが難しい習慣だと考える。break a habitは「習慣を捨てる」という意味。　③　「それ(日本の従業員の考え方)は～できるが，これから激しい議論を数多くすることになるようだ」とあるので，「正しく理解する」だと判断する。　(2)　BVの2つ目の発言で，「実際に使われ，継続して向上するコミュニケーション能力は重要だ」とあり，それを受けFumio Toyama(FT)は2つ目の発言で，「この(コミュニケーション能力の)カテゴリーが極めて重要であることには同感です。それが，私たちが～する理由の1つです」と，重要なので強化するために取り組んでいる内容をthat以下で述べている。　(3)　BVの3つ目の発言にAlso「また」とあり，コミュニケーション能力に加えて，time management is an important categoryだと述べている。さらにBVの4つ目の発言で，I'm also of the opinion that～とあり，もう1つ重視したい考えが述べられている。　(4)　与えられた定義は「正式な情報や証拠を提供し，記録として役立つ資料」という意味。　(5)　FTの4つ目の発言の「多くの従業員は，人は平等に扱われるべきだと信じている」を受けて，BVがその正確な意味を尋ね，それに対しFTが5つ目の発言で，日本の従業員がどう考えているか答えている。

【2】(1)　(解答例)　教科書やシラバスは何を教えるべきか指示できるが，何を学ぶべきかは，生徒を知る教師が計画を立てられるから。(52字)　(2)　(解答例)　語学学習の初期段階に要求の多い授業をすると，児童は外国語に対して不安や恐怖を抱き，求めるものがほとんどない授業をすると語学学習を退屈に感じる。(71字)　(3)　techniques and ideas that clearly work well with children　(4)　(解答例)　助動詞canを用いて，「できること」と「できないこと」を相手に伝えたり，尋ねたりすることができるようになるという，単元を通した目標を立てる。助動詞canを用いた文の構造(肯定文と否定文)を理解し，自分に関して「できること」を言ってみる。その次に「できないこと」を言ってみる。この時点で，canを用いてうまく表現できない生徒には，canを用いた語順整序の問題をしてもらう。〈can＋動詞の原形〉と

〈can't[cannot]＋動詞の原形〉の文を作り，音読してもらうことで，canの文を定着させ，会話に生かせるようにする。疑問文とその答え方の文の構造を理解し，相手の「できること」と「できないこと」を積極的に質問して，聞き出す。相手にもそうしてもらい，自分で答えてみる。うまく対応できない生徒の英文を黒板に書きだし，間違っている個所を本人に指摘してもらい，正しい文を音読して，覚えてもらう。

〈解説〉(1)　下線部は「学習者に合わせた学習目標を設定する必要がある」という意味。その理由は下線部の直後に示されている。　(2)　下線部を行うことが必要な理由は，下線部の直前の文に述べられている。目標を立てるときに，目標を厳選し，段階［等級］に分けることをしないと，要求が多くなったり，要求がほとんどなかったりする授業になり，児童を不安や退屈にさせるのである。　(3)　第4段落を訳出すると，以下のようになる。「初級レベルの語学教室には，学ぶことを教えることと分ける力があり，それはつまり，(教えることではなく,)一般的な初級言語レベルの実践の中から言語材料やアクティビティーを借用することである。この方法論の転換は初級レベルでよく起こり，理由の1つは児童に教えるときの方法論的な真空(方法論が及ばない授業)のためで，また1つには初級レベルの言語の実践には，子どもたちとうまくやっていけるような，本当に良い技術やアイデアがあるからである。つまりそのような転換は悪いことではなく，転換されるときには，それら(子どもたちとうまくやっていけるような，本当に良い技術やアイデア)は，語学学習の新たな目標に合わせる必要がある」。(4)　採点の評価基準として「単元を通して目標を明確にし，生徒の実態を踏まえた段階や課題，副目標を設定すること等に関連した工夫であること」が求められている。解答例では助動詞canの定着を目標に挙げ，語順整序問題やペアワーク等具体的な課題を示している。

【3】(1)　ウ　　(2)　イ　　(3)　ウ　　(4)　エ

〈解説〉(1)「ケンは医者になる過程で，多くの～な状況を克服した」となるので，「不利な，不運な」だと考える。　(2)「観衆は踊り子たちの素晴らしいパフォーマンスに～した」となるので，「魅了された」と考える。 (3)「手伝ってくれてありがとう，トム。いつかあなたに～すると約束します」となるので，「それを埋め合わせる」と考える。(4)「日没の前に町に到着するために，たとえ一日中ハイキングして足が疲れていても，～しなければならないことを知っていた」となるので，「前進し続ける」と考える。

【4】(1)　that Bob lashed out at me like that　(2)　There is nothing I want more than that　(3)　to go on with what I have begun　(4)　If I had read this book ten years ago, my life would be different now.

〈解説〉(1)　be surprised that S+V～.の文を作る。lash out at～は「～を激しく非難する」，like that「あんなふうに」。 (2)　There is nothing I want more thanで「～よりも私の望むことはない」となる。thanの後ろに接続詞のthatを含むthat S+V～のまとまりで，that you should be happyを続ける。 (3)「～する覚悟がある」はbe prepared to do,「～を続ける」はgo on with～,「既に始めたこと」は関係代名詞のwhat「～のこと」を使って，what I have begunとする。 (4)「(過去のある時に)もし～していたなら」は，過去の事実に反することを仮定しているので「仮定法過去完了の形」にし，「今の私の人生は違っているだろう」は現在のことを仮定して言っているので「仮定法過去の形」にする。

【5】(解答例)　(I will tell you about our school.) Our school has 200 students, two classes for each grade. We focus on English education and our students study English hard. They enjoy talking with ALTs in English classes. They are very much interested in you and the country you are from. So, could you introduce yourself in your first class, so that our students can get to know you. We are looking forward to seeing you soon. (68 words)

〈解説〉新しく赴任してくる予定のALTに対するメール文である。「学年」はgrade,「～に力を入れる」は「～に重点を置く」と考え，focus on～とする。

【6】(解答例)　One is to have the students chat on familiar topics to them. It should be conducted in a group with the time set at one minute. Chatting creates a relaxed atmosphere and even students who are reluctant to speak due to a fear of making mistakes will begin to speak English. The other is to have the students listen to "what was in the news?" The teacher talks in English, using the words and grammar the students have already learned. When being asked relevant questions, students should formulate answers in their minds first, and the next speak out. Thus, they will get used to interaction gradually. (106 words)

〈解説〉解答例では，なじみのある話題の選定や話しやすい環境づくり，既習の語彙や文法を使った話を生徒に聞き取らせ，質問に対する答えを組み立てて口頭で答えさせる練習などを挙げている。

【高等学校】

【1】(1)　(解答例)　教育課程や方法論ではassessmentとevaluationを伝統的に最終章で扱うが，その2つは教えるまたは学ぶプロセスで実行される最後の活動という印象を与えるから。　(2)　(解答例)　類似点…evaluationとassessmentはいつでも実施することができ，形式的なものから非形式的なものまで，連続した形で行われる。

相違点…evaluationはより大きな概念で，「講座(や教師)が生徒のニーズをどの程度満たしていたか」という質問に答えることを目的とした一連の手順で構成されている一方で，assessmentの焦点は生徒に直接向けられ，「生徒はどのくらいできたか？」という質問を扱うこと。

(3)　C　evaluation　　D　assessment　　(4)　(解答例)　①　一部の項目ではうまくでき，他の項目ではそれほどうまくいかなかった理由を知るため。　②　教科書が不適切だったのか，教え方に何か問題があったのか，講座のオンライン授業に問題があったのか，生徒のモチベーションが要因だったのかといった問題に関する情報。

〈解説〉(1)　doing soとは最終章でassessmentとevaluationを扱うということ。このことに躊躇する理由は，下線部直後のas「～なので(原因，理由)」以降に述べられている。　(2)　相違点は第3段落3～5文目，類似点は同6文目に述べられている。　(3)　最初のCは講座で使用する教材の選定の話なのでassessment。2つ目のCは生徒のニーズを評価する調査を設計し，同僚にレビューしてもらい，フィードバックを提供する話なのでassessment。それと同時に生徒のニーズの話でもあるので，1つ目のDはevaluationになる。2つ目のDはグループタスクを生徒たちにしてもらい，間違った箇所のメモを取るとあり，生徒のニーズを探る話なのでevaluation。　(4)　①は第4段落3文目，②は同5～8文目をまとめればよい。

【2】(1)　(解答例)　基本的な学習やコミュニケーションを行うことができ，ストレスに迅速に対応できる。　(2)　(解答例)　植物の主体性は，単一の器官や機能に集中しているのではなく，根から葉や新芽に至るまで，植物の体全体に分散している。　(3)　ア
(4)　(解答例)　各種の植物の独特の性質を考慮すると，異なる種や植物の群落を扱うたびに倫理的懸念が生じ，その種ごとに人間がとるべき行動を定める必要があるから。

〈解説〉(1)　第2段落2文目に「植物を生物ではなく装置として扱うことは道徳的に許されるのか」とあり，その理由として，装置ではない生物としての植物の特性が述べられている。　(2)　下線部を含む文は，「細胞・分子植物学の最近の知見では，vegetal what-ness(物質としての植物)とwho-ness(生物としての植物)の食物の嗜好の違いもまた，実質的に区別しなければならない」とあり，「そのような区別の作業が難しいのは～」と，because～以降に区別が困難な理由が述べられている。
(3)　空所を含む文の直前の文で「多年草の再生可能な側面は，植物からの贈り物として人間に受け入れられ，食生活に取り入れられるかもしれない」とあり，「しかし，エンドウ豆や他の一年草の栽培を正当化することは難しいだろう」と，多年草と比べて一年草は～という流れになっている。　(4)　多年生の植物は再生可能な側面もあり，人間が食生活に取り入れてもいいが，一年草の植物は食することを正当化

できないといった倫理的に触発された決定は，すべての植物の抽象的な概念的統一を前提とすることができず，各種の特異性を考慮するので，その都度，倫理的に植物を食べていいか考えるため，倫理的な懸念が消えないと考える。

【3】(1)　(解答例)　・自分の意見を頭に浮かぶままに書き出し，それに対する理由や根拠，具体例，経験など思いつくままに書く。
・展開できそうな意見を採用して，具体的に理由や根拠を2～3くらい挙げ，書き進める。　・主語と動詞の体をなした文になっているか，時制は正しいか，つなぎ言葉(接続詞や接続副詞など)は適切かなどをチェックする。　(2)　①　(解答例)　・興味のあるテーマではない。
・既習の文法や単語で表現しづらい。　・テーマが簡単すぎて，話が広がらない。　・グループ内の生徒の英語のレベルが同程度ではない。　②　同程度の英語レベルの生徒同士でグループを作り，音楽や映画，マンガ，学校生活など，生徒の身近なテーマで話し合う。話し合う前に，テーマに関する資料を読んでもらい，あらかじめ単語や表現を知ってもらう。
〈解説〉(1)　授業の場面を思い出しながら，あるいは想像しながら書く。
(2)　生徒が活動中に英語で話すことを断念しないように，モチベーションを維持できるような事前準備や対応が必要である。

【4】(1)　ア　(2)　エ　(3)　イ　(4)　ウ　(5)　エ
〈解説〉(1)「地方自治体が公共の場での喫煙を禁止する計画はレストラン経営者を～した。支持する経営者もいるが，喫煙者がレストランにこなくなるのでビジネスにダメージを与えるだろうと考える経営者もいる」となるので，「二分した」が適切。　(2)「マコトが特派員としてのキャリアをスタートさせたとき，書くべき記事を命じられた。しかし，かなりの経験を積んだ後，彼は報道すべき内容を選ぶ～をもっと与えられた」となるので，「自由裁量」が適切。give latitude in～「～に関して裁量権を与える」。　(3)「ベイカー氏は彼のスピーチが生

徒たちにやる気を出させると期待していたが，彼のスピーチの後，彼らの顔に浮かぶ～な表情は，彼にそうでないことを伝えていた」となるので，「疑わし気な」が適切。　(4)「会社の経営のしかたについて，3人の重役は～な意見をもっている。それで彼らの会議はしばしば時間がかかる」となるので，「全く異なる」が適切。　(5)「社長の引退が会社の売り上げに～に影響を与えるという恐れがあるにもかかわらず，最も成功した年の1つになった」となるので，「不利に」が適切。

【5】a)　(1)　記号…B　　正しい英語…take　　(2)　記号…D　　正しい英語…which　　(3)　記号…D　　正しい英語…put　　b)　(1)　下線を引く部分…3文目のmany　　正しい英語…a large　　(2)　下線を引く部分…2文目のprefer to　　正しい英語…prefer

〈解説〉a)　(1)「提案する」という意味のsuggestに続くthat節の中の動詞の前にはshouldが隠れているので，動詞は原形のtakeになる。
(2)　関係代名詞のthatはコンマの後では使わない。前出の文の一部を先行詞とする場合は，コンマ＋whichで表す。　(3)　believeに続くthat以下は「もし仮に多くの火山が爆発するなら，壊滅的な地震を引き起こし，日本の多くの地域を灰の下に埋もれさせるだろう」という意味で，仮定法過去のif they were to explodeが倒置した形になっている。
Dは(would)putとなる。　b)　(1)　manyは〈many＋可算名詞の複数形〉で使うが，audienceがいくつもあるわけでなく，1つの聴衆の規模が大きいと考える。　(2)　preferは他動詞なので前置詞toを伴わない。toを不定詞としてとらえてto live in Akita，あるいはpreferのあとに動名詞がきて，prefer living in Akitaでも可。

【6】(解答例)　I will firstly ask ALT to speak a little more slowly and clearly, using simple words, easy grammar, and common expressions which our students already know. I also would like ALT to make sure if our students could follow him/her, by asking some questions in simpler and easier English from time to time. At the same time, before each class, I will explain the today's class content in Japanese to the students who have a problem catching what ALT says, so that they can have some idea of what the class is about. Or, I will stay beside the students during class, explaining what ALT is talking. (107 words)

〈解説〉解答例では，まず，ALTに対して，なるべく簡単な既習の語彙や文法や表現を使い，少しゆっくりはっきり話してくれるように頼む。また，生徒が授業についてきているかを確認するため，さらに平易な英語でALTから生徒にときおり質問してもらうことを挙げている。ALTの英語が聞き取れないという生徒には，あらかじめ日本語で各授業の前に本日の授業内容を知らせておく。または，授業中，聞き取れない生徒のそばに付いていて，ALTが話している内容を説明することを挙げている。

2020年度　実施問題

【中高共通】

【１】リスニングテスト

Part A

(1) Write your answer on your answer sheet.

(2) Write your answer on your answer sheet.

(3) Write your answer on your answer sheet.

(4) Write your answer on your answer sheet.

(5) Write your answer on your answer sheet.

(6) Write your answer on your answer sheet.

Part B

(1) (A) He will drive to the bank first, and then to the train station.
(B) He will take her to the train station and wait for her there.
(C) He will arrive at the bank and leave her there.
(D) He will drive back to her home so that she can get her wallet.

(2) (A) To go on a trip and buy a new bag.
(B) To check his warehouse this weekend.
(C) To repair the bag that she purchased at his shop.
(D) To send her a replacement for the bag.

(3) (A) The woman was 30 minutes late.
(B) The man misunderstood the time they agreed to meet.
(C) They were waiting at different places.
(D) They changed the date to meet.

(4) (A) Because the student often gets to school on time.
(B) Because the student is spirited and sociable enough.
(C) Because both the student and her classmates are reticent.

(D) Because classmates worry about her timidity.

Part C

(1) Write your answer on your answer sheet.
I should (　　).

(2) Write your answer on your answer sheet.
I should (　　).

Part D

(1) 意識調査の結果で，最も低い数値として示されているのは何の割合か。

(2) 外国や外国人に対する関心が薄れることにより，どのようなことが危惧されているか。

(☆☆☆◎◎◎)

【2】次の英文を読んで，(1)～(5)の設問に答えよ。

Scientists at the University of Geneva in Switzerland studied 18 healthy young adults while they slept in the lab for two nights. One night they slept in regular stationary beds; another night they slept in beds that gently rocked from side to side all night. The order of the rocking and stationary nights was randomized, so that each person served as his or her own control.

The researchers found that rocking caused the subjects to fall asleep more quickly and increased their amount of slow-wave deep sleep, a phase of sleep that is associated with feeling refreshed and rested upon waking. They also experienced fewer periods of spontaneous arousal. This was true despite the fact that they were already good sleepers. Rocking did not affect the duration of rapid eye movement or dream sleep.

The study also assessed memory consolidation by having the subjects study word pairs before going to bed. They were tested on their recall of these words in the evening and then again in the morning when they woke up. The subjects showed improved recall on the morning test after the rocking night compared with the stationary night, showing that rocking enhanced the accuracy of their memories.

This study was, of course, quite small. But other studies have reported similar findings, though the size of the effect appears to depend on the frequency and type of rocking.

Whether and to what extent rocking might help people with severe sleep issues is unknown, but these findings are welcome news for our nation of insomniacs — more than 30 percent of adults report that they don't get enough sleep — to say nothing of the rampant use of sleeping pills, which can have harmful effects on cognition and everyday functioning.

<u>It might not be surprising that rocking helps</u>. After all, who hasn't noticed the soothing effects of swinging in a hammock or lying on a raft on the undulating water? And let's not forget that we spend the first nine months of our lives being gently rocked in an amniotic sea.

But *why* does it work?　How exactly does a gentle rhythmic motion change the sleep architecture of the brain?

The researchers found that rocking induced a kind of synchrony in brain wave activity that varied in tandem with the external motion. Rocking also increased the number of brain oscillations specific to sleep, which are critical for memory consolidation and learning. Though the exact mechanism is unclear, the researchers hypothesize that rocking activates motion-sensitive neurons in the inner ear, which then leads to modulation of brain activity.

All this made me wonder: How does physical movement affect the brain more broadly?　It's well known that exercise enhances cognitive functioning, but what about movements like rocking that involve minimal exertion? What effect on the brain do our seemingly purposeless everyday physical movements have — like fidgeting, foot shaking and doodling, among others?

A 2016 study showed that children with A.D.H.D. who were allowed to fidget — bouncing around and moving gently in place — performed better on a concentration task the more they moved.

Another study focused on doodling. Researchers had 40 participants monitor a boring telephone message for the names of people attending a party. Half the group was randomly assigned to doodle — they shaded printed shapes — while listening to the message. The study found that the "doodling group performed better on the monitoring task and recalled 29 percent more information on a surprise memory test."

【出典　*The New York Times*, February 13, 2019】

(1)　調査によって明らかになったrockingの影響を，睡眠について3点，記憶について1点，日本語で書け。

(2)　筆者が下線部のように感じた理由として挙げている例を，70字程度の日本語で書け。

(3)　研究者たちが睡眠に関する調査結果を基に立てた仮説はどのようなものか，40字程度の日本語で書け。

(4)　2016年に行われた研究と，doodlingに関する研究の結果に見られる共通点を，日本語で書け。

(5)　次は，筆者が本記事のまとめとして書いた文の一部である。(　a　)及び(　b　)に入る最も適切な語を，ア～エからそれぞれ一つずつ選び，その記号を書け。

We like to think the brain is (　a　), but it is obvious that it sometimes takes its marching (　b　) from the body.

a:　ア　antiquated　イ　sovereign　ウ　inadequate　エ　humble

b:　ア　functions　イ　permissions　ウ　memories　エ　orders

(☆☆☆☆◎◎◎◎◎)

【中学校】

【1】次の会話文を読んで，(1)〜(6)の設問に答えよ。

McMillan : Some language lovers and scientists are calling for a "slow reading" movement. The idea is to encourage people to develop the habit of reading more slowly and in-depth in order to better comprehend and appreciate complex texts. That can be a <u>tall</u> order, given the frenetic pace of modern life.

Breakstone : This is the crux of a debate that's taking place among educators these days. What exactly does it mean to read in the digital age?　Some say that declining scores by teenagers on standardized reading tests are the result of the endless hours they spend surfing the Net. But there's another school of thought that says the Internet has created a new mode of reading that educators and society shouldn't automatically dismiss.

McMillan : I prefer to be a hidebound traditionalist and stick with the good old-fashioned printed page. I think reading a book, which reflects one author's thoughts with a definite beginning, middle and end, is inherently different from reading online messages and postings on social networking sites. That's because on the Internet you can flit from one text to another without the linear structure or discipline you get when you read a book.

Umemura : I totally agree. I'm sure this sounds dreadfully clichéd, but [　　] for developing the capacity for concentration and contemplation. Settling down with a good book helps you calm down and take a (　　) from this busy world.

Lyons : I agree, Seiji. But on the other hand, in the time it takes to read a 500-page book about a given topic, you can read any number of websites and blog posts about that same subject and potentially be exposed to a much wider range of information and opinion than you'd get from that single book.

Umemura : That's all well and good, Steve. But people who rely on the Internet as their main source of information have a weak spot, namely whether that information is accurate. There's a lot of unfiltered, unverified garbage online passing itself off as the truth or the inside scoop.

【出典　杉田　敏，『実践ビジネス英語　ニューヨークシリーズ　ベストセレクション』，NHK出版】

(1) 下線部とほぼ同じ意味を表す語を，次のア～エから一つ選び，その記号を書け。

ア erroneous　イ firm　ウ entire　エ difficult

(2) インターネットの活用について，教育者の間で議論になっている二つの意見を，それぞれ日本語で書け。

(3) McMillanが，本を読むこととインターネット上のメッセージを読むことは異なると考える理由を，日本語で書け。

(4) [　　]に入る最も適切なものを，次のア～エから一つ選び，その記号を書け。

ア only a few books are worth reading

イ there's nothing like reading a physical book

ウ people face no choice but to borrow books from libraries

エ people can do no better than reading electronic books

(5) (　　)に入る最も適切なものを，次のア～エから一つ選び，その記号を書け。

ア breather　イ commission　ウ question　エ tumble

(6)　文中の人物が主張している，インターネット上で読むことの長所と短所について，「情報」をキーワードとして，それぞれ日本語で書け。

(☆☆☆◎◎◎◎◎)

【2】次の英文を読んで，(1)～(4)の設問に答えよ。

One important element in a school that teaches for intelligence is a staff that values intellect. This means (A)<u>a staff</u> that conveys to students the view that having information and being able to use it to make sense of new information is valuable, and that academic disciplines like math, history, science and language study are powerful tools for making sense of the world. Staff members who themselves value the life of the mind are invaluable for teaching for intelligence. They must, of course, also be able to convey this value to children, but teachers who are "great with children" but lack intellectual values are unlikely to do a great job teaching for intelligence.

A curriculum that teaches for intelligence must include a great deal of factual knowledge, beginning in the earliest years. This is especially true for students who do not receive background knowledge at home. A broad base of factual knowledge is critical to making sense of new information. If a student does not already know something about a subject, he or she cannot investigate the subject. If a teacher asks a student to comment on or research a topic that the student knows little about, the student will have little idea what questions to ask or what explanations make sense; he or she will be intellectually tied to people who do know — in most cases, teachers. Intelligence means intellectual independence, and only someone who is well informed is capable of such independence.

A curriculum that teaches for intelligence must include opportunities to master language and mathematics. This mastery must include drills that help a student to achieve "(B)<u>automaticity</u>," the ability to do many things (such as arithmetic and algebraic computation, spelling, and creation of grammatical sentences) automatically — without conscious thought. Without this automaticity, students will be forever counting on their fingers, struggling with the simplest algebraic equation, looking up spellings, and writing and rewriting the simplest sentences. They will have little time and energy for the complicated mathematical and linguistic expression required for intelligence. Building automaticity is critical and involves some degree of drill and practice.

A curriculum that teaches for intelligence must provide many opportunities for students to use what they have learned in order to investigate, understand, discuss, and comment on significant matters. No student should be asked to investigate or discuss matters about which he or she knows little, or to use math or language beyond the level the student has mastered. However, opportunities for investigation, discussion, and comment should be built into the curriculum as soon as the student has learned enough information and sufficiently mastered language and math to make the exercise authentic. By the end of high school, every student should have achieved sufficient knowledge, mastery, and practice in discussion and expression to, for instance, respond *intelligently* to an article in *The New York Times* on any subject.

A curriculum that teaches for intelligence must prepare students for the inevitable "interdisciplinary" nature of most issues in life. It should do this by helping students develop a strong understanding of the major academic disciplines. The student should understand how, for instance, the natural sciences differ from social science and the humanities disciplines, and how literary study differs from history. Only with this kind of understanding will students be able to evaluate claims and evidence from several disciplines to make judgments about complex issues. In general, "interdisciplinary" instruction should probably come in the early grades (when students cannot be expected to understand what an academic discipline is) and the later grades (after they have achieved that understanding).

Perhaps most of all, teaching for intelligence should be based on respect for students' abilities to acquire information, master math and language, and eventually understand and intelligently comment on complex issues. With this respect, educators can provide the kind of systematic and intellectually serious instruction students need to be intelligent in the real world.

【出典　Barbara Z. Presseisen, *TEACHING FOR Intelligence SECOND EDITION*, CORWIN PRESS】

(1)　下線部(A)が生徒に伝える見方は何か，2点日本語で書け。

(2)　本文では，生徒に知性を身に付けさせるカリキュラムに必要なことが述べられている。その4点を日本語で書け。

(3)　生徒が下線部(B)を身に付けていないことにより生じる問題点は何か，70字程度の日本語で書け。

(4)　知性を身に付けさせる上で教師が最も大切にしなければならないことは何か，70字程度の日本語で書け。

(☆☆☆☆◎◎◎◎◎)

【3】(1)～(4)について，それぞれの英文の[　　]内に入る最も適切なものを，ア～エから一つずつ選び，その記号を書け。

(1)　The box office profits from the movie are expected to [　　] three billion yen.

ア　undergo　　イ　evaporate　　ウ　exceed　　エ　withdraw

(2)　James is terribly busy with his job, but he always makes sure to [　　] time for his son in the evening.

ア　set back　　イ　set off　　ウ　set on　　エ　set aside

(3)　[　　] I am concerned, this is the best Italian restaurant in the town.

ア　As far as　　イ　As soon as　　ウ　As if　　エ　As though

(4)　At the time the conference was scheduled to begin, people were still [　　] in the lobby. The organizers made an announcement urging everyone to come into the room.

ア　backing out　　イ　milling about　　ウ　blasting off

エ　knuckling under

(☆☆☆◎◎◎◎◎)

【4】(1)～(3)について，それぞれの日本語の内容を表すように，[　　]内の語句を並べかえよ。(4)については，日本語の意味になるように英語で書け。

(1)　少女が川岸をジョギングしていたら，突風で帽子が川に飛ばされてしまった。

As the girl was jogging along the riverbank, [of / a / cap / sudden / blew / wind / her / gust] into the river.

(2)　ある国の人たちがどんな服装をするかは，気候によるところが大きい。

Climate decides [wear / people / of / what / country / a / clothing / the].

(3)　ジョンが熱心に勉強したので，友達は彼の成功を確信した。

So [were / study / hard / did / his friends / John / that] convinced of his success.

(4)　教師は，何を教えるかだけではなく，どう教えるかを理解すべきだ。

(☆☆☆◎◎◎◎)

【5】新しく来日したALTに対し，訪問初日の最初の授業で自己紹介をしてほしい旨をメールで伝えることにした。ALTに60語程度の英語でメール文を書け。挨拶等は省略し，依頼したい内容から書き始めることとする。※語数を数えて記入すること。(符号は語数に含めない)

(☆☆☆☆◎◎◎◎)

【6】中学校学習指導要領(平成29年告示)解説には，「小学校までの学習の成果が中学校教育に円滑に接続され，育成を目指す資質・能力を生徒が確実に身に付けることができるよう工夫する必要がある。」という記述がある。このことを踏まえて，あなたは授業においてどのよう

な工夫をするか。例を二つ挙げ，100語程度の英語で書け。※語数を数えて記入すること。(符号は語数に含めない)

(☆☆☆☆☆◎◎◎)

【高等学校】

【1】次の英文を読んで，(1)～(5)の設問に答えよ。

Thinking in a Language

We began this chapter by asking why communication breaks down across cultures and across languages. On the other hand, our culturally dictated experiences color how we tend to think. If we're used to holding our bodies in a particular way or seeing clothes of a particular type and so on, we will construct embodied simulations to understand language that reflect those tendencies. When two people's backgrounds are different, whether it's within or across cultures, the words they use will evoke different embodied simulations in their respective minds, and, to the extent that the task they're using language for relies on the details of those embodied simulations, then communication will be impaired.

That's because language, after all, provides a very narrow aperture through which we communicate thoughts. In speaking, we utter a few quickly selected words, seeds that are meant to produce florid gardens of meaning when they find purchase in the fertile mind of the listener. And yet minds differ because they are made over the course of individual experience. And so the soil in my mind (　A　). What looks like a tomato plant in your mind might produce a seed that grows into a pumpkin when I try to interpret it.

People who speak different languages are also compelled to think differently, because of what their language forces them to attend to and the categorical distinctions it forces them make. This, of course, isn't the exclusive purview of language; (B)<u>people attend and perceive differently for other reasons as well</u>. One important reason is expertise. An expert Starcraft player (Starcraft is a military science fiction real-time strategy video game that may or may not be the software equivalent of methamphetamine) sees the screen differently from a novice; he recognizes nonobvious, high-level patterns and attends to different details than the (C)<u>neophyte</u>. The same is true for the expert birdwatcher, chef, or tennis player.

And if there's anything that birdwatchers do more than watch birds, that chefs do more than cook, it's use language. (It's not however a given that Starcraft experts do anything more than they play Starcraft.) To the extent that any of us are experts in anything, we are experts many times over in our native tongue. And this expertise, in the form of recurrent, obligatory attention to specific contrasts or particular features, produces the somewhat different ways of thinking characteristic of Korean, Russian, Arabic, or English speakers. We are, ultimately, what we speak.

As anyone who has ever tried to learn a second language late in life knows, it's a brutal proposition, a path strewn with the corpses of declensions mangled and tenses tortured. But, further down the path, where grammatical genders are more or less intact, where words and idioms are sturdy and sound, the more advanced second language learner often finds herself immersed in a sort of alternate universe. Yes, the words are different, but that's not the rub. More entrancingly, the farther the learner walks down into the garden of a second language, (D)<u>the more the world itself appears to take on different forms</u>, not because its pieces are called by different names, but because the same tableau is seen to be composed of a different set of pieces, which crosscut and overlap the borders of the jigsaw that she is most familiar with from her native language. Part of what makes learning a second language so difficult is precisely this: the commitment one made early on in life to a particular cutting up of the world at its joints is hard to see as merely one possible commitment among many, and just as it is hard to see, it is hard to let go of.

【出典　Benjamin K. Bergen, *Louder Than Words*, Basic Books】

(1)　二人の背景が異なる場合，どのようなことが起こると筆者は言っているか，具体的に日本語で書け。

(2)　(　A　)に入る最も適切な英文を，次のア～エから一つ選んで，その記号を書け。

ア　would let both of us have the identical fruits in our gardens

イ　might not make simulations blossom the same way yours does

ウ　should provide you with vegetables that you want as quickly as possible

エ　could not bring you different simulation if you are from different countries

(3)　下線部(B)について，どのような点で，母語についてもっている専門的知識が重要な理由の一つであると筆者は言っているか，具体的に日本語で書け。

(4)　下線部(C)と同じ意味で用いられている英語一語を書け。

(5)　下線部(D)のようになるのはなぜか，具体的に日本語で書け。

(☆☆☆☆◎◎◎◎◎)

【2】次の英文を読んで，(1)～(4)の設問に答えよ。

Look around on your next plane trip. The iPad is the new pacifier for babies and toddlers. Younger school-aged children read stories on smartphones; older boys don't read at all, but hunch over video games. Parents and other passengers read on Kindles or skim a flotilla of email and news feeds. Unbeknownst to most of us, an invisible, game-changing transformation links everyone in this picture: the neuronal circuit that underlies the brain's ability to read is subtly, rapidly changing — a change with implications for everyone from the pre-reading toddler to the expert adult.

As work in neurosciences indicates, the acquisition of literacy necessitated a new circuit in our species' brain more than 6,000 years ago. That circuit evolved from a very simple mechanism for decoding basic information, like the number of goats in one's herd, to the present, highly (　A　) reading brain. My research depicts how the present reading brain enables the development of some of our most important intellectual and affective processes: internalised knowledge, analogical reasoning and inference; perspective-taking and empathy; critical analysis and the generation of insight. Research surfacing in many parts of the world now cautions that each of these essential "deep reading" processes may be under threat as we move into digital-based modes of reading.

This is not a simple, binary issue of print vs digital reading and technological innovation. As MIT scholar Sherry Turkle has written, we do not err as a society when we innovate, but when we ignore what we disrupt or diminish while innovating. In this hinge moment between print and digital cultures, society needs to confront what is diminishing in the expert reading circuit, what our children and older students are not developing and what we can do about it.

We know from research that the $_{(B)}$<u>redding circuit</u> is not given to human beings through a genetic blueprint like vision or language; it needs an environment to develop. Further, it will adapt to that environment's requirements — from different writing systems to the characteristics of whatever medium is used. If the dominant medium advantages processes that are fast, multitask-oriented and well suited for large volumes of information, like the current digital medium, so will the reading circuit. As UCLA psychologist Patricia Greenfield writes, the result is that less attention and time will be allocated to slower, time-demanding deep reading processes, like inference, critical analysis and empathy, all of which are indispensable to learning at any age.

Increasing reports from educators and from researchers in psychology and the humanities bear this out. English literature scholar and teacher Mark Edmundson describes how many college students actively avoid the classic literature of the 19th and 20th centuries because they no longer have the patience to read longer, denser, more difficult texts. We should be less concerned with students' "cognitive impatience", however, than by what may underlie it: the potential inablity of large numbers of students to read with a level of critical analysis sufficient to comprehend the complexity of thought and argument found in more demanding texts, whether in literature and science in college, or in wills, contracts and the deliberately confusing public referendum questions citizens encounter in the voting booth.

The possibility that critical analysis, empathy and other deep reading processes could become the unintended "collateral damage" of our digital culture is not a simple binary issue about print vs digital reading. It is about how we all have begun to read on any medium and how that changes not only what we read, but also the purposes for why we read. Nor is it only about the young. The subtle atrophy of critical analysis and empathy affects us all. It affects our ability to navigate a constant bombardment of information. It incentivises a retreat to the most familiar silos of unchecked information, which require and receive no analysis, leaving us susceptible to false information and demagoguery.

【出典　*The Guardian*, August 31, 2018】

(1)　空所(　A　)に入る最も適切な語を，次のア～エから選び，その記号を書け。

ア　elaborated　　イ　primitive　　ウ　pathological　　エ　illiterate

(2)　下線部(B)は環境とどのような関係にあると筆者は言っているか，2点日本語で書け。

(3)　英文学の専門家によると，多くの大学生にどのようなことが起こっていると言っているか，その理由も含めて70字程度の日本語で書け。

(4)　筆者は，批判的分析力や共感する力が衰えると，私たちのどのような能力に影響を与え，その結果，何が起こると言っているか，具体的に日本語で書け。

(☆☆☆☆◎◎◎◎◎)

【3】次の(1)～(2)について，日本語で答えよ。

(1) ①英語の授業において，読んだ内容についてテーマを定め，即興でディベートを行う際に授業者が留意すべきことについて具体的に箇条書きで述べよ。また，外国語によるコミュニケーション能力の育成の観点から，②①の活動を通じて育成することが期待できる生徒の能力について具体的に箇条書きで述べよ。

(2) 中学校との接続及び発信力の育成の観点から，高校の英語の授業において文法や文構造，語彙等の指導を行う際に留意すべきことを述べよ。

(☆☆☆☆☆☆◎◎◎◎)

【4】次の(1)～(5)の(　　)に当てはまる最も適切な語をそれぞれア～エから一つ選び，その記号を書け。

(1) Government officials of the U. S. had never made a notification of the sudden cancelation of the ambassador's visit to Japan and when they (　　) the subject with the Japanese authorities, it was met with more than disappointment.

ア levitated　イ lingered　ウ broached　エ chartered

(2) Even as an elderly entertainer he was famous for his talents and versatility, (　　) at acting, singing and, to my surprise, even ventriloquism.

ア adept　イ intimate　ウ cerebral　エ stubborn

(3) The vitality of the society is threatened by the great (　　) of people with ingenious ideas for solving pressing issues.

ア feasibility　イ subscription　ウ precursor　エ paucity

(4) The professor asked all of the students to (　　) the basic meaning of the thesis she had assigned them to read.

ア exhort　イ recapitulate　ウ placate　エ intercept

(5) A major effort underway in machine translation is to develop (　　) classifications of meaning that will duplicate the knowledge that allows

humans to know which of various meanings a speaker intends.

ア　sophisticated　　イ　jumbled　　ウ　provident

エ　impermeable

(☆☆☆☆◎◎◎◎◎)

【５】a)　次の(1)～(3)の各英文の下線部には，それぞれ誤りが1か所ある。その部分の記号を書き，正しい英語に直せ。

(1)　Some vegetables especially if they are kept properly in a refrigerator, $_{\mathrm{A}}$last longer than $_{\mathrm{B}}$other, $_{\mathrm{C}}$some are eatable for $_{\mathrm{D}}$as long as 10 days beyond the usual limit of consumption.

(2)　The teacher $_{\mathrm{A}}$complimented that her students' reports are $_{\mathrm{B}}$wholly convincing, not only including significant materials but essentially consisting of profound truths $_{\mathrm{C}}$that they could have better $_{\mathrm{D}}$served as academic theses.

(3)　$_{\mathrm{A}}$Although her words are formally polite and her tone is conciliatory, her repute $_{\mathrm{B}}$varies widely, depending $_{\mathrm{C}}$on whom you happen $_{\mathrm{D}}$to talk.

b)　次の(1)，(2)は，以下のタイトルで生徒が書いてきた英文であるが，それぞれ誤りが1か所ある。その部分に下線を引いて指摘し，正しい英語に直せ。ただし，タイトルは訂正しないこと。

(1)　Title: My dream in the future

I want to go to a university in a foreign country after I graduate from high school because it is a very good way to learn foreign languages. I hope I will be able to improve my listening skills if I go abroad. Another good point is that I can feel cultural differences. Although it will take some time to get used to live in a different country, I can touch its culture directly.

(2)　Title: The person I respect

I have a brother who is two years older than I. I respect him very much. He belongs to the baseball club of his high school and practices very hard every day. He is very busy but he helps my homework on weekends. He is very kind and I like him very much.

(☆☆☆◎◎◎◎)

【6】次の質問に，100語程度の英語で答えよ。※語数を数えて記入すること(符号等は語数に含めない)

The Ministry of Education, Culture, Sports, Science and Technology made a research on English skills of high school students. It shows that the students scored less in speaking and writing than in listening and reading. What do you think about this?　What do you think you can do to improve this situation?

(☆☆☆☆☆◎◎◎)

解答・解説

【中高共通】

【1】Part A　(1)　(C)　(2)　(C)　(3)　(B)　(4)　(C)　(5)　(A)　(6)　(C)　Part B　(1)　(A)　(2)　(D)　(3)　(C)　(4)　(B)

Part C　(1)　work until seven o'clock in the evening.　(2)　bring the item in its original condition within 30 days.　Part D　(1)　解答略

(2)　解答略

〈解説〉スクリプトは公開されていない。Part Aは選択肢が印刷されていないため，各選択肢の内容を聞き逃さないように注意したい。Part Bは対話を聞いて選択肢で答える形式と思われる。対話を聞く前に印刷されている選択肢から内容を推測することができる。Part Cは英問英答形式であるが，書く量はあまり多くないことから，ポイントを聞き取れれば解答できると思われる。Part Dは英文を聞いて，あらかじめ印刷されている日本語の質問に答える形式となっている。キーフレーズが採点の主な観点となっているため，キーフレーズを押さえた解答を心がけること。例えば，(1)では，「海外で学んだり働いたりしたい」，

(2)では「外国人に対する誤解」,「外国人とのよい関係づくり」がキーフレーズである。

【2】(1)　(解答例)　睡眠…・すぐ眠りにつくことができること。　・休息感と関わる深い眠りが増えること。　・自然に目覚める回数が少なくなること。　記憶…・記憶の正確さが向上するということ。　(2)　(解答例)　人はハンモックや波打つ水に浮かぶいかだの上で揺られることで,落ち着く感覚が得られること。また,胎児は羊水の中で優しく揺られているということ。(70字)　(3)　(解答例)　揺られることで内耳にある運動を検知するニューロンが活性化し,脳の活動を調整すること。(42字)　(4)　(解答例)　動きながら課題に取り組むことで,パフォーマンスが向上するということ。　(5)　a　イ　b　エ

〈解説〉(1)　睡眠に関する3つの影響については第2段落の1文目と2文目に述べられている。また,記憶に関する影響については第3段落で述べられており,特に,最後の文の後半にあるshowing that rocking enhanced the accuracy of their memoriesが答えになっている。　(2)　下線が引かれた文の直後にある内容をまとめればよい。　(3)　第8段落の最後の文にあるthe researchers hypothesizeに続くthat節の内容をまとめればよい。　(4)　2016年に行われた研究は第10段落に,doodlingに関する研究は第11段落にそれぞれ述べられている。あとは,それぞれの段落の後半にあるperformed betterに着目して共通点をまとめればよい。　(5)　空欄を含んだ文は「私たちは脳が司っていると思いたいが,時に,体から命令を受けていることは明らかだ」の意である。aに入るのは「統治者」の意であるsovereignそして,bに入るのは「命令」の意であるordersである。なお,marching ordersで「出発命令・前進命令」。

【中学校】

【1】(1)　エ　(2)　(解答例)　・10代の子どもたちがインターネットに延々と時間を費やしているため,読解力テストで得点低下が起こって

いるということ。　・インターネットが新しい読み方を生み出したため，インターネットを頭ごなしに否定すべきではないということ。

(3)　(解答例)　本を読むときは直線的な構造や秩序を理解する必要があるが，インターネット上のメッセージは次々と飛びながら読むことができ，その必要がないから。　(4)　イ　(5)　ア

(6)　(解答例)　長所…500ページの本を読むのにかかる時間で，1冊の本から得られるよりも広範囲な情報や意見を得ることができること。短所…インターネット上の情報が正確かどうかの問題があること。

〈解説〉(1)　下線部の後に「現代生活の慌ただしさを考慮すると」とあるので，下線部の前にあることは「難しい注文」である。

(2)　Breakstoneの最初の発話に着目し，3文目と4文目をそれぞれまとめればよい。　(3)　2回目のMcMillanの最後の発話にThat's becauseとあり，それ以降をまとめればよい。　(4)　1回目のUmemuraの最初の発話にI totally agree.とあるように，UmemuraはMcMillanに同意している。したがって，集中や熟考のためには「物理的な本(＝紙に印刷された本)を読むことに勝るものはない」を選ぶ。　(5)　空欄を含む文は「良い本を手に腰を落ち着けることは，気持ちを落ち着かせ，この忙しい世界で一息つくのに役立つ」の意である。take a breather「一息つく，一休みする」。　(6)　Lyonsと2回目のUmemuraの発話に着目する。それぞれ，インターネットで文書を読むことの長所と短所が述べられている。

【2】(1)　(解答例)　・既存の情報を活用して新しい情報を理解することは価値があるという見方。　・数学，歴史，理科，言語などの学問は世界を理解するための強力なツールであるという見方。

(2)　(解答例)　・最初はたくさんの事実に基づく知識を扱うこと。

・言語や数学を習得させる機会を与えること。　・重要な事柄を検証，理解，議論そして意見するために，既習事項を活用する機会を与えること。　・人生におけるほとんどの問題が様々な学問分野にまたがる学際的なものであり，それに備えさせること。

(3)　(解答例)　生徒は単純な計算や単純な文を書くことでさえ苦労するため，知性に必要とされる複雑な数学や言語表現を習得する時間や気力がなくなってしまうこと。(69字)　　(4)　(解答例)　生徒の，情報を入手する能力や，数学や言語を習得する能力，そして最終的には複雑な問題を理解して知的に意見する能力を尊重するということ。(66字)

〈解説〉(1)　下線部の直後にconveys to students the viewとあり，それ以降にある2つの見方をまとめればよい。　(2)　第2段落から第5段落まで，知性を身に付けさせるためのカリキュラムに必要なことが述べられている。各段落の1文目をまとめればよい。　(3)　下線部の次の文にあるWithout this automaticityから始まる文と，次に続く文をまとめればよい。字数制限を超えないよう簡潔に書きたい。　(4)　最後の段落の1文目にあるPerhaps most of all以降の部分をまとめればよい。

【3】(1)　ウ　　(2)　エ　　(3)　ア　　(4)　イ

〈解説〉(1)　設問文は「その映画の興行収入は30億円を超える見込みである」の意である。アは「経験する」，イは「蒸発する」，エは「引く，引き出す」。　(2)　設問文は「Jamesは仕事で非常に忙しいが，いつも夕方は息子と過ごす時間を取っておくようにしている」の意である。アは「戻す」，イは「出発する」，ウは「攻撃する」。　(3)　設問文は「私の個人的な考えでは，ここがその町で最高のレストランである」の意である。As far as I am concerned は，個人的な意見を述べるときに使用する定型表現である。イは「～するやいなや」，ウ・エは「まるで～であるかのように」。　(4)　設問文は「その会議が始まる予定だった時刻に，人々はまだロビーをうろうろとしていた。主催者は皆が部屋に入るよう促す案内をした」の意である。アは「後ずさりしながら出る」，ウは「発射する，飛び出す」，エは「屈服する」。

【4】(1)　a sudden gust of wind blew her cap　　(2)　what clothing the people of a country wear　　(3)　hard did John study that his friends were

(4) Teachers should understand not only what to teach but also how to teach.

〈解説〉(1) 並べ替える部分を「突風が彼女の帽子を飛ばした」と考えるとよい。 (2) 並べ替える部分を「ある国の人がどんな服を着ているか」と考えるとよい。 (3) 「とても…なので～」の意のso … that ～の構文を使用することは容易に浮かぶと思われるが，今回は文頭にSoがあることから，倒置が生じていることに注意が必要である。
(4) 「AだけではなくB」という表現としてはnot only A but also B が浮かぶと思われる。あとは，AとBに入る内容として，「何を教えるか」と「どう教えるか」を疑問詞＋不定詞を用いて表現する。

【5】(解答例) I would like to talk to you about the first English class. Can I ask you to introduce yourself to the students on the first day? I would appreciate it if you could tell me your plan by the day before class. We will discuss with each other how to conduct the class in the morning of the class day. (60 words)

〈解説〉最初の授業でALTに自己紹介を依頼するということから，Can I ask you to introduce yourself? やI would like you to introduce yourself.といった表現は欠かせない。制限語数には比較的余裕があるので，設問文にある「新しく来日したALT」や「訪問初日の最初の授業」といった条件を踏まえ，当日の授業までの準備や事前打ち合わせに関する内容を書くとよいだろう。

【6】(解答例) In order to make sure that junior high school students acquire knowledge and skills in English, I have two possible approaches as follows. First, I will help my students to learn new things by activating their existing knowledge. I also will encourage my students to use grammar and vocabulary that they learned in elementary schools. Second, I will give them a lot of opportunities to engage in language activities in which they communicate with others using their knowledge and skills. I will try to make the activities as practical as possible so that the students can develop their English proficiency actively. (101 words)

〈解説〉小学校の外国語活動および外国語科を踏まえ，資質・能力の確実な定着を図る方法を論じることが求められている。解答例では，新しい内容を学習する際に既存の知識との関連づけや活用を促すことと，実践的な言語活動を通して英語の運用能力を高めることを述べている。

【高等学校】

【１】(1)　(解答例)　お互いが使用する言葉から，双方が異なることを想定するため，コミュニケーションがうまくいかなくなる。　(2)　イ　(3)　(解答例)　特定の差異や特徴に目を向けることができ，他言語話者のようなどこか違った考え方を生み出すことができるということ。　(4)　novice　(5)　(解答例)　同じ情景であっても，自分がよく知っているものとは異なる要素で構成されているように見えるため。

〈解説〉(1)　設問文の「二人の背景が異なる場合」に対応する記述を探すと，第1段落4文目にWhen two people's backgrounds are differentとある。挿入されているwhether節の次から始まる主節の内容をまとめて書けばよい。　(2)　第2段落は第1段落で述べてきたことを植物にたとえて説明している。具体的には，言葉が植物の種，人の心(背景)が土壌，そして言葉の意味や解釈が成長した植物にたとえられている。空欄を含む前の文では，人の心が異なることが述べられていることから，空欄に入るのは，イの「必ずしも同じ植物が生長しないかもしれない」である。　(3)　設問文にある「専門的知識」に対応する単語を探すと，下線部の次の文にexpertiseがある。しかし，その後，第4段落の2文目までは，Starcraft playerやbirdwatcherなどの具体例が続いており，第4段落4文目にand this expertiseという表現がある。ここに着目して，それ以降の内容をまとめればよい。　(4)　単語の意味は「初学者」であるが，この単語の意味を知っている人は少ないと思われる。その直前にあるthanに着目して，比較対象がexpertであることがわかれば，同じ段落内で対比されている表現を探せばよい。　(5)　この文の直後にnot because...but because～の表現があるため，but because以下の内容をまとめて書けばよい。

【2】(1)　ア　　(2)　(解答例)　・発達させるためには環境が必要であるということ。　・環境が要求するものに適応するということ。
(3)　(解答例)　多くの大学生がより長く，より内容が濃く，そしてより難しい文章を読む忍耐力がないため，19世紀や20世紀の古典文学を意識的に避けているということ。(70字)　　(4)　(解答例)　能力…絶え間ない情報をうまく処理することができなくなる。　　起こること…馴染みのある未確認の情報に逃げやすくなり，誤った情報やデマに流されやすい状態になる。

〈解説〉(1)　空欄部を含んだ文のfrom...to～の構文に着目すると，「基礎的な情報を解読する非常に単純な回路から，非常に精巧な脳に進化した」の意になる。　(2)　下線部に続く英文から，environmentを含んだ箇所をまとめればよい。1つはlanguage;以下の節であり，もう1つはこれに続く次の文である。　(3)　設問文の「英文学の専門家」に対応する記述を探すと，第5段落2文目にEnglish literature scholar and teacher Mark Edmundsonとある。その後のbecauseと明示されている箇所を和訳すればよい。　(4)　設問文の「批判的分析力や共感する力が衰えると」に対応する記述を探すと，第6段落4文目にThe subtle atrophy of critical analysis and empathyとある。その後の内容をまとめればよいだろう。能力への影響については同段落5文目に，そして，起こることについては6文目にそれぞれ述べられている。

【3】(1)　①　(解答例)　・読んだ内容を共有することで，生徒が自分の意見を形成できるよう配慮する。　　・必要に応じて，生徒が自分の意見を即興で表現できるように段階的に指導する。　　・司会者の役割やディベートの流れを含めた手順を明確に示す。　　・必要に応じて，ディベートで使用する定型表現の指導を行う。　　・ディベート

を円滑に進められるよう，形式面に限らず内容面を含めたフィードバックを工夫する。　②　・目的や場面，状況などに応じて主体的に必要な情報を読み取る力。　・既存の知識を活用して即興でやり取りを行う力。　・読むこと，話すこと(やり取り)を中心に受容技能と発信技能を統合的に活用する力。　・情報や考えなどを論理の構成や展開を工夫して伝える力。　(2)　(解答例)　生徒に文法や文構造および語彙等を定着させるだけに留まらず，それらの知識をコミュニケーションにおいて活用させることに主眼をおいた授業を展開する。具体的には，中学校までに学んだ文法や文構造および語彙等を言語活動の中で繰り返し活用させる。その際，語彙に関しては，受容語彙を含め中学校までに学んだ語彙を発信語彙として活用させる機会を設ける。また，文法や文構造を扱う際は，具体的な言語の使用場面における働きを意識しながら指導する。

〈解説〉(1)　新学習指導要領に関する問題であり，高等学校学習指導要領解説を幅広く理解しておく必要がある。具体的には「英語コミュニケーションⅠ・Ⅱ・Ⅲ」の「読むこと」に関する解説や，「論理・表現Ⅰ・Ⅱ・Ⅲ」の「話すこと(やり取り)」に関する解説に基づいて書けばよい。　(2)　この問題も高等学校学習指導要領解説を網羅的に理解しておくことが求められる。総説や総論に加え，「英語コミュニケーションⅠ」ならびに「論理・表現Ⅰ」に示されている「語，連語及び慣用表現」と「文法事項」に関する解説に基づいてまとめるとよいだろう。

【4】(1)　ウ　(2)　ア　(3)　エ　(4)　イ　(5)　ア

〈解説〉(1)　設問文は「アメリカの政府官僚は大使が日本訪問を突然中止したこと，そして日本当局にその件を切り出す時期を通知しなかったが，そのことは非常に遺憾であった」の意である。アは「空中浮遊させる」，イは「残存する」，エは「借り切る・特許を与える」の意である。　(2)　設問文は「彼は年配のエンターテイナーであるが，熟練した演技，歌唱，そして驚くべきことに，腹話術といった多彩な才能で有名である」の意である。adept at～は「～に熟練する」を意味する定型表現である。イは「親密な」，ウは「脳に関する」，エは「頑固な」の意である。 (3) 設問文は「社会の活力は喫緊の課題を解決する妙案を出す人の不足によって脅かされる」の意である。アは「実現可能性」，イは「定期購読，寄付」，ウは「先駆者」の意である。 (4) 設問文は「その教授は学生全員に対して，課題として読ませた論文の基本的な意味を要約するように言った」の意である。アは「熱心に進める」，ウは「なだめる」，エは「妨害する」の意である。 (5) 設問文は「機械翻訳で進行中の主要な努力は，様々な意味の中から話し手の意図を知ることができる知識を複製する洗練された分類方法を開発することである」の意である。イは「ごちゃごちゃの」，ウは「先見の明がある」，エは「不浸透性の」の意である。

【5】a) (1) 記号…B 正しい英語…others (2) 記号…C 正しい英語…that could (3) 記号…D 正しい英語…to talk to

b) (1) 下線を引く部分…4文目のlive 正しい英語…living

(2) 下線を引く部分…4文目のmy homework 正しい英語…me with my homework

〈解説〉a) (1) 主語のSome vegetablesに着目すると，比較対象はother vegetablesであるため，otherではなくothersに直す必要がある。

(2) 下線部Cのthatを関係代名詞と考えると，that節は名詞が欠けた不完全な形になるはずである。しかし，that節は完全な文になっており，that節内の主語であるtheyを削除する必要がある。 (3) 下線部Cが引かれているwhomに着目すると，下線部Dが引かれているtalkの対象が欠けていることがわかる。talkは自動詞であることから，対象をとるためにtoを加える必要がある。 b) (1) used toにはused to＋原形で「昔は～したものだ」の用法と，be (get) used to＋～ingで「～に慣れている(慣れる)」の用法がある。今回は「異なる国に住むことに慣れる」の意であることから，get used to livingの形に直す必要がある。

(2) helpを「助ける」の意味で使用する場合，help＋人＋with＋名詞

(手伝う内容)もしくはhelp＋人＋to不定詞(手伝う内容)という形になる。そのため，今回はme with my homeworkの形に直す必要がある。別解としてme to do my homeworkとしてもよい。

【６】(解答例)　I think that Japanese high school students do not have enough experience of speaking and writing in English. One of the reasons could be that traditional English classes have focused on developing receptive skills, especially reading skills, and the instructors did not implement communicative language activities in the classroom. Therefore, it is important for learners to work on communicative activities where they can improve productive skills as well as receptive skills. For instance, I will give students many opportunities to use integrated language skills. They should express their thoughts and opinions based on the knowledge obtained through listening or reading activities. (101wolds)

〈解説〉日本人高校生の発信技能(話す・書く)が低いことについて，自身の考えと対策を論じる問題である。論点自体は新学習指導要領の「改訂の趣旨」などにも書かれているため，馴染みがある内容だと思われる。解答例では，日本人高校生が発信技能上達のための言語活動を十分に経験していない現状に加え，受容技能(読む・聞く)と発信技能を統合的に活用する授業展開の重要性について述べている。

2019年度　実施問題

【中高共通】

【1】リスニングテスト

Part A

(1) Write your answer on your answer sheet.

(2) Write your answer on your answer sheet.

(3) Write your answer on your answer sheet.

(4) Write your answer on your answer sheet.

(5) Write your answer on your answer sheet.

(6) Write your answer on your answer sheet.

Part B

(1) (A) At or after 1 p.m.
(B) At about 11:30 a.m.
(C) Every twenty minutes.
(D) Before 12:50 p.m.

(2) (A) The stock price.
(B) The price of a computer.
(C) The woman's contact information.
(D) The time the woman will come again.

(3) (A) Go to a bank.
(B) Cook dinner at home.
(C) Search for other restaurants.
(D) Ask about payment methods.

(4) (A) To cancel a reservation.
(B) To reschedule his gym booking.
(C) To invite her to the club activities.

(D) To sign up for a training session.

Part C

(1) Write your answer on your answer sheet.
I should (　　).

(2) Write your answer on your answer sheet.
I should (　　).

Part D

(1) このシステムでは，津波の状況や被害を迅速に予測するために，どのような方法を用いているか。

(2) このベンチャー企業が予定している情報配信先はどこか。

(☆☆☆◎◎◎◎)

【2】次の英文を読んで，(1)～(4)の設問に答えよ。

Humans may not always get along, but the fact is, we can't get enough of one another. There are 7.6 billion of us in the world, but we inhabit only about 10% of the planet's land, and roughly 50% of us live on just 1% of that land.

"We evolved to depend on social connections," says Dr. Vivek Murthy, a former U.S. Surgeon General, "so much so that if we are feeling disconnected, that places us in a physiologic stress state." According to Murthy, that state is as dangerous to our health as smoking 15 cigarettes a day, increasing the risk of cardiovascular disease, cancer and more.

It's hard to come by a firm count of how many $_{\text{(A)}}$intentional communities exist in the U.S. Only about 160 of them have been built from the ground up, but the Fellowship for Intentional Community now lists 1,539 groups that have used existing homes to establish cohousing arrangements.

There are communities like *Commonspace in many major cities. There is Milagro in Tucson, Ariz., 28 homes built around a central green with a shared community center and other facilities. There is Village Hearth Cohousing, a similar setup in Durham, N.C., intended for the LGBTQ community.

The Commonspace model is the simplest. "We set everything up with a town-square feel so that when you come out of your door there's not a long, dark hallway like in most apartment buildings," says Troy Evans, a Commonspace co-founder.

Nearly all of the people who call Commonspace home are millennials, and they tend to be transitory, with the average length of tenancy just eight months. (B)Things are different at communities like Milagro in Tucson. There, the buy-in is typically for life. The investment in house and land means an equal investment in the community.

"For families with very young children, we do baby-care trades," says (C)Brian Stark, a married father of two who has lived in Milagro since 2003. "And having a supportive community to help as you grow older is also a wonderful alternative to assisted-care living."

The physical benefits of human connections are well established — provided they're real. Murthy worries about the number of people whose social lives are reduced to social media, which can be isolating and even dangerous. In a recent meta-analysis, (D)Julianne Holt-Lunstad, a professor of psychology and neuroscience at Brigham Young University, found that adults who are lonely have a 50% greater risk of dying within a given period than people who are more connected. The cause is stress triggered by loneliness, which weakens the immune system and other bodily functions.

Certainly, not everyone who is lonely dies from the condition — but they hardly thrive either. Intentional communities, in their quiet way, may heal both the body and the mind with the simple balm of other people.

(注)　* Commonspace: a cohousing community in Syracuse, N. Y.

【出典　*TIME*, November 27, 2017】

(1) 下線部(A)について，次の問いに答えよ。

① 英語で次のように説明するとき，(a)及び(b)に入る最も適切な語をア～エからそれぞれ一つずつ選び，その記号を書け。

clusters of (　a　) made up of a few dozen apartments or homes built around central squares or common spaces with the goal of keeping people (　b　)

a ：　ア　functions　　イ　arrangements　　ウ　residences
　　　エ　cities

b ：　ア　concealed　　イ　connected　　ウ　despondent
　　　エ　independent

② 筆者はこれがもつ可能性について，本文の中でどのように述べているか，40字程度の日本語で書け。

(2) 下線部(B)について，CommonspaceとMilagro in Tucsonの居住者の傾向にどのような違いが見られるか，日本語で書け。

(3) 下線部(C)が自身の住むコミュニティについて述べている具体的な事柄を，2点日本語で書け。

(4) 下線部(D)が最近の研究で発見したことと，その原因と影響について，それぞれ日本語で書け。

(☆☆☆◎◎◎◎)

【中学校】

【１】次のA(外国人)とB(日本人)の会話文を読んで，(1)～(6)の設問に答えよ。

A : People talk a lot about food security these days. The world population is growing rapidly, and there's a rapid increase in per capita food (　①　), reflecting an increase in middle-class families in emerging countries.

B : I read an article that world agricultural production needs to increase by around 60% by 2050 to meet these challenges.

A : Really? <u>It</u> may be achievable, but we really need to think about food security. I hear that [　Ⅰ　]. Is it true?

B : Yes, that's true. The self-sufficiency rate was as low as 39% in 2015. The government says that Japan has one of the lowest rates among the major economies.

A : Indeed. (②) the top of my head, the US rate is above 90%, and Canada and Australia are even more higher, above 120%.

B : You're right. The trick is, most of the countries release the figures by production value, while Japan calculates the ratio on a calorie-intake basis. If it was calculated from the output value, our country's rate would jump to 66%.

A : I see. Do you think it's appropriate to use calorie-based numbers as a major yardstick in the nation's agricultural policy?

B : It can be misleading. For example, livestock raised in Japan with imported feed are not counted as part of the domestic supply. Also, vegetable farming is (③), but it counts for less in calorie than in production value. In terms of the output-based rate, [Ⅱ].

A : That's not bad at all. So, what do you think is important for Japan in terms of securing diversified sources of food for its people?

B : I think three things are vital: maintaining an open trade system, increasing production efficiency, and just in case, building emergency food reserves.

【出典　柴田真一，『知識と教養の英会話』，DHC】

(1) (①)～(③)に入る最も適切な語を，次のア～ウからそれぞれ一つずつ選び，その記号を書け。

① ア production　イ consumption　ウ promotion

② ア Off　イ On　ウ Over

③ ア affordable　イ fragile　ウ competitive

(2) 文中の下線部(It)の表す内容を，日本語で書け。

(3) [Ⅰ]，[Ⅱ]に入る最も適切なものを，次のア～エから一つずつ選び，その記号を書け。

ア Japanese customers are well-educated, sophisticated, and demanding

イ Japan's exports of agricultural products will be the highest in 2050

ウ Japan is similar to Germany and Switzerland, and higher than the UK

エ　Japan's food self-sufficiency rate is quite low

(4)　日本の食料自給率の計算の仕方について，諸外国との違いを明確にして40字程度の日本語で書け。

(5)　国民に様々な食料を確保するために，日本にってどのようなことが重要であると述べられているか，日本語で書け。

(6)　次の(a)，(b)の説明にそれぞれ該当する1語を，文中から抜き出して書け。

(a)　a piece of writing about a particular subject in a newspaper or magazine

(b)　giving the wrong idea or impression and making you believe something that is not true

(☆☆☆◎◎◎◎)

【2】次の英文を読んで，(1)～(4)の設問に答えよ。

Teachers should not assume that transfer will automatically occur after students acquire a sufficient base of information. Significant and efficient transfer occurs only if we teach to achieve it.

——David Sousa (1995), *How the Brain Learns*

Sousa (1995) refers to the brain's process of making connections between old and new learning as transfer. (A)The strength of this process is dependent on two factors. First, the effect of the past learning on the new learning and second, the degree to which the new learning will be useful in the future. When new information is introduced to working memory, a search is conducted in long-term memory for past learning that connects to the new learning. When those connections are made successfully, Sousa says that greater achievement is possible. He refers to this as (B)positive transfer. Negative transfer occurs when past learning interferes with new learning. Sousa uses the example of learning to drive a standard shift car after driving only an automatic shift car in the past. The skill of leaving the left foot on the floor of the car for driving an automatic shift car can be a hindrance if transferred to the standard shift car where the left foot must be moved onto the clutch for shifting.

What if there are no prior experiences or knowledge of the subject to be taught? We have said that the brain is a seeker of connections. We have all had the experience of being in a room where something is being discussed about which we have no knowledge. There is confusion and frustration while we work to find a connection or hook for the new information. For some students (C)this is a daily occurrence. What this means in the classroom is that we cannot assume that students come to us with the structures already in place to learn new material. We must first establish what they know and understand and, where there are no previous connections, supply them for the student. John Bruer (1993) makes a strong case for the relevance of prior knowiedge: "A good teacher will consciously capture attention and relate it to prior knowledge because how we understand and remember new material depends on what we already know. Our brains make sense of what we experience by actively connecting it with prior knowledge." Pyle and Andre (1986) echo these findings: "What a student acquires from instruction is determined as much by what the student already knows as by the nature of the instruction. Using previous knowledge to elaborate upon the presented information facilitates its transfer into long term memory." When the student relates new information to old information already in long-term memory, the student is more likely to learn and remember the new information. Prior to the introduction of new material, we must first find out if the prerequisite knowledge is there.

【出典 Donna Walker TILESTON, *10 BEST Teaching Practices How Brain Reserch, Learning Styles, and Standards Define Teaching Competencies,* CORWIN PRESS, INC.】

(1) 下線部(A)を左右する要因を，2点日本語で書け。

(2) 下線部(B)について，80字程度の日本語で説明せよ。

(3)　下線部(C)を，60字程度の日本語で説明せよ。

(4)　この論旨を踏まえ，中学校の英語の授業で新しい文法を導入をするとき，あなたはどのような工夫をするか。文法事項を一つ設定して，指導の工夫の具体例を日本語で書け。

(☆☆☆◎◎◎◎)

【3】(1)～(4)について，それぞれの英文の[　　]内に入る最も適切なものを，ア～エから一つずつ選び，その記号を書け。

(1)　Although [　　] as “the great scientist on the wheelchair”, he was not initially successful academically.

ア　know　　イ　knew　　ウ　known　　エ　knowing

(2)　Mr. Smith was shocked to see his [　　] damaged apple orchard after the hurricane went away.

ア　extend　　イ　extension　　ウ　extensive　　エ　extensively

(3)　The government will make a number of [　　] to reflect better data since the original figures were released.

ア　budgets　　イ　revisions　　ウ　procedures　　エ　allocations

(4)　If she [　　] ten more votes in the last election, she would be the first female president of the student council now.

ア　receives　　イ　received　　ウ　has received　　エ　had received

(☆☆◎◎◎◎)

【4】(1)～(4)について，それぞれの日本語の内容を表すように，[　　]内の語句を並べかえよ。

(1)　あなたが話している相手は，あなたが完璧な英語で話しているかどうかなんて気にしていない。

The person you [you / couldn’t / whether / to / care / talking / are] speak perfect English or not.

(2)　あんな体験をするのは，もう二度とごめんだ。

Never [through / I / an experience / like / go / do / want to] that again.

(3) 私の弟と妹は，どちらが電車の通路側の席に座るかでけんかした。

My brother and sister argued over [the aisle / them / one / get / would / which / of] seat on the train.

(4) 農作業を体験することで，子どもたちは労働の尊さについて，真剣に考えさせられた。

Exposure [the children / the value / to / thinking / about / left / farm work] of labor seriously.

(☆☆◎◎◎◎)

【5】ある中学3年生が，英語のノートに英語でのコミュニケーションに関する悩みを書いてきた。この内容に対して，英語教師としてのアドバイスを50語程度の英語で書け。※語数を数えて記入すること。(符号は語数に含めない)

Our ALT, Mike, always talks to us very friendly. I enjoy talking with him. But I sometimes stop talking because I don't know what to talk about. So he asks me questions and I just answer them. How do I keep a conversation going?

(☆☆☆☆◎◎◎◎)

【6】中学校学習指導要領(平成29年3月告示)には，「授業は英語で行うことを基本とする」という記載がある。英語による指示や説明を中学生に理解させる上で，有効と思われる具体的な手立てについて，100語程度の英語で書け。※語数を数えて記入すること。(符号は語数に含めない)

(☆☆☆☆◎◎◎◎)

【高等学校】

【1】次の英文を読んで，(1)～(4)の設問に答えよ。

Before choosing whether to participate in a particular conversation, we can pay attention to several characteristics of that conversation: ***time frame***, ***topic***, and ***attitude***. When we choose conversations that are more balanced within each of these areas, our lives will be more balanced as well.

First, we can notice (A)the time *frame* of the conversation — whether it is about the past, the present, or the future. Most people focus much of their conversation on the past. Often they are blaming ("If she wasn't such a jerk, I wouldn't be in this mess"), justifying ("I would have been on time, but between my crazy kids and the crazy traffic, I had a terrible morning"), or regretting ("If only I had bought that land before they started to develop it").

Conversations about the past can be fan and valuable. They can help us learn from our mistakes, celebrate our successes, grieve over our losses, and enjoy fond memories. The problem arises when our conversations are out of balance. When the majority of our conversations are about what has already happened, then both our thoughts and our actions become predominantly influenced by the past. With so much focus and attention on what has gone before, our future could become little more than a repetitive variation of the past.

An alternative is to balance our conversations, making a conscious effort to include the present and the future, as well as the past. Shifting conversations to the present offers many benefits. Much of our pleasure comes from paying attention to what we're doing in the present moment — enjoying great food, performing well in sports, or becoming lost in captivating music. As we engage in conversations about what is currently happening around us, we enhance the richness and quality of our lives.

Benefits also come from conversations about the future. These conversations help us create the most wonderful life possible. Instead of worrying, we can use our planning skills to make our vision of the future a reality.

In looking for ways to balance our conversations, we can select among four *topics* :things, others, self, or "us." Most conversations fall into one of these categories. Like the time frame of conversations, (B)the topics of most conversations are unbalanced. Most people talk about things (cars, houses, trips, football games, weather) and others (politicians, actors, neighbors, kids, coworkers) far more than they talk about themselves or about their relationships.

Of course, there is no problem in having conversations about things and others. But when we talk mostly about things and others, we neglect the rich intimacy that comes from revealing ourselves to another person. When we choose our conversations thoughtfully, we can share our heartfelt desires, fears, joys, and celebrations. We can also choose to talk about the quality of our relationships and how they can be improved.

Depending on our ***attitude***, we can choose conversations that dwell on problems, or we can choose conversations that focus on finding solutions. Most people's conversations are out of balance in this area. They spend about 90 percent of their time $_{(C)}$complaining and talking about what is not working. And they spend only about 10 percent of their time looking for solutions and celebrating what *is* working.

We can reverse these percentages. We can spend about 10 percent of our conversation space looking at and defining problems. Then we can invest the rest of our time discussing solutions, exploring new possibilities, discovering exciting new passions and potentials, and achieving amazing results.

【出典　Dave Ellis, *Becoming a MASTER STUDENT Tenth Edition*, Houghton Mifflin Company】

(1)　人生がよりバランスのとれたものになるのは，どのような会話を選んだ場合だと筆者は述べているか，日本語で書け。

(2)　下線部(A)が「現在」である場合の良い点は何か，日本語で書け。

(3)　下線部(B)について，筆者が述べている具体例と，その問題点をそれぞれ日本語で書け。

(4)　下線部(c)に費やす時間の割合を少なくすることで我々は何ができるようになるか，具体的に日本語で書け。

(☆☆☆◎◎◎◎)

【2】次の英文を読んで，(1)～(5)の設問に答えよ。

One of the most painful issues facing Indigenous peoples globally is the loss of Indigenous languages occurring in especially European settler-colonial societies in North and South America, Oceania, and Southern Africa, where English or French assume (　A　) and Indigenous children are miseducated into believing that their mother-tongues are valueless and aspire toward becoming fluent European language speakers. Felipe Molina, a traditional Yoeme (Yaqui) teacher in Tucson, Arizona, laments this crisis among young people in the Yoeme nation when he observes that "in Arizona many young Yoeme people do not speak the Yoeme language anymore so this makes it more difficult to learn about the Yoeme truth." Richard Grounds, an Indigenous Yuchie scholar and a colleague formerly at the University of Oklahoma, has been involved in Indigenous language teaching and training among college students in the persevering movement to reclaim and retain Indigenous Indian languages.

In post-apartheid South Africa/Azania, for example, many parents of Indigenous African children are demanding that their children be instructed in the English language since they view European languages as the languages of the future and the key to economic success, a belief that is reinforced by the post-apartheid African National Congress government's embracing of the ideology of globalization and foreign investment. Though Indigenous African languages are encouraged within all curricula in schools where non-Indigenous languages take precedence, the former are not required as mandatory for all students. (B)<u>This policy of voluntary schooling in Indigenous African languages</u> inevitably marginalizes Indigenous cultures since it presupposes that dominant European languages like English or Afrikaans (from the Dutch settler-colonialist legacy) are primary ***lingua franca*** for South Africa/Azania.

The lethal side effects of colonization of Indigenous peoples in Africa and the world has compelled the internalization of negative values about and

(C) of their languages and cultures. Though there are elements within government circles that are seriously committed to the instruction and training of children in African languages, the rhetoric of the Western market capitalist system holds sway in the minds of parents as they reflect upon needs for economic security in the future. (D)I was shaken too during a visit to a travel agent in Fez, Morocco, in June 2006, when the Moroccan travel agent whose mother tongue was Arabic opted to communicate in French with her fellow Moroccan who was also Arabic-speaking. The hegemonic role that English (and other European languages like French play) is destructive for the preservation of Indigenous languages. Today, there are only about 20 speakers of the Indigenous Kara/Mapuche language in Chile's Patagonia region left and the struggle is to continue such language lines by teaching children in their Indigenous mother tongues. One of the fundamental pitfalls of globalization, as with colonialism in the past, is the rush toward maintaining the supremacy of languages like English even though it is not the first language or mother tongue of most people in the world. Indigenous languages preserve the profound and subtle nuances of their cultures, and translation into English from these languages does not capture the cultural distinctiveness of such languages in which deep meanings are embedded. (E)Tsitsi Dangerembga articulates this point in her classic work, *Nervous Conditions*, when she describes villagers communicating in Shona in Zimbabwe as opposed to English, the language of formal education in the country.

【出典 Julian E. Kunnie, *The Cost of Globalization DANGERS TO THE EARTH AND ITS PEOPLE*

McFarland & Company, Inc., Publishers】

(1) 空所(A)に入る最も適切な語を，次のア～エから選び，その記号を書け。

ア submission イ reparation ウ primacy エ frailty

(2) 下線部(B)の具体的な内容を，日本語で書け。

(3) 空所(C)に入る最も適切な語を，次のア～エから選び，その記号を書け。

ア　expansion　　イ　anticipation　　ウ　formation

エ　deprecation

(4)　下線部(D)のように筆者が感じた出来事について，具体的に日本語で書け。

(5)　下線部(E)の人物は，土着の言語を英語に翻訳することをどう考えているか，具体的に日本語で書け。

(☆☆☆◎◎◎◎)

【3】次の(1)，(2)について，日本語で答えよ。

(1)　英語の授業において観点別評価を行うに当たり，その観点の一つである①「外国語表現の能力」において，評価の対象となるのはどのような能力か説明せよ。また，教科書の内容に基づいたテーマについて，②自分の考えを，英語を用いて口頭で発表する活動を行う場合に評価する点について，具体的に箇条書きで答えよ。

(2)　英語の授業において，「読むこと」の指導を行う場合に，①概要や要点をとらえるための言語活動を行う際の留意点を述べよ。また，②概要や要点をとらえることを目的とした，英語による言語活動を一つ取り上げ，その内容と実施の手順を書け。

(☆☆☆☆◎◎◎◎)

【4】次の(1)～(5)の(　　)に当てはまる最も適切な語をそれぞれア～エから一つ選び，その記号を書け。

(1)　Men with brain damage on the right side lose most or all of their (　　) skills—the ability to think in three dimensions and to rotate objects in the mind to picture how they look from different angles.

ア　chronological　　イ　spatial　　ウ　empirical　　エ　numerical

(2)　Under natural conditions, plants capture solar energy, and absorb carbon dioxide and water for (　　), which creates nutrients necessary for life and yields oxygen into the air.

ア erosion　イ hibernation　ウ synchronization
エ photosynthesis

(3) At the speech contest one of my students Mika made such a splendid delivery that she was (　　) by all the audience present.

ア acclaimed　イ provoked　ウ censured　エ dejected

(4) The growing number of foreign visitors to Japan has lifted the country's annual travel balance (　　) to a record high.

ア subtraction　イ statement　ウ surplus　エ recession

(5) There was no screen in the room. We hastily (　　) one out of an old blanket.

ア improvised　イ retained　ウ reiterated　エ assimilated

(☆☆☆◎◎◎◎)

【5】a) 次の(1)～(3)の各英文には，それぞれ誤りが1か所ある。その部分の記号を書き，正しい英語に直せ。

(1) Several years ago, as I $_{A}$was looking over my travel itinerary for a business trip, I $_{B}$noticed that I $_{C}$would have some time at the airport in Dallas before $_{D}$having caught my connecting flight.

(2) Just before $_{A}$the night falling, all the States were on alert $_{B}$due to the extreme snow, but I hurried to a supermarket to buy milk and cookies. $_{C}$Despite Mom told me to keep warm at home in such weather. I was getting ready to welcome Mr. Claus. $_{D}$That was why I caught a severe cold after all.

(3) He was constantly complaining that he was so busy $_{A}$dealing with his work every day. I knew that he didn't have enough time. $_{B}$Hoping him to take a mental break, $_{C}$I suggested to him that $_{D}$he have some time to do exercises.

b) 次の(1)，(2)は，以下のタイトルで生徒が書いてきた英文であるが，それぞれ誤りが1か所ある。その部分に下線を引いて指摘し，正しい英語に直せ。ただし，タイトルは訂正しないこと。

(1)　Title:　Our school trip to Nara

On the second day, we visited some temples and saw the Great Buddha in Nara. We were amazed because the Buddha was very big. Also, deer in Nara Park were very cute and we fed them. We bought a nice souvenir to our ALT. We had a very good time.

(2)　Title: My tennis advisor

These days, I have been practicing very hard for the city tennis tournament this weekend. My older sister was a champion of the tournament two years ago. So I ask many questions. She is very kind and always answers to them. I know it is really hard to win the tournament, but I enjoy working hard.

(☆☆◎◎◎◎)

【6】次の質問に，100語程度の英語で答えよ。※語数を数えて記入すること。(符号等は語数に含めない)

You have team-teaching lessons with an ALT. One day he says that each class has its own atmosphere and that one of your classes is silent and difficult to have the students speak out. What do you say to the ALT to cope with this problem?

(☆☆☆☆◎◎◎◎)

解答・解説

【中高共通】

【1】Part A　(1)　(A)　(2)　(C)　(3)　(B)　(4)　(B)　(5)　(C)　(6)　(A)　Part B　(1)　(A)　(2)　(C)　(3)　(D)　(4)　(B)
Part C　(1)　talk to Mr.Kato before I leave.　(2)　contact the Information Desk to sign up by Saturday.　Part D　(1)　解答略　(2)　解答略

〈解説〉スクリプトは公開されていない。Part Aは選択肢が印刷されておらず，音声のみのテストである。Part Bは対話文を聞いて選択肢で答える形式。難しい内容ではないと思われる。Part Cは英問英答形式である。Part Dは英文を聞いて，あらかじめ印刷されている日本語の質問に答える形式となっている。(1)は「気象庁からの地震データ」や「スーパーコンピュータで」等のキーフレーズ，(2)は「医療機関」，「地方自治体」等のキーワードが採点の主な観点となっている。例えば(1)では「気象庁からの」という文言をきちんと拾い，キーワードを充実に再現して解答するよう心がけること。

【2】(1) ① a ウ b イ ② (例) 意図的なコミュニティは，他者がいるという慰めにより，体と心の両方を静かに癒やしてくれる。(44字) (2) (例) コモンスペースには一時的に居住する人が多いが，ツーソンのミラグロでは，住人は家や土地に投資し通常終生暮らす。 (3) (例) ・小さい子供のいる家族のために子守をする。
・年齢を重ねていくと介護施設の代用として役立つ。
(4) (例) 発見したこと…孤独な人は，そうではない人に比べて一定期間内に命を落とす危険性が50%高いこと。 原因と影響…孤独によるストレスが原因で，それが免疫システムや身体機能を低下させる。
〈解説〉(1) ① 意図的なコミュニティとは「人々を結び付けておくことを目的に，中央広場や共用スペースのまわりに建てられた数十のアパートや家からなる住宅の集まり」となる。 ② 意図的なコミュニティが持つ可能性については，まとめとして最終段落に記述がある。
(2) 第6段落の内容を拾う。for life「死ぬまでずっと」。 (3) 第7段落を参照。baby-care「子守」。assisted-care「介護」。 (4) 第8段落の後半から解答する。trigger「引き金となる」。immune system「免疫システム」。bodily function「身体機能」。

【中学校】

【1】(1)　①　イ　②　ア　③　ウ　(2)　(例)　世界の農業生産量を2050年までに60％程度増加させること。　(3)　Ⅰ　エ　Ⅱ　ウ　(4)　(例)　諸外国では生産額による数値を発表するが，日本はカロリー摂取量に基づき自給率を計算する。(43字)　(5)　(例)　開かれた貿易システムを維持すること，生産効率を上げること，そして，万が一に備えて緊急のための食糧備蓄をすること。　(6)　(a)　article　(b)　misleading

〈解説〉(1)　①　空欄を含む文の意味は「世界の人口は急速に増加している。そして新興国の中流家庭の増加を反映し，一人あたりの食料消費量が急速に増加している」となる。per capita「一人あたりの」。②　off the top of one's head「今(即座に)思いつく限りでは」。　③　空欄を含む文の意味は「また野菜栽培も他に負けないが，生産額においてより，カロリー(摂取量)においては，ほとんど意味がない」となる。(2)　前文の新聞記事の内容を指している。　(3)　Bの応答からⅠには，日本の食料自給率の低さについての文が入る。Aの応答からⅡには，生産高ベースの率から見ると日本もそれほど悪くないという内容が入る。　(4)　Bの3度目のせりふより解答する。production value「生産額」。calorie-intake「カロリー摂取量」。　(5)　Bの最後のせりふ，I think three things are vital:「3つのことが極めて重要だと思う」以降の文から解答する。　(6)　(a)「新聞や雑誌で特定の話題について書かれているもの」は「記事」。　(b)「間違った考えや印象を与え，正しくないことを信じさせる」は「誤解を招く恐れのある」。

【2】(1)　(例)　・過去の学習が新しい学習へ与える影響。　・新しい学習が将来役に立つ度合い。　(2)　(例)　新しい情報が作業記憶に伝えられると，新しい学習に関連する過去の学習の長期記憶の中で検索が行われ，その2つの学習の関連付けがうまくいくと，よりよい成果を挙げられること。(83字)　(3)　(例)　知識のないことについて議論されているところに身を置き，その新しい情報への関連や手がか

りを見つけようとして混乱や挫折を感じる経験。(64字)

(4) (例) 従位接続詞として，例えばwhen I was a childを導入する場合，日本語の影響を受け，I was a child whenというような誤文はよく見られる。前置詞が後続の語句とセットとなり機能することを復習しながら，従位接続詞が前置詞同様に，後続の文と意味のまとまりをもつ語であることを確認する。前置詞でもあり接続詞でもあるbeforeやafterなどを例に挙げながら説明することが理解を助ける。

〈解説〉(1) 次文のfirst, secondで始まる文を解答として挙げる。

(2) positive transfer「正の転移」については第1段落の4～5文目を参照。

(3) Cを含む文意は「何人かの生徒にはこのことは日常よく起きる」。第2段落の3～4文目が「このこと」の説明にあたる部分である。

(4) 採点の主な観点は「既にある知識を活用すること等に関連した工夫であること」である。解答例以外でも，受動態やbe going to ～など，疑問文や否定文がbe動詞の文のルールに則っているものなど，同種，同ルールで説明がつくものを整理しながら教えることが考えられる。

【3】(1) ウ　(2) エ　(3) イ　(4) エ

〈解説〉(1) 「車いすの科学者として知られているが，元々彼は学問的に優れていなかった」。分詞構文。　(2) 「スミスさんはハリケーンが通り過ぎた後，広範囲に渡り被害を受けたリンゴ園を見てショックを受けた」。extensively「広範囲に」。　(3) 「最初の数値が発表されたので，政府はよりよいデータを反映するために多くの見直しをするだろう」。make a revision「修正する」。　(4) 「もし彼女がこの前の選挙でもう10票獲得していたら，今ごろは生徒会初の女性会長なのだが」。if節は仮定法過去完了，主節は仮定法過去。

【4】(1) are talking to couldn't care whether you　(2) do I want to go through an experience like　(3) which one of them would get the aisle

(4) to farm work left the children thinking about the value

〈解説〉(1) the person you are talking toが主語で，the personはtoの目的語

である。　(2)　neverが強調のため文頭に置かれ，その後は疑問文と同じ語順となる。go through an experience「経験する」。　(3)　which one of them「弟と妹の(うちの)どちら」。aisle seat「通路側の席」。
(4)　exposure to ～「～に接すること，～を体験すること」。farm work「農作業」。leave O C「OをCにしておく」。

【5】(例)　If you talk more, you'll have something in common to talk about. Otherwise, tell him what you are interested in. When he doesn't know much about it, you can explain it. Or ask him questions that starts with who, what when and so on. It'll bring more information and you can keep it going. (54 words)
〈解説〉ALTと何を話していいのか分からないので会話が中断するというのが悩みのようである。解答例では，自分の興味のあることをALTに説明したり，詳しい内容の質問をしたりして会話を続ける工夫をすることをアドバイスしている。

【6】(例)　As for instructions in English, it's important to use classroom English repeatedly so that the students get familiar with those expressions. When we explain a new material to the students, we should pay attention to how much they understand by interacting. If they don't understand the vocabulary in the explanation, we can rephrase it. Or sometimes the use of non-verbal tips is useful. If they seem to understand the explanation unclearly, we should let them acquire it by presenting more examples or taking small steps again from the basic ones already introduced. Having a lot of exposure to English will lead to their deep understanding. (105 words)
〈解説〉解答例では，クラスルームイングリッシュを繰り返し使うことで，決まった表現に慣れること，言い換え，非言語の手段，更なる例示や既習事項から段階を踏みなおすことなどを挙げている。

【高等学校】

【1】(1) (例) 時間枠，話題，姿勢のそれぞれの範囲内でバランスのとれた会話を選んだ場合。 (2) (例) 人生の豊かさや質を高めることができるところ。 (3) (例) 具体例…自分自身や人間関係より，事物や他人について話すことがはるかに多い。 問題点…自分自身のことを他の人に話すことで生まれる深い親密さを無視することになること。 (4) (例) 解決策を話し合う，新しい可能性を探求する，わくわくするような新しい感情や潜在能力を発見する，びっくりするような成果をあげることなどに時間をかけることができる。

〈解説〉(1) 第1段落の2文目，conversations that are more balanced within each of these areasが解答にあたる。these areaとは前文の，time frame, topicとattitudeを指す。 (2) 第4段落の最後の文，we enhance the richness and quality of livesに注目する。 (3) 会話の話題は4つで，事物，他人，自分自身，自分たちの人間関係。どのようにアンバランスであるかは下線部Bの次文に，その問題点は次段落にある。 (4) 最終段落の最後の文を拾う。

【2】(1) ウ (2) (例) 土着の言語は学校のカリキュラムで奨励されてはいるが，全生徒に対して必須ではない。 (3) エ

(4) (例) アラビア語を母語とする旅行業者の人が同じくアラビア語を話す同僚とフランス語を選び意思疎通をしていたこと。

(5) (例) 土着の言語は意味深く微妙な文化のニュアンスを保持しているので，その文化的特殊性を表現することはできない。

〈解説〉(1) 空欄前後の内容は「ヨーロッパ人の植民社会では，英語やフランス語が絶対だと見なされている」。primacy「第1位」。 (2) 下線部Bは「土着のアフリカの言語の教育は強制ではないとする政策」。前文に具体的な内容が示されている。 (3) 植民地化の副作用について述べている部分である。自分たちの言語や文化に対して，否定的価値観と卑下する気持ちを，強制的に植え付けたことが挙げられている。deprecation「見下すこと」。 (4) I was shaken.「私は衝撃を受けた」。

モロッコの旅行業者を訪れたときの出来事が解答にあたる。　(5)　下線部Eの前文を参照する。

【3】(1)　(例)　①　音声，語彙，文法，語法，言語の背景にある文化などに係る知識を活用して，実際に話したり書いたりすることにより，英語で表現することのできる能力。　②　・発表内容(オリジナリティ，論理展開，文法)　・発表方法(発音，リズム，イントネーション，声量，スピード，表情，アイコンタクト)　(2)　(例)①　読む目的を明らかにし，それに応じた読み方を選択させることや読みとるべきポイントをあらかじめ明示して理解を促す工夫をする。
②　内容…個々に概要や要点をとらえて読む活動を行った後，グループで話し合う活動を通して，全文の要約として正しい順序となるよう並び替える。完成後全体を通して再度読み，内容や構成についての理解を深めたり，個の要約文について振り返ったりする。　実施手順…グループのそれぞれのメンバーが，英文のエッセイやストーリーの一部を読み，それぞれが要約する。要約文を順次発表し，話し合うことで全体を完成させる。

〈解説〉(1)　①「評価規準の作成，評価方法等の工夫改善のための参考資料(高等学校 外国語)」(平成24年7月　国立教育政策研究所　教育課程研究センター)における「第2編　外国語科における評価規準の作成，評価方法等の工夫改善」が参考となる。　②　発表の内容と発表の方法に分けてそれぞれ挙げるとよい。発表の方法については，原稿を読んだり内容を暗記したりするのではなく，内容を理解しアウトラインやポイントを書いたメモに基づいて発表しているかなども評価できる。　(2)　①　主題文・支持文・まとめ文など基本的な文章構成についてあらかじめ学習しておくことも挙げられる。　②　複数のグループが同題材で同活動をすれば，要約文を比較し合うなども可能となる。

【4】(1)　イ　(2)　エ　(3)　ア　(4)　ウ　(5)　ア

〈解説〉(1)「右側の脳に損傷を持つ人は，ほとんどまたは全ての空間認識力，即ち3次元で考え，物体が他の角度からどのように見えるか描くために，物体を頭の中で回転させる能力を失う」となる。spatial「空間の」。 (2)「自然の条件下で植物は太陽エネルギーを得て，光合成のため二酸化炭素と水を吸収する。それは生きるのに必要な栄養素を作り，空気中に酸素を放出する」となる。photosynthesis「光合成」。
(3)「スピーチコンテストで生徒の一人のミカはすばらしい発表をしたので，彼女はそこにいる観客全員に称賛された」となる。acclaim「称賛する」。 (4)「日本への外国人観光客数の増大で，国の年間旅行収支の黒字は過去最高まで上向いた」となる。surplus「黒字」。
(5)「部屋にはスクリーンがなかった。私たちは大至急古い毛布で作った」となる。improvise「即席でつくる」。

【5】a) (1) 記号…D 正しい英語…catching (2) 記号…C 正しい英語…Although (3) 記号…B 正しい英語…Hoping that he would take b) (1) 下線を引く部分…4文目のto 正しい英語…for (2) 下線を引く部分…4文目のanswers to them 正しい英語…answers them
〈解説〉a) (1)「私は乗り継ぎ便に乗る前にダラスの空港でしばらく時間があると気づいた」。主節との時制のずれを直す。 (2) despiteは前置詞。「～だけれども」という意の接続詞を置く。 (3) hopeは「hope＋O＋to～」という文型をとらない。 b) (1) buyを第3文型で使う場合，前置詞はfor。 (2)「彼女はいつも親切で，質問に答えてくれる」。answerは他動詞であり前置詞は不要。

【6】(例) I think it's hard to have every student to speak out in the same way or at the same rate but it's true that increasing students' participation is our goal. First, we should ensure a comfortable classroom environment in which students are given positive feedback and not laughed at when making mistakes or performing poorly. Second, giving a range of activities that target different types of learners will help. And ideally, they are designed to have students take turns when working in groups or pairs so that all students are required to participate. We should plan accordingly and encourage them to speak more in class. (104 words)

〈解説〉「生徒が授業で発言しない」という課題を感じているALTがいる。この問題に対処するため英語教師として何と言うかという問題である。課題解決に向けた提案をいくつか述べることが必要である。解答例では，雰囲気づくりと様々な活動の提供を挙げている。と様々な活動提供を挙げている。

2018年度　実施問題

【中高共通】

【1】リスニングテスト

Part A

(1) Write your answer on your answer sheet.

(2) Write your answer on your answer sheet.

(3) Write your answer on your answer sheet.

(4) Write your answer on your answer sheet.

(5) Write your answer on your answer sheet.

(6) Write your answer on your answer sheet.

Part B

(1) (A) To translate books into Italian.

(B) To work for an Italian restaurant.

(C) Because she has a plan to take a trip to Italy.

(D) Because she is interested in reading about Italian food and cooking.

(2) (A) Consider an option.

(B) Prepare for the exam.

(C) Stop using his smartphone altogether.

(D) Promise not to use his smartphone for more than an hour a day.

(3) (A) The convention center is not so near.

(B) The man must be late for the meeting.

(C) Other people have got lost in Sendai.

(D) There are not many tourists from abroad in Sendai.

(4) (A) Find a book to buy for himself.

(B) Buy a science fiction DVD.

(C) Use the coupon to buy a CD.

(D) Look for a new magazine for himself.

Part C

(1) Write your answer on your answer sheet.

(2) Write your answer on your answer sheet.

PartD

(1) あるアメリカ人の学生は，どのような方法で「エコ・ソープ」を作っているか，日本語で書け。

(2) (1)のアメリカ人の学生が，「エコ・ソープ」を作る活動を通して，カンボジアの人々に望んでいることは何か，日本語で書け。

(☆☆☆☆◎◎◎◎)

【2】次の英文を読んで，(1)～(4)の設問に答えよ。

The robots are coming, but the march of automation will displace jobs more gradually than some alarming forecasts suggest.

A measured pace is likely because what is technically possible is only one factor in determining how quickly new technology is adopted, according to a new study by the McKinsey Global Institute. Other crucial ingredients include economics, labor markets, regulations and social attitudes.

(A)<u>The report</u>, which was released Thursday, breaks jobs down by work tasks — more than 2,000 activities across 800 occupations, from stock clerk to company boss. The institute, the research arm of the consulting firm McKinsey & Company, concludes that many tasks can be automated and that most jobs have activities ripe for automation. But the near-term impact, the report says, will be to transform work more than to eliminate jobs.

Globally, the McKinsey researchers calculated that 49 percent of time spent on work activities could be automated with “currently demonstrated technology” either already in the marketplace or being developed in labs.

That, the report says, translates into $15.8 trillion in wages and the equivalent of 1.1 billion workers worldwide. But only 5 percent of jobs can be entirely automated.

"This is going to take (①)," said James Manyika, a director of the institute and an author of the report. "How automation affects employment will not be decided simply by what is technically feasible, which is what technologists tend to focus on."

The report, a product of years of research by the McKinsey group, adds to the growing body of research on automation and jobs.

(B)Conclusions about the relationship between the two vary widely. Examining trends in artificial intelligence, Carl Benedikt Frey and Michael A. Osborne, researchers at Oxford University, estimated in a widely cited paper published in 2013 that 47 percent of jobs in the United States were at risk from automation.

By contrast, a report published last year by the Organization for Economic Cooperation and Development concluded that across its 21-member countries, 9 percent of jobs could be automated on average.

Differing assumptions, and sheer uncertainty about the future, explain the conflicting outlooks.

Throughout history, times of rapid technological progress have stoked fears of jobs (②). More than 80 years ago, the English economist John Maynard Keynes warned of a "new disease" of "technological unemployment."

Today, it is the rise of artificial intelligence in increasingly clever software and machines that is stirring concern. The standard view is that routine work in factories and offices, like bookkeeping or operating basic machinery, is most vulnerable to automation.

But A.I. software that can read and analyze text or speech — so-called natural language processing — is encroaching on the work of professionals. For example, there is a lot of legal work that is routine, said Frank Levy, a labor economist at the Massachusetts Institute of Technology. But that routine work, sifting through documents for relevant information, is wrapped in language, which had protected lawyers from the effects of automation. (C)<u>But no longer</u>.

"Natural language processing opens the door to doing more and more work that was beyond automation until recently," Mr. Levy said.

The McKinsey report cites natural language processing as a key technology: The faster it develops, the more that tasks can be automated; a slower pace means less automation.

【出典　*The New York Times*, January14-15, 2017 】

(1)　下線部(A)が結論付けている内容を，70字程度の日本語で書け。

(2)　(　①　)，(　②　)に入る最も適切な語を，ア～エからそれぞれ一つずつ選び，その記号を書け。

①　ア　turns　　イ　decades　　ウ　actions
　　エ　responsibilities

②　ア　measures　　イ　data　　ウ　losses
　　エ　reports

(3)　下線部(B)が示す内容を，具体的に80字程度の日本語で書け。

(4)　下線部(C)が表す内容を，具体的に日本語で書け。

(☆☆☆☆◎◎◎◎)

【中学校】

【１】次の会話文を読んで，(1)～(5)の設問に答えよ。

Charlie　: That's precisely the topic I wanted to talk to you about. I will show you the (　①　) results right here ... It turned out that ICX is not necessarily chosen by men — not all the time anyway — after all. Up to 65％ of the time, the final purchase decision is made by female companions of the car owners — wives or girlfriends. Women love to drive that car and absolutely love to be seen in that car. Historically,

	[I] and this market segment has been completely ignored. It's almost scary. It's time for us to wake up and pay attention to (A)those real decision makers!
Rebecca :	That's amazing, but you know, in a way, I am not surprised. I personally love that car, too. I love the way people look at me when I drive an ICX. I can easily come up with a couple of commercials to specifically target women who feel the same way. Let me tell you, they are out there.
Andrew :	Hold on a minute. As I said, I know this brand inside and out more than anyone else in this company. Folks, this car isn't made for women. It is a car that successful (B)[when / they / businessmen / have / feel / crave / they] "arrived," you know? As I said, [II] to turn our backs on this loyal customer base. I think it's suicidal.
Charlie :	I tell you what is suicidal. To stick to the (②) − *that's* suicidal. Pretty soon, GX, our perennial competitor from Company G, will surpass us if we don't do this. They have been (③) at our market share, and I heard a rumor that they are coming up with a killer design change and marketing strategy to go with it. Unless [III], ICX will be history. The market will pass us by. Look at the chart of this market-share change over the past five years.

【出典　ロッシェル・カップ　小野智世子　増田真紀子　外国人との交渉に成功するビジネス英語　語研】

(1) (①)～(③)に入る最も適切な語を，次のア～カから一つずつ選び，その記号を書け。

ア launching　イ survey　ウ status quo　エ nibbling
オ promotion　カ prototype

(2) [I]～[III]に入る最も適切なものを，次のア～オから一つずつ選び，その記号を書け。

ア　it is a big mistake

イ　we go through a complete makeover

ウ　this particular segment responds very well

エ　this was not well known

オ　this may be the last opportunity

(3)　下線部(A)が表す内容を，具体的に20字程度の日本語で書け。

(4)　下線部(B)を，意味が通るように並べかえよ。

(5)　次の(a)，(b)の説明にそれぞれ該当する1語を，会話文中から抜き出して書け。

(a)　to be even better or greater than someone or something else

(b)　a planned series of actions for achieving something

(☆☆☆☆◎◎◎)

【２】次の英文を読んで，(1)～(4)の設問に答えよ。

"A fundamental change is needed in the way we think about education's role in global development, because it has a catalytic impact on the well-being of individuals and the future of our planet. ... Now, more than ever, education has a responsibility to be in gear with 21st century challenges and aspirations, and foster the right types of values and skills that will lead to sustainable and inclusive growth, and peaceful living together. "

(A)Irina Bokova, Director-General of UNESCO

"Education can, and must, contribute to a new vision of sustainable global development."(UNESCO, 2015)

Embarking on the path of sustainable development will require a profound transformation of how we think and act. To create a more sustainable world and to engage with sustainability-related issues as described in the SDGs*, individuals must become sustainability change-makers. They require the knowledge, skills, values and attitudes that empower them to contribute to sustainable development. Education, therefore, is crucial for the achievement of sustainable development. (B)<u>However, not all kinds of education support sustainable development</u>. Education that promotes economic growth alone may well also lead to an increase in unsustainable consumption patterns. The now well-established approach of Education for Sustainable Development (ESD) empowers learners to take informed decisions and responsible actions for environmental integrity, economic viability and a just society for present and future generations.

ESD aims at developing competencies that empower individuals to reflect on their own actions, taking into account their current and future social, cultural, economic and environmental impacts, from a local and a global perspective. Individuals should also be empowered to act in complex situations in a sustainable manner, which may require them to strike out in new directions; and to participate in socio-political processes, moving their societies towards sustainable development.

ESD has to be understood as an integral part of quality education, inherent in the concept of lifelong learning: All educational institutions — from preschool to tertiary education and in non-formal and informal education — can and should consider it their responsibility to deal intensively with matters of sustainable development and to foster the development of sustainability competencies. ESD provides an education that matters and is truly relevant to every learner in the light of today's challenges.

ESD is holistic and transformational education that addresses learning content and outcomes, pedagogy and the learning environment. Thus, ESD does not only integrate contents such as climate change, poverty and sustainable consumption into the curriculum; it also creates interactive, learner-centred teaching and learning settings. What ESD requires is a shift from teaching to learning. It asks for an action-oriented, transformative pedagogy, which supports self-directed learning, participation and collaboration, problem − orientation, inter − and transdisciplinarity and the linking of formal and informal learning. Only such pedagogical approaches make possible the development of the key competencies needed for promoting sustainable development.

(注) *SDGs: Sustainable Development Goals

【出典 *Education for Sustainable Development Goals Learning Objectivies*: UNESCO 2017】

(1)　下線部(A)が述べている現在の教育のもつ責任を，2点日本語で書け。

(2)　下線部(B)の例として，筆者はどのような教育を取り上げているか，日本語で書け。

(3)　筆者はESDがどのような教育をもたらすと述べているか，40字程度の日本語で書け。

(4)　筆者はどのような教育の手法が，持続可能な発展の推進に必要な能力の育成を可能にすると述べているか，70字程度の日本語で書け。

(☆☆☆☆◎◎◎◎)

【3】(1)～(4)について，それぞれの英文の[　　]内に入る最も適切なものを，ア～エからそれぞれ一つずつ選び，その記号を書け。

(1)　Paul is normally [　　], so it's surprising when he tells a joke.

ア　talkative　　イ　gossipy　　ウ　energetic　　エ　reserved

(2)　When Satoshi walked onto the stage to give his presentation in English, he suddenly [　　]. He couldn't say anything at first.

ア　called out　　イ　chilled out　　ウ　froze up　　エ　cried up

(3)　Mr. Smith is an [　　] sumo fan. He never misses watching sumo on TV.

ア　avid　　イ　adept　　ウ　invalid　　エ　ignorant

(4) One of the jobs we are always asked to do as teachers is to evaluate our students. [　　], we are required to show how good they are.

ア　Notoriously　　イ　Incidentally　　ウ　In other words

エ　By no means

(☆☆☆☆◎◎◎◎)

【4】(1)～(4)について，それぞれの日本語の内容を表すように，[　　]内の語句を並べかえよ。

(1) 自分が10年後に何をしているか，思い描くことができない。

[what / can't / I / I'll / doing / be / visualize] ten years from now.

(2) 直美は，2年間海外留学し無事帰国した。

Naomi [nice / overseas / homecoming / had / studying / a / after] for two years.

(3) 彼らは，まず精神的要素を強くする必要がある。

They need [go / to / have / the / stuff / strong / mental] first.

(4) 私たちは，女性が人権を侵されない世界を実現していかなければならない。

We must realize the kind of world [women / rights / free / are / human / from / where]　abuses.

(☆☆☆◎◎◎◎◎)

【5】次の英文は，ある中学3年生が書いた英語学習に対する振り返りである。この内容に対して，英語教師としてのアドバイスを50語程度の英語で書け。

I've studied English for five years. I like English very much and I study it hard. But I'm not good at speaking. I need to practice it more. I want to speak English better. I'm very happy if you tell me what I should do. I'll try everything to improve my English.

(☆☆☆◎◎◎◎)

【6】中学校の英語の授業において，自分の考えや気持ちなどを英語で伝え合う活動を行う上での指導上の留意点を2点取り上げ，70語程度の英語で書け。

(☆☆☆☆◎◎◎◎)

【高等学校】

【1】次の英文を読んで，(1)〜(4)の設問に答えよ。

The ethics of the global commons are explicitly cosmopolitan in the sense that they refer to the earth's environment as a single biological community that creates a human community of (　A　). This ethics emphasizes that national gains or advantages need to be sacrificed or moderated if the environmental problems are to be solved and the 'tragedy of the commons' is to be avoided.

Global warming (GW) is a good example of both positive and negative duties. At face value it seems reasonably clear that there are negative duties for those countries that have contributed most to GW, and that will do so in the future, to cease doing so. Most people would agree that we should all take responsibility for harming someone else, especially if we have benefited from it. In the case of GW $_{(B)}$<u>this</u> would mean that there is a proportionate responsibility on the part of the advanced industrial countries, especially the USA, Europe, Japan, and Canada, to reduce their greenhouse gas emissions (GHGE) and to take financial responsibility for the harms that their past and future emissions will cause others. There are also positive duties on the part of the richer states to aid the poorest states and populations, who will be disproportionately affected and who have done the least to (　①　). We can think, for instance, of countries like Pacific island states, which are barely industrialized but which are likely to be the first to disappear. If we have harmed someone, we ought to help them overcome the harm we have caused them, especially if they are unable to do so unassisted. That is, there is not only a negative duty to (　②　), but also a positive duty to (　③　). This is an issue of retributive justice — a duty to aid those most affected by one's harms.

The overall cost to rich states of addressing GW, including the likely impacts of rising sea levels and other environmental consequences, are proportionally lower than for poor states. This issue is of course complicated by the fact that the production of GHGE is so central to economic growth, especially in industrializing countries. (C)Poorer countries are at a disadvantage in both regards. Any attempt to curtail their output implies a restriction on the prospects for economic growth in those countries that perhaps need it most. Indeed, there is even an argument that the 'people in the developing world need to increase their emissions in order to attain a minimally decent standard of living for themselves and their families' (Singer and Gregg 2004: 57). In addition, for rich states, dealing with climate change might only affect the luxury or non-necessary end of their quality of life, whereas for poor states reducing emissions will more probably affect the basic necessities of life and survival.

【出典 JOHN BAYLIS, STEVE SMITH, AND PATRICIA OWENS, *THE GLOBALIZATION OF WORLD POLITICS An introduction to international relations Sixth Edition;* OXFORD UNIVERSITY PRESS】

(1) 空所(A)に入る最も適切な語を，次のア～エから選び，その記号を書け。

ア interdependence　イ dependence　ウ self-dependence

エ independence

(2) 下線部(B)が示す内容を日本語で書け。

(3) 文中の(①)～(③)に入る最も適切な句を，次のア～ウから一つずつ選び，その記号を書け。ただし，同じ記号を2回以上書かないこと。

ア cease or reduce GHGE　イ contribute to GW

ウ redress the damage done

(4) 下線部(C)にとって，地球温暖化対策への取組はどのような影響をおよぼす可能性があると本文では述べられているか，2点日本語で書け。

(☆☆☆☆◎◎◎◎◎)

【2】次の英文を読んで，(1)～(4)の設問に答えよ。

In the past, famine was often misunderstood as an inadequate food supply. Now we have grasped that — notwithstanding the alarming implications of a soaring global population, climate change and the effects of current farming practices — the key question is who can access food. People die because of (　A　) governments as well as poor rains. In each of the current cases, the problem has complex roots, but the striking common thread is conflict: the impact of jihadist group Boko Haram in northern Nigeria, the civil war in South Sudan and a war — fuelled in part by British and US bombs — that has destroyed and paralysed Yemen's ports, to devastating effect in a country which imported 90% of its food. In Somalia, the primary immediate cause is drought, but decades of conflict have left it vulnerable.

So these crises are in large part manmade; and (B)they were seen coming. Agencies began warning about the risks in South Sudan almost two years ago. In November, Médecins Sans Frontières warned that malnutrition appeared to have wiped out young children in parts of Borno state, Nigeria. Yet even now, attention is minimal and the response limited. Our unwillingness to recognise such creeping disasters — compared with, say, earthquakes — is remarkable; one expert has described it as " 'no corpses, no food aid' myopia". Their gradual nature gives us a greater opportunity to intervene but seems to reduce our inclination to do so.

When the pictures of starving children with bloated bellies appear, we have already failed. In 2011, "the best chronicled descent into mass starvation in history" saw a quarter of a million people die in Somalia, many of them before the famine was declared, despite scores of warnings. Never again, people said — but here we are again, and the indifference is equally pronounced. The UN says it needs $4.4bn by the end of March to avert a catastrophe. So far, it has $90m in hand. Pledges need to be fulfilled, and quickly; and much more is needed. The department for international development announced £100m in "new humanitarian support" for South Sudan, but it soon emerged that the money had already been allocated to the country.

(C)Those at risk need more than emergency support of course. The international community must continue to pursue peace and, in the meantime, do their utmost to ensure aid can be delivered. Supporting longer-term development work is essential.

The shortfall must also be put into context: there have been massive increases in global humanitarian aid, but they have not kept up with the rising tide of need. Even the best-intentioned perhaps feel too overwhelmed by the world's other woes to register this fresh human misery. Populist politicians such as Nigel Farage grumble that "charity begins at home", meaning it should end there too. There are concerns that the United States, currently Nigeria's biggest donor, will scale back aid in Africa. In the UK, Conservative MPs seek to end the commitment to spend 0.7% of national income on aid.

Defenders say that it is in the developed world's own interests to promote the well-being and stability of other communities, but it is also a question of basic human decency. As the UN secretary-general António Guterres stated, there is no excuse for inaction in a world of plenty. The growing food crisis not only has the makings of a tragedy, as he warned, but of a scandal.

【出典　*The Guardian*, 23 February 2017】

(1)　空所(　A　)に入る最も適切な語を，次のア～エから選び，その記号を書け。

ア　coalition　　イ　disintegrating　　ウ　established　　エ　settled

(2)　下線部(B)の状況にもかかわらず人々の反応が鈍いのはなぜか，日本語で書け。

(3)　下線部(C)について，必要とされているものは何か，具体的に日本語で書け。

(4)　世界の人道的援助はどのような現状であると述べられているか，日本語で書け。

(☆☆☆☆◎◎◎◎◎)

【3】次の(1)，(2)について，日本語で答えよ。

(1)　英語の授業を通して，「積極的にコミュニケーションを図ろうとする態度を育成する」ことは重要なことである。具体的には生徒のどのような態度を育成したらよいか，箇条書きで答えよ。

(2)　高等学校学習指導要領において「英語表現Ⅰ」で示されている言語活動の一つに，「与えられた話題について，即興で話す」とある。このことを踏まえ，①「即興で話す」活動を授業で実施する際に授業者が留意すべきことについて具体的に箇条書きで答えよ。また，②ある話題について，互いの考えを口頭で「即興でやり取りをする」活動の例を一つ取り上げ，その内容と実施の手順を書け。

(☆☆☆☆◎◎◎◎◎)

【4】次の(1)～(5)の(　　)に当てはまる最も適切な語をそれぞれア～エから一つ選び，その記号を書け。

(1)　I (　　) the opportunity to go to France as an exchange student on a scholarship.

ア　seized　　イ　delegated　　ウ　hurled　　エ　denigrated

(2)　Ami had a (　　) day at the office. Three members in her section got cold and there were only two poeple working there today.

ア　stingy　　イ　blatant　　ウ　hectic　　エ　transient

(3)　This reference book is (　　), so it is good for a learner to read.

ア interminable　イ interstitial　ウ intangible
エ intelligible

(4) Customer: Excuse me, I'm looking for a magazine containing an (　　) of the interview with the coach of the Japanese national soccer team.
Clerk: Let me see... Here you are.
ア excerpt　イ exponent　ウ agenda　エ offshoot

(5) After five days away from home, Elizabeth found that her cherry tomato plants in the porch had (　　) because it had been so hot and dry.
ア disgraced　イ tangled　ウ withered　エ unprecedented

(☆☆☆◎◎◎◎)

【5】a) 次の(1)～(3)の各英文には，それぞれ誤りが1か所ある。その部分の記号を書き，正しい英語に直せ。

(1) The Japanese rugby team $_{A}$performed very well in the match. They $_{B}$won the South African team. On that day, many Japanese people $_{C}$were delighted and $_{D}$celebrated the victory.

(2) He wished to resign on $_{A}$the reason that he was ill. But I $_{B}$persuaded him out of resignation. I advised him to take $_{C}$a few days off and see $_{D}$a doctor.

(3) Satoshi has to $_{A}$return the city library the books today. As it is rainy and windy, he $_{B}$has no choice but walk to the library. It $_{C}$takes him about ten minutes to get there on foot. He $_{D}$can't be bothered to walk all the way in such weather.

b) 次の(1)，(2)は，以下のタイトルで生徒が書いてきた英文であるが，それぞれ誤りが1か所ある。その部分に下線を引いて指摘し，正しい英語に直せ。ただし，タイトルは訂正しないこと。

(1) Title:　My Future Job

I want to contribute to my community. There are many elderly people in this area, so I hope supporting their happy lives. I want to work for my hometown and find solutions to aging problems in the future.

(2)　Title:　My Summer Vacation

I went to Hokkaido to see a rock concert. The concert was taken place outside. There was a large audience. It was so exciting. I never forget my experience this summer.

(☆☆☆☆◎◎◎◎◎)

【６】次の質問に，100語程度の英語で答えよ。

A group of senior high school teachers from abroad visit your school and ask you what the merits of club activities for students are or what they can learn from club activities. How do you explain them to the foreign teachers?

(☆☆☆☆☆◎◎◎◎◎)

解答・解説

【中高共通】

【１】PartA　(1)　(C)　(2)　(A)　(3)　(C)　(4)　(B)　(5)　(B)　(6)　(A)　PartB　(1)　(D)　(2)　(B)　(3)　(C)　(4)　(A)

PartC　(1)　(I should) get a numbered ticket at the information desk.

(2)　(I should) post my responses on the conference website.

PartD　(1)　解答略　(2)　解答略

〈解説〉スクリプトが公表されていないので，一般的な注意になるが，数字や名詞には注意すること。放送回数が2回ならば1回目で概要をつかみ，2回目でチェックできるが，1回しか放送されない場合には集中して聞くことが必要である。なお，Part Bについては問題用紙に選択肢があるので，放送を聞く前に4つとも読んでおくと，どういう話題の英語を聞き取るのか事前に把握することができる。(1)はイタリアに関する話題で，おそらく女性が何かをする理由を聞かれている。(2)はスマートフォンを使い過ぎて，勉学に励む時間が取れないというような話題かと思われる。(3)は男性が仙台で行われる会議に遅れて，その理由を聞かれているかもしれない。(4)は書店かどこかに行って何をするかその目的を問われているかもしれない。

【2】(1)　多くの職務は自動化が可能で，ほとんどの仕事は自動化に適した作業を含んでいる。また短期的な影響は，仕事を排除するというより仕事に変化をもたらすだろう。(74字)　(2)　①　イ　②　ウ　(3)　自動化の可能性について，オクスフォード大学の推定では米国の仕事の47パーセント，OECDの報告では21加盟国の仕事のうち平均9パーセントとなった。(79字)　(4)　今やAIソフトウェアが弁護士の仕事を侵食している。

〈解説〉(1)　第3段落の2文目に(報告書を作成した)研究機関が結論付けたとあり，concludes that 以下が報告書の結論となるが，3文目に短期的な影響についても述べられているので，これも結論に加えたい。

(2)　①　第4段落の1文目で「仕事に費やす時間の49パーセントが自動化される可能性がある」と試算されているが，3文目では「完全に自動化できるのは，仕事のわずか5パーセントだろう」とある。自動化される仕事は予想よりもはるかに低いので，空欄は「何十年もかかるだろう」という意味になると判断する。　②　空欄を含む文は，「歴史を通して，急速な科学技術の進歩の時代は～の不安を煽っている」と述べているので，「仕事の喪失」が不安を煽ると考える。

(3)　第7段落1文目には，「調査結果について自動化と職種の関係についての結論は大きく異なる」という意味のことが述べられている。結論のひとつは同2文目の「アメリカの仕事の47パーセントは自動化の危険にさらされている」で，もうひとつの結論は第8段落の「一方，21加盟国で，平均して仕事の9パーセントが自動化される可能性がある」である。この2つの具体例を加えて書くとよい。　(4)　第12段落の1文目に「文字の解読や音声の解析ができるAIソフトウェア，いわゆるNLP(自然言語処理)は，専門家の仕事を侵食している」と現在の状況を述べている。3文目では，「弁護士は情報を求めて大量の文書をふるいにかけなければならないが，言語の特殊性から，この分野の仕事を自動化するのは困難だった」という意味のことが述べられている。しかし「今やそうではない」と続くと考える。

【中学校】

【1】(1)　①　イ　②　ウ　③　エ　(2)　Ⅰ　エ　Ⅱ　ア　Ⅲ　イ　(3)　車の所有者の妻や女友達といった連れの女性(20字)

(4)　businessmen crave when they feel they have　(5)　(a)　surpass

(b)　strategy

〈解説〉(1)　①　空欄の後の文で「ICXを購入の際，65パーセントまでは車の所有者の連れである女性が最終の決定をする」とあり，具体的な数字を挙げて説明していることなどから，調査結果(the survey result)を述べていると判断する。　②　Andrewの発言の5～6文目の「この得意客の層(男性層)に背を向けることは大きな間違いである。これは自殺行為だと思う」という意見を受けて，Charlieは「何が自殺行為か教えてあげよう。～に固執すること―それが自殺行為だ」とあるので，今まで通り男性客に固執すること，つまり「現状(ウstatus quo)に固執すること」と考える。　③　Charlieの最後の発言の3文目に「女性層をターゲットにしないと，我々の永遠のライバル車のGXは，私たちを追い抜くだろう」とあり，その次に実際「彼らは私たちのマーケットシェアを～している」とあるので，「エのnibbling『ちびちび食べる』→少しずつシェアを奪っている」と考える。　(2)　Ⅰ　空欄の直後に「このマーケット層(女性層)は完全に無視されてきた」とあり，等位接続詞のandで結ばれているので，同じような内容の「このこと(車購入の最終決定権が女性にある)はあまり知られていなかった」がくる。

Ⅱ　Andrewの発言の3文目に「この車は女性のために作られていない」とあり，男性層をターゲットと考えている。「この得意客の層(男性層)に背を向けることは～」とあるので「大きな間違いである」だと判断する。　Ⅲ　Charlieの最後の発言の4文目の半ばに「彼らはすごいデザインチェンジと，それと一緒に市場戦略を考え出している」とある。

それを受け「もし～しないならば，ICXは過去のものとなるだろう」と危機感を表しているので，「完全な作り変え(ターゲットを男性から女性に移す)をしないと～」と考える。 (3) Charlieの発言の4文目に「ICXを購入の際，65パーセントまでは車の所有者の連れである女性が最終の決定をする」とあり，女性が車を購入する際の本当の意思決定者だとわかる。 (4) 「出世したビジネスマンが，自分は成功したんだと感じる時，強く欲しがるものが車である」という意味。It is～that …の強調構文。craveは「強く欲しがる」，arriveは「成功する」という意味。 (5) (a)は「他の誰かあるいは何かよりもずっとよい，あるいはずっとすばらしい」という意味。 (b)は「あることを達成するための，計画的な一連の行動」という意味。

【2】(1) ・21世紀の課題や願いに向けて準備をする責任 ・持続可能で包括的な成長と，平和的な共存に向かうであろう正しい価値観や技能を育む責任 (2) 持続不可能な消費パターンを増幅する方向に向ける可能性が高い経済成長のみを促進する教育 (3) 現在と未来の世代の経済成長などに，十分な情報を得て責任ある行動をとる力をつける教育 (41字) (4) 行動指向的で，変容可能な教育で，自律学習や参加，協力，問題志向型で，多分野にまたがって，公式学習と非公式学習のつながりを求める教育の手法。(69字)

〈解説〉(1) Irina Bokovaのスピーチの2文目のNow, more than ever以下に「今はこれまで以上に，教育が～の責任を持っている」とある。responsibilityのあとにto be in gear with 21st century challenges …と(to) foster the right types of values and skills that …と2つ責任が述べられている。 (2) 下線部(B)は「しかしながら，すべての教育が持続可能な発展を支えるわけではない」という意味。その次の文に具体的な教育の例としてEducation that promotes economic growth alone may well also lead to an increase in unsustainable consumption patterns.と述べており，持続不可能な消費パターンを増幅する教育があることから判断する。

(3) 第1段落7文目に「しっかり確立した持続可能な発展のための教育

は～」と，ESDがどういう教育か説明しているので，その箇所をまとめる。　(4)　第4段落の最後の文に「そのような教育の手法だけが持続可能な発展の推進に必要な重要な能力の育成を可能にする」とあるので，「そのような教育の手法」が指す箇所が答えとなる。第4段落の3文目に「持続可能な発展のための教育に必要なことは，教える(教育の)手法から学ぶ(教育の)手法へのシフトである」とあるので，学ぶ手法がそのような教育の手法になる。そしてその学ぶ手法は，続く4文目のIt asks for ～以下に述べられているので，この箇所をまとめるとよい。

【3】(1)　エ　(2)　ウ　(3)　ア　(4)　ウ

〈解説〉(1)　問題文の後半で，「それで彼が冗談を言った時は驚きだった」とあるのでふだんは「控えめだ」と考える。　(2)「Satoshiが壇上に上がると突然～になった」とあり，その結果「最初何も言うことができなかった」と続くので，「固まった」と考える。　(3)　2文目は「彼は決してテレビで相撲を見損なうことはない」とあるので「熱心な」相撲ファンだと考える。　(4)　空欄の後は「彼ら(生徒)がどんなによいかを示すことを求められる」とあり，「生徒を評価すること」を別の表現で述べているので，「言い換えると」が入ると考える。

【4】(1)　I can't visualize what I'll be doing　(2)　had a nice homecoming after studying overseas　(3)　to have the mental stuff go strong
(4)　where women are free from human rights

〈解説〉(1)「私は思い描くことができない」を作り，その後でvisualizeの目的語として「自分が10年後に何をしているか」を続ける。
(2)「2年間留学した後」と「直美は無事帰国した」の2つの意味のまとまりに分けて考えるとよい。後半にfor two yearsがあるので，after studying overseas for two yearsを意味のまとまりとして作る。前半の動詞はhadがあるので，had a nice homecoming「よい帰国(無事な帰国)を経験した」と考える。　(3)「精神的要素」はthe metal stuff,「強くする」はgo strongにする。haveはこの場合使役動詞(have＋目的語＋動詞の原形)で「精神的要素が強くなるようにする」と考え，have the metal stuff go strongにする。　(4) 「女性が人権を侵されない世界」→「女性が人権侵害から自由である世界」と考える。worldのあとに関係副詞whereを続け，その後にwomen are free from ～「女性が～から自由である」がきて，fromの目的語にhuman rights abusesとなる。

【5】There are two things you should do to improve your speaking skills. The first is to expand your vocabulary so that you can more easily express your opinions and ideas. The second is to read aloud to become familiar with English words and English grammar structure. These two will make your English sound more fluent. (55words)

〈解説〉I'm not good at speakingとあることから，スピーキングを改善するアドバイスをするとよい。2点なので，The first ～. The second ～のように2つのアドバイスを明確に述べるようにする。

【6】There are two things you should keep in mind when teaching how to communicate in English. Students tend to use the model sentences they learn automatically. So you should have them describe what they feel or think in their own words. Thus students will be able to convey their messages properly. And while listening and speaking, you should encourage students to keep their eye contact with each other, which shows they are interested in the topic. Using some gestures is also an effective way for good communication. (86words)

〈解説〉「自分の言葉で会話させる」と「相手に興味を示し，効果的にメッセージを伝える」などの留意点を2つ決め，その留意点に対する解決方法などを述べる。

【高等学校】

【1】(1)　ア　(2)　私たちはみな誰かほかの人に危害を加えたことに対

し，特に私たちがその危害から恩恵を受けている場合，責任をとらなければならないと，たいていの人は同意するだろう。　(3)　①　イ　②　ア　③　ウ　(4)　・温室効果ガスを削減するどんな試みも，おそらく経済成長を最も必要とする国の経済成長の可能性を制限する。　・貧しい国にとって，温室効果ガスの削減は，おそらく彼らの生活と生存のための基本的な必需品に影響を与える。

〈解説〉(1)　空欄を含む文は「グローバル・コモンズという倫理観は，～の人間社会を作るひとつの生物群集としての地球環境に関連するという意味では，明白に地球市民的な考え方である」という意味。そしてこの倫理観が強調しているのは「国家の利益や国家的優位性は，環境問題が解決され，～しなければならないならば，犠牲にされるか，抑えられる必要がある」とある。したがって，様々な国が共存する地球は，「お互いに依存している」のであり，地球規模の環境問題などは一国の利益を優先してはいけないと考える。　(2)　第2段落3文目から，地球温暖化の問題で他国に危害を加え，恩恵を受けている先進工業国に応分の責任をとってもらうことを意味すると考える。　(3)　第2段落2文目に「地球温暖化の大きな原因となっていて，将来も原因となるであろう国々が原因になることをやめるという消極的な義務がある」とあり，消極的な義務は「温室効果ガス排出をやめるか削減する」と考える。また，同5文目には積極的な義務として最貧国の救済が挙げられている。　(4)　第3段落の4文目から，経済成長した先進国は温室効果ガスを削減して，経済成長を遅らせてもそれほど影響がないが，貧しい国は生産を削減すると経済成長の可能性がつぶれることを汲み取る。また5文目の中ほどの内容から，温室効果ガスを削減し，結果として生産を減らす貧しい国では，経済成長だけでなく生存に必要な基本的必需品にも影響を受けてしまうと考える。

【2】(1)　イ　(2)　死者がいなければ食料支援は必要ないという近視眼的考えで，徐々に進行する大惨事を認めたがらないから。

(3)　国際社会は継続して平和を追い求め，最善を尽くして確実に援助が行われるようにしなければならない。長期的な開発事業を援助することが絶対必要である。　(4)　世界規模の人道的援助が大きな広がりを見せているが，援助をますます必要とする情勢に追いついていない。

〈解説〉(1)　人々が死ぬ理由として第1段落の4文目以降に，共通の原因は紛争で，ナイジェリア北部のボコハラムの聖戦を行うグループの影響，南スーダンの内戦，イエメンの港湾を破壊し，麻痺させた戦争などが挙げられている。政府が「崩壊して」，こうした争いが起きると考える。　(2)　第2段落の5文目の半ば以降に，「専門家は，それを『死者がいなければ食料支援は必要ないという近視眼的考え』と述べている。徐々に進行するという紛争の性質は，私たちに介入する機会を多く与えるが，そうしようという気持ちを減少させるようである」という反応の鈍さが述べられている。　(3)　下線部を含む文以降に，緊急支援以外に何が必要か述べられている。　(4)　第5段落の1文目に「不足も考慮されなければならない」とあり，それ以降に人道的援助が不足している現状が述べられているので，それをまとめる。

【3】(1)　コミュニケーションは自分と相手がいるので，自分は具体的な場面や状況に合った適切な表現を，例文のパターン練習にならないよう，自ら考えて言語活動できるようにする。相手に対しては，注意深く聞いて相手の思いを理解しようとする態度が重要である。また，言葉だけでなくジェスチャーや表情なども使って積極的にコミュニケーションすることが必要である。　(2)　①　・与えられた話題について即興で話すとき，生徒は当然，不安や緊張を抱くので，間違えても大丈夫という環境を作ること。　・どんな内容でも思っていることを自由に言える環境を作ること。　・間違いはあっても，何とか英語で自分の考えを伝えることができるという達成感と自信を持たせること。　②　「部活動」や「趣味」，「買い物」，「週末の過ごし方」，「家族のこと」など身近な話題で行う。リアクションや相づち，アイコンタクトをしながら話すように指導する。つなぎ言葉を事前に用意

し，いろいろな疑問詞を用いて相手に質問しながら話を進める。質問に答えるときには，相手の質問内容を確認したりするよう指導する。また答えだけでなく，その後に感想や具体例などを加えて答えるように指導する。

〈解説〉(1)　コミュニケーションの積極さとは，覚えた例文をただ繰り返す受け身の態度ではなく，自分の言葉で積極的に話すことであり，相手の言うことを積極的に聞くことであり，相手の言うことに積極的に応じることである。　(2)　①　事前の準備なしで英語を使って話すので，生徒はパニックになり，不安になりがちである。それを少しでも緩和するよう配慮することがとても大切である。　②　即興でやり取りすると，どうしても話が続かず，沈黙することが多くなる。それをどう防ぎ，たくさん英語を話してもらえるか工夫することが重要である。

【4】(1)　ア　(2)　ウ　(3)　エ　(4)　ア　(5)　ウ

〈解説〉(1)　「私は奨学金で交換留学生として，フランスに行く機会を～」とあるので「捉えた」と判断する。　(2)　2文目に「彼女の課の3人が風邪をひいて今日そこで仕事をしたのはわずか2人だった」とあるので，「大忙しの日」だと考える。　(3)　「この参考書は～，それで学習者が読むのにはいい」とあるので，「理解できる」と考える。

(4)　空欄を含む文は「日本の代表サッカーチームの監督とのインタビューの～を含む雑誌を探している」とあるので，「抜粋」が適当。

(5)　前半に「家を5日留守にした後」とあり，because以下に「とても暑く乾燥していたので」とあるので，プチトマトは「枯れた」と判断できる。

【5】a)　(1)　記号…B　正しい英語…beat　(2)　記号…A　正しい英語…the grounds that　(3)　記号…B　正しい英語…has no choice but to walk　b)　(1)　下線を引く部分…2文目のsupporting　正しい英語…to support　(2)　下線を引く部分…2文目のwas taken place　正しい英語…took place

〈解説〉a)　(1)　win the game「その試合に勝つ」, beat the team「チームを負かす」のように使う。　(2)「～の理由で」は, for the reason that S＋V ～, on the grounds that S＋V～である。　(3)「～せざるを得ない」はhave no choice but to doとto不定詞になる。　b)　(1)　hope to doで「～することを望む」という意味。　(4)　take placeと能動態で用いて「行われる」という意味。

【6】It is believed to be ideal to take part in both academic learning and club activities in Japan. It's called "Bunbu Ryodo". Through club activities, students learn some important things other than getting good grades. One is to learn human relationships, including ones between superior and inferior and social skills among people from different backgrounds. Another is to learn to work together towards a common goal and show respect for coaches, captains and one another. Also, club activities provide students a good opportunity to relieve stress. Students can enjoy the activities they like after a busy school day. (98 words)

〈解説〉問題文の意味は「外国から高校教師の団体があなたの学校を訪れ, 生徒にとって部活動の良いところは何か, あるいは部活動から生徒は何を学ぶことができるかと尋ねたら, あなたは外国人教師にどのように説明するか」である。解答例は「日本では, 学業と部活動の両方に参加することが理想だと信じられている。それは文武両道と呼ばれている。部活動を通して, 生徒はよい成績をとる以外に大切なことをいくつか学ぶ。ひとつは異なる環境からきた人たちの間で, 上下関係を含む人間関係や社交術を学ぶことである。もうひとつは共通の目標に向かって協力することと, コーチやキャプテンやお互いを尊重することである。また, 部活動は, 忙しい授業の後に好きなことをしてストレスを発散するよい機会となる」という趣旨である。

2017年度　実施問題

【中高共通】

【1】リスニングテスト

Part A

(1) Write your answer on your answer sheet.

(2) Write your answer on your answer sheet.

(3) Write your answer on your answer sheet.

(4) Write your answer on your answer sheet.

(5) Write your answer on your answer sheet.

(6) Write your answer on your answer sheet.

Part B

(1) (A) Shut down his computer without any problems.
(B) Save the file successfully.
(C) Ask the woman for help.
((D) Call Technical Support.

(2) (A) Because he was caught in a traffic jam.
((B) Because he lost his way.
(C) Because there was a building under construction.
(D) Because he went there by train.

(3) (A) Drive her daughter to the daycare.
(B) Turn the lights on.
(C) Pick up her daughter at the daycare.
(D) Have her car serviced because the battery is dead.

(4) (A) She has misplaced the staff's information.
(B) She will be late for the appointment.
(C) She has not received the documents yet.
(D) She cannot confirm the departure time.

Part C

(1) Write your answer on your answer sheet.

(2) Write your answer on your answer sheet.

Part D

(1) 特別な支援を必要とするこの受験生が，高校入試の際に許可されたことを，箇条書きで全て答えよ。

(2) 専門家によると，この法律が教育に求めているものは何か。

(☆☆☆☆◎◎◎◎)

【中学校】

【1】次の会話文を読んで，(1)～(5)の設問に答えよ。

A member of the HR department, Laura Brown, interviews an applicant for an open position.

Brown : What interests you most about this job?

Applicant : What interests me most is the opportunity to work in a large, [Ⅰ]. By "opportunity," I mean the high potential for career development.

B : I see. Could you be more (①) about what you call "potential for career development"?

A : Yes. My career goal is to become a bilingual professional. And (A)<u>the advertised job</u> would allow me to add to my knowledge and skills in my chosen field while actively participating in that kind of work.

B : Right. Now tell us a little about yourself. What's your greatest strength?

A : While I'm good with facts and (②), my greatest strength is in communication, both written and oral. Things like drafting memos (B)[<u>easily to / reports / always / and / come / have</u>] me.

B : Hmm. In what areas of your current job are you weakest?

A : I don't have any major weaknesses that [Ⅱ]. Maybe one

thing I should mention is that I'm a detail person and [　Ⅲ　]—but I know where to draw the line between being meticulous and being unproductive.

B：Do you have any questions?

A：Will there be a second interview?

B：Yes, shortlisted (　③　) will be invited to a second and final interview. Thank you for coming. You'll hear from us next week.

A：Thank you for your time.

【出典　日向清人　即戦力がつくビジネス英会話　DHC】

(1)　[　Ⅰ　]～[　Ⅲ　]に入る最も適切なものを，次のア～オから一つずつ選び，その記号を書け。

ア　interfere with how I do my work

イ　assembled company around here

ウ　tend to overdo things

エ　don't care how things are going on

オ　developed organization such as this

(2)　(　①　)～(　③　)に入る最も適切な語を，次のア～カから一つずつ選び，その記号を書け。

ア　abstract　　イ　candidates　　ウ　figures　　エ　specific

オ　habits　　カ　employers

(3)　この応募者は下線部(A)の仕事に就く利点をどのようなものであると考えているか，40字程度の日本語で答えよ。

(4)　下線部(B)を，意味が通るように並べかえよ。

(5)　次の(a)～(c)の説明にそれぞれ該当する1語を，会話文中から抜き出して書け。

(a)　having or showing the capacity to develop into something in the future

(b)　belonging to the present time; happening or being used or done now

(c)　showing great attention to detail; very careful and precise

(☆☆☆☆◎◎◎)

【2】次の英文を読んで，(1)～(4)の設問に答えよ。

Students' academic achievement is, without doubt, the first and most important goal of schools. Frequently, teachers struggle to balance the time needed to teach academic content related to standardized tests—student performance on standardized tests is often an important component of their own professional performance evaluation—and the time needed to teach social skills. However, the dichotomy between (A)these two classroom priorities is somewhat artificial, and in fact they usually interact and overlap with one another. Social competence and academic achievement influence each other, and children need both to succeed academically and socially and, later in life, professionally (Welsh, Parke, Widaman, & O'Neil, 2001). When teachers fail to educate students about appropriate and inappropriate social behaviors, they will probably spend an enormous amount of time managing student misbehavior at the expense of academic content.

The most successful administrators and teachers frequently use a comprehensive approach that promotes both positive behavior and academic performance (Flay, 2002; Flay & Allred, 2003). Research supports this comprehensive approach, indicating that prosocial behavior (e.g., cooperation, assistance, empathy) can have a strong impact on increasing academic achievement (Caprara, Barbaranelli, Pastorelli, Bandura, & Zimbardo, 2000).

Strong teaching and motivational skills reduce behavioral problems in the classroom and promote a positive classroom climate (Hein, 2004; Pianta, 1999; Pierce, 1994). We have found that many students bully their peers when they do not understand classroom content and when they are frustrated because of their lack of academic skills. (B)These bullies often get caught in a downward spiral: bullying others because they are afraid of being called stupid, and then being disciplined in ways that put them further behind academically (e.g., office referrals, detention, suspension). Bullies who are frustrated with learning also tend to be unprepared for class, avoid working in class, challenge school authority, interrupt others in discussions, and display flippant attitudes about learning. Unfortunately, these inappropriate behaviors usually thwart the bully's ability to establish a relationship with the teacher, who is less likely to provide special attention to the bully's academic needs after having his or her authority challenged and class time wasted.

In an extensive review of the literature conducted by the U.S. Department of Health and Human Services (2001), excellence in teaching was identified as a primary method for the prevention of violence. In particular, two teaching strategies were highlighted as successful for increasing academic success: continuous progress programs and (C)cooperative learning. Continuous progress programs present students with a hierarchy of skills; students progress from the beginning level to the advanced level as they master each unit. Cooperative learning groups are composed of students with different skill levels who work cooperatively on academic tasks. The report concluded that cooperative learning can improve academic achievement, race relations, and positive attitudes toward school. Thus, this strategy appears to be promising for helping bullies reduce academic failure and learn skills for working and interacting cooperatively.

In addition to these two strategies to increase academic success, teachers have recommended using diverse teaching strategies to accommodate different learning styles; dividing the solution to a problem into small, achievable steps; providing positive reinforcement for effort and achievement; and providing age-appropriate examples that are interesting to students.

【出典　Pamela Orpinas, Arthur M. Horne, *BULLYING PREVENTION Creating a Positive School Climate and Developing Social Competence,* American Psychological Association】

(1)　下線部(A)の指導において，教師に見られがちな行動を，50字程度の日本語で答えよ。

(2)　下線部(B)について，次の問いにそれぞれ40字程度の日本語で答えよ。

①　どのようなときに，級友をいじめるか。

② いじめた結果，どのような状況に陥りがちであるか。

(3) 下線部(C)は，いじめにおいてどのような効果があると考えられるか，60字程度の日本語で答えよ。

(4) 学力向上のために推奨されてきた，多様な学び方に対応する教育的手立てについて，三つの具体例をそれぞれ30字程度の日本語で答えよ。

(☆☆☆☆◎◎◎◎)

【3】次の英文を読んで，(1)～(4)の設問に答えよ。

This was the year the global movement of people fleeing conflict finally burst onto the world's political agenda. With 20 million refugees crossing borders in 2014 and 40 million people displaced within their own countries, 1 in every 122 people on the planet has been forced from their home by conflict.

Yet for all the complaints about asylum seekers in the richer parts of the world, more than 8 in 10 refugees are actually living in developing countries—and that (①) is wearing those countries down. We know what a failed state is; the disasters of Libya and Yemen come to mind. But there are a larger number of states where the delivery of basic services or the enforcement of the rule of law have been compromised by a lack of state capacity, will or legitimacy, or simply the sheer scale of the problems. They are (A)<u>fragile states</u>, and they are the human and development challenge of 2016.

Fifty fragile and conflict states account for 20% of the world's population but 43% of the extreme poor (living on less than $1.25 a day). Nearly two-thirds of fragile states have failed to meet the Millennium Development Goal of halving extreme poverty by the end of 2015. And just a fifth have secured universal primary education for their children.

A New Deal for fragile states—agreed to in 2011 in the South Korean city of Pusan and endorsed by over 40 countries, development partners and civil society—produced a set of principles guiding policy and practice in fragile and conflict-affected states. But while the principles behind it are good, the

New Deal has not gotten the global (②) it needs to drive improved social and economic outcomes at the national and international levels.

There are three immediate priorities. First, aid. U.N. humanitarian appeals are currently only 50% funded. The result is misery and the onward flow of refugees—especially into Europe. The United Kingdom recently announced that half its overseas-aid budget of around $18 billion would in the future be devoted to helping fragile and conflict states. Other donors need to follow this example.

Second, (B)host populations as well as refugees need help. With 59% of refugees living outside of camps among local communities in cities like Beirut, it is essential to offer broad-based help. The best route is to use cash vouchers as a humanitarian and economic tool. A study by the International Rescue Committee, of which I am the CEO, showed that $1 distributed in Lebanon delivered $2.13 to the local economy. Yet cash provision makes up less than 6% of the global humanitarian budget. Before services are delivered, we should ask whether cash could do the job better.

Third, we need (③), not just social services. It is scarcely believable that the World Bank's work is limited in Jordan and Lebanon—with over 2 million refugees between them—because they are officially middle-income countries. International institutions created in a different time need to be adapted to the modern geography of poverty and need.

The World Humanitarian Summit taking place in May is a chance to bring these issues to the fore. U.N. Secretary-General Ban Ki-moon has rightly called for innovation and determination. The focus needs to be on fragile places—or they will become the failed places of tomorrow. With head as well as heart, we should respond to their call for a renovation of our efforts to help them. After all, in a global village, when we help them we help ourselves.

【出典　TIME, December 28, 2015—January 4, 2016】

(1) (①)～(③)に入る最も適切な語句を，次のア～エからそれぞれ一つずつ選び，その記号を書け。

① ア custom イ outflow ウ burden
エ agreement
② ア constraint イ traction ウ condemnation
エ ethics
③ ア imposition イ dynamics ウ social network
エ economics

(2) 下線部(A)について，次の問いに答えよ。
① 筆者は，ここではどのような国家であると説明しているか，60字程度の日本語で答えよ。
② これらの国々のミレニアム開発目標に対する達成状況について，2点日本語で答えよ。

(3) 下線部(B)に対して，筆者は具体的にどのような支援を提案しているか，20字程度の日本語で答えよ。

(4) 筆者は，今後どのような姿勢で支援を進めていくべきだと述べているか，日本語で答えよ。

(☆☆☆☆◎◎◎◎)

【4】次の(1)～(4)について，それぞれの英文の[ ]内に入る最も適切なものを，ア～エからそれぞれ一つ選び，その記号を書け。

(1) He made [ ] on his promise to visit his old friends when he went to London.
ア away イ up ウ good エ through

(2) Please give us your good ideas to break this [ ] economic growth.
ア sluggish イ ambiguous ウ subsequent エ brisk

(3) Japan's victory over two-time world champions South Africa was hailed as the biggest [ ] in rugby history.
ア grief イ upset ウ composure エ emotion

(4) This English teaching material provides students with many useful listening and speaking activities, and [ ], they have come to learn English more actively.

ア　on the contrary　　イ　by the way　　ウ　as a result
エ　on the other hand

(☆☆☆☆◎◎◎◎)

【5】次の(1)～(4)について，それぞれの日本語の内容を表すように，[　　]内の語句を並べかえよ。

(1)　彼は自分の子どもに多くを期待しがちだ。

He [expect / too / to / is / much / of / apt] his children.

(2)　彼女のフランス語の発音は，ほとんど理解できないものだった。

Her pronunciation in Franch was [practically / to / that / such / it / impossible / was] understand her.

(3)　ジョンは新しいポジションで働けば働くほど，仕事をこなしやすく感じるようになった。

The longer John warked in his new position, [he/ in / comfortable / felt / the / carrying / more] out his new business.

(4)　中途半端に知っているよりも，全然知らない方がよい。

One way [know / a thing / at / as / all/ not / well] as know it incompletely.

(☆☆☆◎◎◎◎◎)

【6】8月に来日する新任のALTから，秋田県や勤務校についての問い合わせの電子メールが届いた。その電子メールへの返信として，あとの〈伝える内容〉を含んだ80語程度の英語を指示された書き出しに続けて書け。

ただし，あなたはALTの勤務校の英語担当教員であるとし，ALTへの挨拶やあなたの自己紹介などの英文は省略するものとする。

(書き出し)　I will introduce Akita Prefecture and our school.

〈伝える内容〉
○　秋田県について
・日本の北部に位置する。
・自然が豊かで，四季折々の景色やスキーなどのスポーツを楽しむことができる。
○　勤務校について
・秋田県の中央部に位置する。
・生徒は文武両道の精神の下，勉強と部活動に一生懸命に励んでいる。
・来年，創立50周年を迎える。

(☆☆☆◎◎◎◎)

【7】あなたが英語を指導する上で，授業で大切にしたいことを二つ取り上げ，100語程度の英語で書け。

(☆☆☆☆◎◎◎◎)

【高等学校】

【1】次の英文を読んで，(1)～(7)の設問に答えよ。

As an inner-city public school, Boston Arts Academy deals with the academic challenges facing every school with a large proportion of economically disadvantaged students. For this school, the poverty level is very high: 65 percent of the students qualify for free and reduced-cost lunch. In addition, a third of the school's incoming students arrive reading below grade level, often far below grade level. Yet 94 percent of their graduates go to college, a dramatically higher percentage than the national norm. Interestingly, most Boston Arts Academy graduates do not go on to an arts college, largely because of leadership that opens up a larger world to the students. "Among our graduates, the top majors they choose are design and engineering," headmaster Anne Clark told me. "Those are things they never would have understood if they weren't being taught in an interdisciplinary way, where they could see they had this strength."

"We're operating from a different sense of what education should and could be, and (A)a different sense of success. It's not narrowly defined through standardized assessments, but also through the types of things the arts teach, like persistence and collaboration and creativity and vision and voice. We have found that many of our students who were not successful before coming to Boston Arts Academy find their way to engaging with school through the arts, because school isn't just another thing that they hate and are bad at."

Still, Boston Arts Academy is a public school and, like all other public schools in Massachusetts, they are required to administer standardized tests. For the staff and the administration, that means doing some teaching to the test.

"We would be doing our students a disservice if we didn't prepare them for the tests," Anne said. "We're *always* preparing them for the tests. By the time they finish their state-required tests, we have to switch gears and prepare them for the SAT, which is a very different kind of test."

The school offsets this requirement with an environment that keeps students inspired even in the face of high-stakes testing. "Students are generally here from eight to four. If it's during a performance period or a portfolio period, they could be here much later. They spend half their day in the arts, and half in academics. They do a full academic program, though we teach through the arts and through interdisciplinary modes as much as possible. We teach math, humanities, world languages, and science. Then they all have an art major: music (instrument or vocal), dance, theater, visual arts. They mostly have to focus on one, but there are times during the day when the underclassmen especially get to explore other majors."

While every student at the school is an individual, what unites them is their passion for the arts. And this is what influences their approach to every element of their education. Anne Clark was one of the founding teachers at the school before taking a leadership role, and she has seen the value of this passion more times than she can say.

"The kids are happy to be here, and that makes a big difference for all of us. Most of our academic faculty has an arts background, and they teach in both arts and academics. When I was a teacher, one of the things I did was teach reading to (B)the lowest readers. These were seventeen-year-old young men reading on a third-grade level. If they get to spend two to three hours a day on the thing that lets them show their strengths, it's a lot easier to work with them one-on-one on the thing that makes them feel most disempowered. A parent said to me recently, 'This is the only school that started with what my daughter could do, not what she couldn't do.' The school is about showcasing the student's gifts and strengths. It changes the conversation."

The Boston Arts Academy model substantiates what I've seen in all my work with schools around the world: building the curriculum around students' interests leads to them performing at higher levels in all areas. There's something else too. Because it is an arts-based program, and because artists are accustomed to receiving criticism and responding to that criticism quickly, the school is also creating students far better prepared for what will be asked of them once they leave school.

"(C)Creativity and interdisciplinary thinking are what the world demands. I think that's why our graduates are so successful. That's what we've heard from colleges. Our kids are willing to take risks, imagine, work hard, work collaboratively. They take critique, which is a really important part of an arts-based education. Formal revision, review, and feedback is inherent to the arts. I worry about my biological children growing up in a world of 'Is it right? Well, I'll find out when the test grader tells me.' Our students are being invited to imagine their own answers, defend them through critique, and revise — but not just because there's some standard to meet. That's the kind of thinking that we need. When your whole education is based on learning a specific way, filling in bubbles, and then waiting for your number, (D)you don't learn the same way."

"There's a member of our board who is a high-ranking executive. He said that he's here because when he's hiring, he always wants to look for the violinist. He's looking for someone with an arts background because he knows that person is creative and imaginative. That person has been trained to meet problems with fresh eyes. That's what an arts-based education provides."

Far more students want to attend Boston Arts Academy than there are slots. The school admits about 120 new students a year and gets more than 500 applications. The school looks at each application carefully, but (E)there is one thing it ignores completely when making its selections.

"We're unique among art schools in the country because we're academic-blind," Anne said. "We don't look at previous grades, test scores, or anything else. We believe that an arts-based education should be accessible to all. One would never say, 'You can't study history because your math scores stink.' Why would we say you can't study art because your math scores stink? Functionally, that's what happens around the country. They'll include academic records in admissions, or they say they won't, but they'll say something like you have to have Algebra 1, and that becomes a functional barrier."

"We choose through auditions. But if we only took kids who knew how to do a formal audition, we wouldn't get a population that's reflective of the city of Boston, which is our mission. We're looking for students who are responsive and invested, but not necessarily formally skilled. I like to say we're looking for the kid who (F) *not* dance. Most of our students have not had formal training, because the resources aren't there in the Boston public schools. We have a lot of musicians who can't read music; a lot of visual artists who haven't had many art classes, because those have been cut from the lower grades. A lot of dancers who danced in the community but never had any formal ballet training. We're looking for the kid who would flourish with the opportunity for formal training, but hasn't necessarily had that before."

What Anne is describing is the heart of a principal's role: appreciating the individuality of the student body, seeking potential at every turn, and constantly striving to move the school forward in the face of constant change.

【出典　KEN ROBINSON and Lou Aronica, *CREATIVE SCHOOLS Revolutionizing Education from the Ground Up*, ALLEN LANE】

(1)　下線部(A)について，Boston Art Academyでは，どのようなもので示されているか，日本語で答えよ。

(2)　下線部(B)への対応の仕方について，Anne校長はどう述べているか，日本語で答えよ。

(3)　下線部(C)に対して，Boston Arts Academyの生徒たちがどのような意欲をもって取り組んでいるか，具体的に日本語で答えよ。

(4)　下線部(D)のような状況に陥るのは，どのような教育の場合か，日本語で答えよ。

(5)　下線部(E)について，Boston Arts Academyの方針を，50字程度の日本語で答えよ。

(6)　空所(　F　)に入る最も適切な語を，次のア～エから選び，その記号を書け。

ア　shouldn't　　イ　cannot　　ウ　needn't　　エ　mustn't

(7)　本文の内容を踏まえて，次の問いに30語程度の英語で答えよ。

What do you think is important as a role of homeroom teacher?

(☆☆☆☆◎◎◎◎◎)

【2】次の(1)，(2)について，日本語で答えよ。

(1)　スピーキングテストにはいくつかの形式があるが，インタビュー形式及びディスカッション形式について，それぞれの<u>①実施する際の留意点</u>と<u>②評価する際の留意点</u>を箇条書きで述べよ。

(2)　「コミュニケーション英語Ⅰ」の目標は，「英語を通じて，積極的にコミュニケーションを図ろうとする態度を育成するとともに，情報や考えなどを的確に理解したり適切に伝えたりする基礎的な能力を養う。」である。このことを踏まえ，①「読むこと」の指導を行う際の留意点を述べよ。また，②「読むこと」と他の技能とを関連付けた活動を一つ取り上げ，その内容と実施の手順を書け。

(☆☆☆☆☆◎◎◎◎◎)

【3】次の(1)～(5)の(　　)に当てはまる最も適切な語を，それぞれア～エから一つ選び，記号を書け。

(1) They tried to falsify the accounting records to (　　) the tax, but in vain.

ア undergo　イ extract　ウ evade　エ justify

(2) Studying abroad offers you an (　　) study experience and creates lifelong memories. You can build wonderful relationships with peers from around the world.

ア intricate　イ invitable　ウ intuitive　エ invaluable

(3) The lake is 280 meters deep on average and 6 kilometers in (　　). It takes about 30 minutes to go around by car.

ア diameter　イ luminosity　ウ latitude　エ density

(4) Many people were (　　) at the news of the sudden death of the legendary singer.

ア offended　イ mortified　ウ fascinated　エ astounded

(5) The number of schools is not as large as it was in the past because of the (　　).

ア retribution　イ consolidation　ウ segmentation
エ dissension

(☆☆☆◎◎◎◎)

【4】a) 次の(1)～(3)の各英文には，それぞれ誤りが1か所ある。その部分の記号を書き，正しい英語に直せ。

(1) Many people $_{A}$wondered why the store $_{B}$will be closed $_{C}$for remodelling $_{D}$since tomorrow until New Year's Day.

(2) Not only Jim's father but also his mother $_{\mathrm{A}}$<u>are</u> so excited that $_{\mathrm{B}}$<u>neither</u> of them seems to want to stop talking about their son all the way $_{\mathrm{C}}$<u>home</u> though it takes another 30 $_{\mathrm{D}}$<u>minutes</u> to get there.

(3) I $_{\mathrm{A}}$<u>haven't been</u> to my hometown since I was in school. It has a lot of beautiful $_{\mathrm{B}}$<u>scenery</u> $_{\mathrm{C}}$<u>where</u> I want to $_{\mathrm{D}}$<u>go back</u> and see someday.

b) 次の(1)，(2)は，「今年の思い出」というテーマで生徒が書いてきた英文であるが，それぞれ誤りが1か所ある。その部分に下線を引いて指摘し，正しい英語に直せ。ただし，タイトルは訂正しないこと。

(1) Title: School Trip

We went to Kyoto on a school trip. I saw many things. It was a great fun taking pictures with my friends. I wished I had more time in Kyoto.

(2) Title: The First Tournament

I was chosen as a regular member of our volleyball team. I was worried because I was not certain if I could play well. But I was encouraged by the coach that I should relax and do my best. I practiced hard. Finally, we won the game.

(☆☆☆☆◎◎◎◎◎)

【5】次の質問に，100語程度の英語で答えよ。

According to the result of a survey conducted in 2015 by the Ministry of Education, Culture, Sports, Science and Technology, many students answered that they are studying English mainly because they have to take English tests in order to enter a college or a university. What do you think about this? How do you motivate those students to continue learning English after they graduate from high school?

(☆☆☆☆◎◎◎◎)

解答・解説

【中高共通】

【１】Part A　(1)　(C)　(2)　(B)　(3)　(B)　(4)　(A)　(5)　(A)　(6)　(C)　Part B　(1)　(D)　(2)　(A)　(3)　(C)　(4)　(B)　Part C　(1)　(I should) write it down on the card provided and hand it to the staff.　(2)　(I should) call the customer service soon during the day on a weekday.　Part D　(1)　解略　(2)　解略

〈解説〉スクリプトが公表されていないので，一般的な注意になるが，数字や名詞には注意すること。放送回数が2回ならば1回目で概要をつかみ，2回目でチェックできるが，1回しか放送されない場合には集中して聞くことが必要である。なお，Part Dについて公式解答の評価基準では，(1)は「「別室受験」や「口述筆記」などのキーワードを主な観点として相対的に評価する」，(2)は「「異なる方法で」や「合理的な配慮」などのキーフレーズを主な観点として相対的に評価する」としている。

【中学校】

【１】(1)　Ⅰ　オ　Ⅱ　ア　Ⅲ　ウ　(2)　①　エ　②　ウ　③　イ　(3)　自分自身の知識及び技能，また書くこと及び口頭でのコミュニケーション能力を伸ばすことができる。(46字)　(4)　and reports have always come easily to　(5)　(a)　potential　(b)　current　(c)　meticulous

〈解説〉(1)　Ⅰ　「この会社のような大きな組織」の意味である。応募者は面接を受けている会社について述べているので，イは適切ではない。assembled company「聴衆。来場者」。　Ⅱ　自分の弱点について聞かれたので，「仕事を妨げるものはない」と答えているのである。
Ⅲ　直前で「細かいことを気にする」と言っているので，「物事をやりすぎる」と考えればよい。　(2)　①　質問者は「あなたが「キャリア開発」と言っているものについてもっと詳しく述べよ」と言っている。 ② facts and figures「正確な情報」。 ③ shortlisted candidatesとして「絞り込まれた応募者」と考えればよい。 (3) 応募者は「バイリンガルの専門家」が最終目標と答えていて，採用されれば「職場での知識と技術が蓄積できる」ことと「書くことと口頭でのコミュニケーション」が得意だと回答している。 (4) 下線部(B)を含む1文は「簡単なメモや報告書が常に成果をもたらしてきた」という意味である。 (5) (a) 説明は「将来的に何かを発展させる可能性を持っている」の意味である。Applicantの最初の発言中にあるpotentialは「可能性のある。見込みのある」という意味。 (b) 説明は「現在の，現在起こっている」の意味である。Brownの4つ目の発言中にあるcurrentが同義。 (c) 説明は「細かな点に注意を集中する，非常に注意深くて几帳面な」の意味である。Applicantの4つ目の発言中にあるmeticulousが同義。

【2】(1) 社会的規範の教育に失敗すると，学業指導の時間を犠牲にして生徒の社会生活上の生活指導を行う。(45字) (2) ① 授業の内容が理解できない時や，勉強の仕方がわからずにいらだちを感じるとき。(37字) ② 馬鹿だと思われないためにさらに他人をいじめて，その結果学力がさらに低下する。(38字) (3) 学業不振の改善や学校に対する積極的な態度など，いじめが原因の学力低下を防いで，協調的に作業をする技術を学ぶ助けになる。(59字) (4) ・達成可能な小さなステップに分けた問題を難易度順に出題する。(29字)
・努力や達成に対して積極的にほめて，生徒のやる気を育てる。(28字) ・生徒の年齢に適した出題で，興味・関心を持たせて学習を進める。(30字)

〈解説〉(1) 第1段落最後の文で，学業指導と生活指導に対する教員の役割を記述している。at the expense of …「…を犠牲にして」。
(2) ① 第3段落2文目many以下で，いじめを行う2つの場合が記述されている。 ② 第3段落3文目bullyingからacademicallyまでで，いわゆる悪循環に陥ることが記述されている。　(3)　第4段落最後の2文目に記述されている。最後の文のhelpingからfailureまでは「いじめをなくすことが学力の低下を減少させる」という意味になる。　(4)　第5段落のセミコロンで区切られた3つのまとまり，dividing ～steps, providing ～ and achievement, and providing ～ studentsのそれぞれの内容をまとめればよい。

【3】(1)　①　ウ　②　イ　③　エ　(2)　①　社会生活上の基本的サービスや法律支配の実効性，国家の余力，意欲，合法性のなさ，または単に問題の深刻さに責任転嫁をする。(59字)　②　・2015年末までに極貧を半減させるという目標は，ほぼ3分の2の国々で未達成である。　・子どもたちの5分の1に世界で普遍的な教育を受けさせるという目標が未達成である。　(3)　人道的および経済的道具としての金券の支給(20字)　(4)　人道的観点と同時に経済的な観点で，助けを必要とする人々の声に応える援助

〈解説〉(1)　①　第2段落1文目8 in 10からcountriesまでで「難民のうち10人中8人が発展途上国在住である」と述べている。このことを空欄①で言い換えているので，ウ「負担，重荷」が適切である。wear「疲弊させる」。　②　空欄②のすぐ後ろのto drive以下がヒントである。「国家または国際レベルでの社会的経済的な成果を引き出す」という意味なので，イ「牽引力」が適切である。　③　空欄③の直後の意味は「単なる社会的サービスではない」である。したがって，対応するのはエ「経済学，経済的な考え方」が適切である。　(2)　①　下線部(A)は，1文前(第2段落3文目)の内容を指示している。　②　第3段落2，3文目で大きく2点説明している。fail to ～「～することに失敗する。～できない」。　(3)　第6段落3文目で具体策として記述されている。
(4)　第8段落最後から2文目で述べられている。with head as well as heart「心だけでなく頭も使って」とは，ここでは「人道的な面と経済的な面の両方で」という意味になる。

【4】(1) ウ　(2) ア　(3) イ　(4) ウ

〈解説〉(1) make good one's promiseで「約束を守る，履行する」の意味。keep one's promiseでも同義。(2) sluggishはslow-movingの意味である。sluggish economic growthは「鈍い経済状況」と訳せばよい。
(3) big upsetで「大番狂わせ」の意味である。最上級にすることで意味を強めている。(4) as a result「結果として」。

【5】(1) is apt to expect too much of　(2) such that it was practically impossible to　(3) the more comfortable he felt in carrying　(4) as well not know a thing at all

〈解説〉(1) be apt to ～「～する傾向がある」。(2) such that ～で「～のようなもの。～の状態」の意味である。(3) the＋比較級 ～, the＋比較級 …で「～すればするほど…」の意味である。The more, the better.は「多ければ多いほどよい」の意味。(4) may as well A as Bで「BするくらいならAする方がましだ」の意味である。「不完全に知っているくらいなら，全く知らないほうがましだ」と考えればよい。

【6】(I will introduce Akita Prefecture and our school.) 1　Akita Prefecture: Akita Prefecture is situated in northern part of Japan and is filled with nature. You can enjoy seasonal scenes and such sports as skiing. 2　Our school: Our school is situated in the central area of Akita Prefecture. The students of our school are very active both in studying and doing club activities with the spirit of scholarships and martial arts. Next year is the 50th anniversary year since the school was founded. (76語)

〈解説〉「北部」と「中央部」は，それぞれの文脈で考えれば単語は異なる。「楽しむ」は，風景とスポーツの両方にenjoyを使える。「文武両道」は「勉学と武道」と考えればよい。

【7】My target is the following: The first is to enhance and develop students' abilities by way of applauding their activities positively. When they make mistakes in the class, I'll say, "OK, but you had better say …" or "OK, well, how about …" and so on. The second is to make the class active for the purpose of getting students' interests and concerns forward. For example, in a class of English Communication Ⅰ, after students read text or essays, I instruct them to write down a summary, and some of them present their summary individually. That's my way of making class active. (105 words)

〈解説〉解答例では，「生徒の能力を積極的に伸ばすこと」と「生徒の興味・関心を伸ばす活動的な授業」の2つを取り上げている。「2つ」とあるので，the firstとthe secondという対照表現を用いている。前者では暗黙的(implicit)な対応をして，後者では「読むこと」と「話すこと」を有機的に関係づけた活動を示している。

【高等学校】

【1】(1)　標準的な評定ではなくて，芸術が教える内容，つまり，追求，協調，創造，見通しそして願望のようなもの。　(2)　17歳の読書能力第3段階の生徒たちで，自分の強みを表現することに1日に2時間から3時間費やせば，最も弱みだと感じることにずっと簡単に取り組めると教えた。　(3)　生徒たちは困難に積極的に取り組み，想像力を働かせ，熱心に協力して作業をする。また，芸術を基盤にした教育では本当に重要な批評というものを受け入れる。　(4)　教育の全課程が決められた内容の学習に基づき，穴埋め問題を解いて自分の順位を待つような教育内容の場合。　(5)　過去の成績は全く不問が大きな特徴であり，芸術を基盤とする教育を誰もが享受できることを信条とする。(48字)　(6)　イ　(7)　I think it is to enhance and guide individual students who may have brilliant hidden abilities, even if they were not good at studying and social skills. (27 words)

〈解説〉(1)　第2段落2文目で「標準的な評定ではなくて，芸術を基盤としたものである」ことが記述されている。　(2)　下線部(B)の直後の2文(第7段落4，5文目)で具体的な内容を述べている。また，その後ろにある保護者のことばも訳出の参照になるだろう。　(3)　第9段落4，5

文目で，生徒たちの具体的な活動の様子が描写されている。be willing to ～「よろこんで～する」。　(4)　第9段落最後の文の下線部(D)の直前までで，この学校の特徴的な内容と正反対の様子(現行の大多数の学校)が記述されている。　(5)　第12段落1～3文目で，この学校の信条が記述されている。　(6)　第13段落3文目に入学させたい生徒について記述されていて，この直後の1文で「ダンスができない，本当にできない」ということを強調しているのである。この*not*は強調と考えればよい。　(7)　解答例の概要は，「生徒の過去の実績にとらわれずに，個人の可能性を引き出す指導をすること」である。

【2】(1)　インタビュー形式　①　評価を行う目的の明確化(CAN-DO記述文などを参照してテストを作成する)。テスト内容の受験者への事前周知。テストの実施。受験者への配慮事項。採点と評価。妥当性の確認。　②　評価基準を統一する。評定者間の信頼性を確保する。評定者内の信頼性を確保する。採点手順を決定する。　ディスカッション形式　①　インタビュー形式の①と共通の内容に加え，試験官は，受験者との応答の中で，各受験者の多面的な能力を引き出すようにする。発言が特定の受験者に集中しないようにする。　②　評価基準を統一する。評定者間の信頼性を確保する。評定者内の信頼性を確保する。採点手順を決定する。　(2)　①　主に事実に基づいて書かれた文章や一定の筋をもった文章などが教材になることが多いが，その際には，全体の要旨を理解したり，登場人物の言動やその理由等を文章に即してとらえたりすることが重要である。実際の指導においては，個人，ペア，グループ，クラス全体など，活動の目的に合った形態で音読を行うように工夫したり，読んだ内容について意見を述べたり，簡単な感想を述べたりする活動も併用することが大切である。
②　例えば，読んだ内容を基にして，賛成や反対の意見を述べるディベートなどは有効である。実施の手順は，読んだ内容を整理する時間，それに基づいて賛成または反対のどちらかの主張をする時間，主張を聞いてそれぞれが反論を準備する時間，それに基づいて再び賛成また

は反対の主張をする時間，などの手順が考えられる。
〈解説〉(1)　授業の一環として，4技能のうち「話すこと」の評価の一環としてスピーキングテストを行う場合の実施と評価についての出題である。ここでは，実際に学校でテストを行う際の実践的な内容と考えてよい。インタビュー形式もディスカッション形式も，試験官(教員またはALT)は1人だが，受験者(生徒)はそれぞれ異なる。「グループ・ディスカッション」とは表記されていないが，出題の意図を考えれば，グループと捉えるのが妥当であろう。なお，実施の前提として，「学習指導要領に基づいた内容であること」，「テストの要求するタスクが指導内容と関連していること」，「テストの要求するタスクが習熟度指標(proficiency guideline)や評価指標に沿っていること」の3点を満たす必要がある。　(2)「コミュニケーション英語Ⅰ」は，中学校におけるコミュニケーション能力の基礎を養うための総合的な指導を踏まえて，4技能について関連する技能を結び付けながら総合的に指導することが必要である。ディベートなどの他には，読んだ内容について概要をまとめさせたり，概要を口頭で発表させたりするなどの指導も有効である。

【3】(1)　ウ　(2)　エ　(3)　ア　(4)　エ　(5)　イ
〈解説〉(1)　evade the taxで「課税を逃れる」という意味である。in vain「無駄に」。　(2)　invaluableは「計り知れない」の意味で，ここではextremely usefulというニュアンスで用いている。　(3)　diameter「直径」。ここでは，湖の最大幅について述べている。なお，この文は秋田県にある田沢湖の説明になっている。　(4)　astoundは「びっくりさせる。衝撃を与える」の意味である。at the news of …「…の知らせに接して」。　(5)　consolidationは「統合再編，統廃合」の意味である。

【4】a)　(1)　記号　D　正しい英語　from　(2)　記号　A　正しい英語　is　(3)　記号　C　正しい英語　which　b)　(1)　下線を引く部分　3文目のa great　正しい英語　great　(2)　下線を引く

部分　3文目のthat I should　　正しい英語　to

〈解説〉a)　(1)　下線部D以下は「明日から元旦まで」の意味になるので，起点を表すfromが正しい。sinceは「…以来ずっと」の意味である。(2)　not only X but also Yの場合は，Yに動詞を一致させる。　(3)　2文目冒頭のItはmy hometownのことである。したがって，先行詞はwhichでなければならない。　b)　(1)　funは不可算名詞なので，不定冠詞のaは誤りである。　(2)　encourageという動詞の使い方が誤りである。encourage＋人＋to ～が正しい。The coach encouraged me to relax …と考えればわかりやすい。

【５】I am afraid that young students are unable to know about their future. We live in Information and Communication Technology world which will become more and more complicated, therefore global communication will be essential and we must learn an international language. In Japan, the international language almost means English. Many people are communicating with each other through English, and without it, we cannot cooperate with foreign people. Furthermore, we must access necessary information to live daily lives anywhere on the earth. Though I don't know where students live in the future, they surely take responsible positions if they can use English. Accordingly, I believe they had better learn English after graduate. (111 words)

〈解説〉問題文の意味は，「2015年の文部科学省の調査によれば，多くの生徒たちが，主として大学入試のために英語を勉強していると回答した。あなたはこのことについてどう思うか。彼らが卒業後も英語を勉強し続けるようにするには，どのように動機づけるか。100語程度の英語で答えよ」である。解答例は，「現代はICTの複雑な世界になっていて，情報のやり取りには英語が必要である。また，英語が使えないと世界中の人々とコミュニケーションができない。逆に，英語が使えれば，将来責任ある立場につくことができる。したがって，生徒たちは英語を卒業後も学ぶ必要がある」という主旨である。

2016年度　実施問題

【中高共通】

【１】リスニングテスト

Part A

In Part A, you will hear a question or a statement followed by three responses. Choose the best response to each question. The question and the responses will be spoken only once.

(3秒)

(1) Do you have your evaluation sheet for this lesson?

(A) Fill in the blanks.

(B) I'm sorry, I left it in my room.

(C) I think she works very hard.

(5秒)

(2) When will the presentation be over?

(A) All right, see you then.

(B) In the hall over there.

(C) In about an hour.

(5秒)

(3) I'm going on a ten-minute break.

(A) OK, I'll join you.

(B) Don't worry. The problem will be fixed.

(C) Thanks, but I don't need your help.

(5秒)

(4) Do you know who has the Key to the meeting room?

(A) No, I didn't meet him in the room.

(B) He's in the teachers' room.

(C) Mr. Takeda must have it.

(5秒)

(5) Why don't we prepare the gym for the assembly?

(A) Because we already arranged the chairs in the gym.

(B) That's not a bad idea. How long will it take?

(C) It'll be held during the fifth period in the gym.

(5秒)

(6) Don't you think we should start looking for a few more volunteers?

(A) Yes, I also think we should.

(B) I'm not looking for a different job.

(C) No, we need much more volunteer work.

(10秒)

Part B

In Part B, you will hear four short conversations between two people. Each conversation will be followed by one question. Choose the best answer from among the four choices written on your test sheet. Conversations and questions will be spoken only once.

(3秒)

(1) M: Why are you in such a hurry?

W: We have a meeting with our ALT at eight fifteen this morning.

M: You're supposed to have a meeting so early?

W: Yes, he has classes all day today, so it's the only time he's available.

Question: Why can't the woman see her ALT later?

(10秒)

(A) Her ALT will be busy teaching.

(B) She is sick and will go home soon.

(C) She will be away from school later.

(D) Her ALT has some other meetings.

(2) M: Meg, you're using your smartphone again. Have you finished your homework yet?

W: No, not yet, but a message has come from Ken. I must reply to him first.

M: You can answer when you're finished. The first thing you should do is to finish your homework.

W: I know, but... OK, Dad.

Question: Why doesn't the father like his daughter using her smartphone?

(10秒)

(A) Because she uses it to talk with her boyfriend.

(B) Because she always uses it to do her homework.

(C) Because it interferes with her study.

(D) Because the bill will be very expensive.

(3) M: I'd like to borrow these books.

W: Yes, sir. Do you have your library card?

M: No, it's my first time here. Will it take time to make one?

W: No, but a driver's license or some ID is required to register.

Question: What will the man do next?

(10秒)

(A) Go home to bring his library card back.

(B) Present his driver's license to the librarian.

(C) Show his driver's license instead of his library card.

(D) Renew his driver's license soon.

(4) M: I missed my connecting flight to Las Vegas because my inbound flight was delayed. I'd like to get a seat on the next flight.

W: I'm so sorry, but all the economy seats on the last flight to Las Vegas are full. You can get a seat in business class, but you have to pay an additional charge.

M: That's unreasonable. The delay is the airline's fault, not mine. I need to arrive there today.

W: Well... then, I'll see if we can get you one without any extra charge.

Question: What is the woman going to do for the man?

(10秒)

(A) Reserve him an economy seat.

(B) Give him a refund for the ticket.

(C) Arrange a flight on the next day.

(D) Get him on the last flight.

Part C

In part C, you will hear two short passages. Each passage will be followed by one question. Write the answer to each question in English. Both answers should begin with "I should." Passages and questions will be read twice.

(3秒)

(1) Good evening, ladies and gentlemen. Welcome to the Opera Theater. Since the copyright of the performance is strictly protected by the law, we ask that all guests refrain from taking photos and videos throughout. We would also ask that all mobile phones be turned off before the curtain opens. Thank you for your cooperation and enjoy the show.

Question: After this announcement, what should you do while the performance is in progress?

(15秒)

(2回目)

(20秒)

(2) This is your first visit to our clinic, isn't it? Right then, before Dr. Robert can examine you, you'll have to fill in this medical interview sheet. Please remember to include a list of all medications you are taking. After you have finished, take your temperature, and bring the sheet and the thermometer back to me.

Question: What information should you include on the interview sheet?

(15秒)

(2回目)

(20秒)

Part D

In Part D, you will hear a passage. Two questions are written in Japanese on your test sheet. Answer these questions in Japaraese. The passage will be read twice.

Gender equality is th concept that men and women have exactly the same opportunities and rights in society, that they aren't discriminated against based on gender. This can include what people are allowed to do, where they work, what they're paid－these all factor into gender equality.

Women in the United States have it better than many in the world. They aren't forced into marriage at a young age. They can leave the house without their husbands' permission. They can pursue an education, serve on a jury and vote.

But there are ways the U.S. lags behind other nations. For starters, roughly 84 percent of countries, including Afghanistan, guarantee gender equality in their constitutions. The U.S. Constitution does not.

Then, there's paid maternity leave. Studies show it's good for families and for businesses, which is why many countries insist on it. In France, for example, women are guaranteed at least 16 weeks paid maternity leave, 26 weeks if it's their third child. New moms in Estonia get two full years of paid leave. Only four countries in the world do not guarantee any form of paid maternity leave. The United States is one of them. It's the only high income developed country that doesn't.

(15秒)

(2回目)

(30秒)

問い

(1)　世界の多くの女性より，米国の女性の方が男女間において平等である具体例を全て書け。

(2)　男女平等について，米国が他国に後れを取っている面を二つ書け。

This is the end of the listening test.

(☆☆☆◎◎◎)

【2】次の英文を読んで，(1)～(5)の設問に答えよ。

Not the glittering weapon fights the fight, says the proverb, *but rather the hero's heart.*

Maybe this is true in any battle; it is surely true of a war that is waged with bleach and a prayer.

For decades, (A)Ebola haunted rural African villages like some mythic monster that every few years rose to demand a human sacrifice and then returned to its cave. It reached the West only in nightmare form, a Hollywood horror that makes eyes bleed and organs dissolve and doctors (①) because they have no cure.

But 2014 is the year an outbreak turned into an epidemic, powered by the very progress that has paved roads and raised cities and lifted millions out of poverty. This time it reached crowded slums in Liberia, Guinea and Sierra Leone; it traveled to Nigeria and Mali, to Spain, Germany and the U.S. It struck doctors and nurses in unprecedented numbers, wiping out a public-health infrastructure that was weak in the first place. One August day in Liberia, six pregnant women lost their babies when hospitals couldn't admit them for complications. Anyone willing to treat Ebola victims ran the risk of becoming one.

(B)Which brings us to the hero's heart. There was little to stop the disease from spreading further. Governments weren't equipped to respond; the World Health Organization was in (②) and snarled in red tape. First responders were accused of crying wolf, even as the danger grew. But the people in the field, the special forces of Doctors Without Borders / Médecins Sans Frontières (MSF), the Christian medical-relief workers of Samaritan's Purse and many others from all over the world fought side by side with local doctors and nurses, ambulance drivers and burial teams.

Ask what drove them and some talk about God; some about country; some about the instinct to run into the fire, not away. "If someone from America comes to help my people, and someone from Uganda," says Iris Martor, a Liberian nurse, "then why can't I?" Foday Gallah, an ambulance driver who survived infection, calls his (　③　) a holy gift. "I want to give my blood so a lot of people can be saved," he says. "I am going to fight Ebola with all of my might."

MSF nurse's assistant Salome Karwah stayed at the bedsides of patients, bathing and feeding them, even after losing both her parents — who ran a medical clinic — in a single week and surviving Ebola herself. "It looked like God gave me a second chance to help others," she says. Tiny children watched their families die, and no one could so much as hug them, (C)because hugs could kill. "You see people facing death without their loved ones, only with people in space suits," says MSF president Dr. Joanne Liu. "You should not die alone with space-suit men."

Those who contracted the disease encountered pain like they had never known. "It hurts like they are busting your head with an ax," Karwah says. One doctor overheard his funeral being planned. Asked if surviving Ebola changed him, Dr. Kent Brantly turns the question around. "I still have the same flaws that I did before," he says. "But whenever we go through a devastating experience like what I've been through, it is an incredible opportunity for redemption of something. We can say, How can I be better now because of what I've been through? To not do that is kind of a shame."

【出典　TIME, December 22, 2014】

(1)　筆者は下線部(A)を何に例えているか，40字程度の日本語で書け。

(2)　(　①　)～(　③　)に入る最も適切な語を，次のア～エからそれぞれ一つずつ選び，その記号を書け。

①　ア　delight　　イ　despair　　ウ　deceive

エ　determine

② ア　denial　　イ　prospect　　ウ　progress

エ　detail

③ ア　personality　　イ　mentality　　ウ　continuity

エ　immunity

(3)　筆者が下線部(B)のように表現するに至った当時の具体的な医療の状況について，直前の段落で述べられている内容を100字程度の日本語で書け。

(4)　下線部(C)の内容を以下のように具体的に述べたとき，次の(　　)内に入る適切な1語を書け。

because, through physical contact like hugs, the children could be (　　) with Ebola and die

(5)　Dr. Kent Brantlyは自身の経験をどう捉え，今後どうしていきたいと考えているか，70字程度の日本語で書け。

(☆☆☆◎◎◎)

【中学校】

【1】次の会話文を読んで，(1)～(6)の設問に答えよ。

Mrs. Beck is meeting with her son's teacher, Ms.Rendon. Her son is usually good student, but his grades have been slipping in English class and she's a little worried about him.

Mrs. Beck: Hello, Ms. Rendon, I'm Laura Beck, James' mother. How are you?

Ms. Rendon: Mrs. Beck, so nice to meet you. Yes, have a seat. I've just been reviewing James' work. Let's see.

Mrs. Beck: Yes, James has always been such a good student. I don't know what's happened to him.

Ms. Rendon: Honestry, a lot of kids' grades go down around their sophomore or junior year, especially boys.

Mrs. Beck: I don't know whether to be comforted by $_{(A)}$<u>that</u> or not, but high school is when his G.P.A. is the most important. He wants to go to a university, but if he keeps getting grades like this he'll have to go to a junior college first.

Ms. Rendon: Well, sometimes kids need a little time to (①) before going to a university. Maybe a J.C. isn't such a bad thing for some kids.

Mrs. Beck: His father and I both went straight to universities; [Ⅰ].

Ms. Rendon: OK, well, he hasn't been doing his homework. That's one problem. I don't have many entries for homework assignments, and [Ⅱ]. His exam scores are a little lower than they used to be. His lower grade this (B)[<u>not / homework / a / consequence / semester / of / is / in / turning / his</u>] and not scoring well on tests. He hasn't done much participating in classroom discussions either. He probably isn't reading his assignments or maybe he just doesn't understand what he's reading. I've asked him about it, but he just shrugs his (C)――, so I'm not sure what the problem is. Sometimes it's not the class or the material. Sometimes it's not the subject [Ⅲ] or not do well in class.

Mrs. Beck: Everything's fine at home. We have a very close family, so I don't think it has anything to do with his home life.

Ms. Rendon: Have you spoken to his counselor?

Mrs. Beck: No.

Ms. Rendon: Well, have you asked James why he's not doing well in class?

Mrs. Beck: I've tried, but he just gives me a (②) response. I can't get anything out of him.

Ms. Rendon: If he won't tell me and he won't tell you, then (D)――

Mrs. Beck: OK, I think I'll do that. I'm also going to talk to him about his assignments. Do you have a syllabus with the assignments?

Ms. Rendon: Yes, I'll get you one. Remember that he may have some issues going on in his life [Ⅳ]. Kids at this age really start keeping their problems to themselves. Other than his grades going down, he's a good kid. I'm sure this is just a (③) concern.

Mrs. Beck: OK, Ms. Rendon, I appreciate all your help.

Ms. Rendon: No problem. Take care.

【出典 Barbara Raifsnider, *FLUENT ENGLISH*, LIVING LANGUAGE】

(1) 下線部(A)が示す内容を，30字程度の日本語で書け。

(2) (①)～(③)に入る最も適切な語を，次のア～カから一つずつ選び，その記号を書け。

ア pressing イ vague ウ passing エ ferment

オ mature カ distinct

(3) [Ⅰ]～[Ⅳ]に入る最も適切なものを，次のア～カから一つずつ選び，その記号を書け。

ア that causes a student to lose interest

イ that you may not know about

ウ the homework prepares the kids for the exams

エ we expect James to do the same

オ he applies himself to his homework

カ that he may not be concerned with

(4) 下線部(B)を，意味が通るように並べかえよ。

(5) 下線部(C)に入る体の部位を，最も適切な形で書け。

(6) 下線部(D)に入る最も適切なものを，次のア～エから一つ選び，その記号を書け。

ア would you mind if I take him to his counselor?

イ you might want to talk to his counselor.

ウ you might not blame him too much for his grades.

エ could you see whether he has read his assignments yet?

(☆☆☆◎◎◎)

【2】次の英文を読んで，(1)～(4)の設問に答えよ。

Educators have come to realize (A)<u>that learners come in different styles</u>. Some students learn best by seeing someone else do it. Usually, they like carefully sequenced presentations of information. They prefer to write down what a teacher tells them. During class, they are generally quiet and seldom distracted by noise. These ***visual*** learners contrast with ***auditory*** learners, who often do not bother to look at what a teacher does, or to take (　①　). They rely on their ability to hear and remember. During class, they may be talkative and are easily distracted by noise. *Kinesthetic* learners learn mainly by direct involvement in activity. They tend to be impulsive, with little patience. During class, they may be fidgety unless they can move about and *do*. Their approach to learning can appear haphazard and random.

Of course, few students are exclusively one kind of learner. Grinder(1991) notes that in every group of 30 students, an average of 22 are able to learn effectively as long as a teacher provides a blend of visual, auditory, and kinesthetic activity. The remaining 8 students, however, prefer one of the modalities over the other two so strongly that they struggle to understand the subject matter unless special care is taken to present it in their preferred mode. In order to meet these needs, (B)<u>teaching has to be multisensory and filled with variety</u>.

Educators also have been noticing changes in their students' (　②　) styles. For the past fifteen years, Schroeder and his colleagues(1993) have been giving the Myers-Briggs type Indicator(MBTI) to incoming college students. The MBTI is one of the most widely used instruments in education and business today. It has been especially useful for understanding the role of individual differences in the learning process. Their results indicate that approximately 60 percent of entering students have a *practical* rather than a *theoretical* orientation toward learning, and the percentage grows year by year. Students prefer to be involved with immediate, direct, concrete experiences rather than learning basic concepts first and applying them later on. Other MBTI research, Schroeder points out, shows that high school students prefer learning activity that is ***concrete active*** to activity that is ***abstract reflective*** by a ratio of five to one. From all this, he concludes that active modes of teaching and learning create the best match for today's students. To be effective, teachers should use all she following: small-group discussion and projects, in-class presentations and debates, experiential exercises, field experiences, simulations, and case studies. In particular, Schroeder emphasizes, today's students "adapt quite well to group activities and collaborative learning."

These findings come as no surprise if you consider the active pace of modern life. Students today grow up in a world where things happen quickly and where many choices are presented. Sounds come in clever "bites," and colors are vibrant and compelling. Objects, both real and virtual, move quickly. The opportunity to change things from one state to another is everywhere.

【出典　Mel Silberman, *Active Learning 101 Strategies to Teach Any Subject*, Allyn and Bacon】

(1)　下線部(A)の内容について，三つの具体例を80字程度の日本語で書け。
(2)　文中の(　①　)，(　②　)に入る最も適切な英語1語を，それぞれ文中から抜き出して書け。
(3)　下線部(B)の理由を，80字程度の日本語で書け。
(4)　今日，以前に比べ多くの学生に好まれるようになった学び方と，そうなった背景をそれぞれ40字程度の日本語で書け。

(☆☆☆◎◎◎)

【３】(1)～(3)について，それぞれの英文の[　　]内に入る最も適切なものを，ア～エからそれぞれ一つずつ選び，その記号を書け。また，(4)については，[　①　]と[　②　]に入れるのに最も適切な組合せを選び，その記号を書け。

(1) I couldn't concentrate on studying because all that noise was very [　　].

ア restricting　イ detracting　ウ distracting
エ dismissing

(2) [　　] been in our team, we would not have won the pennant this year.

ア Had he not　イ Hadn't he　ウ He had not
エ He not had

(3) He was [　　] as anyone could have had.

ア as a patient teacher　イ a teacher as patient
ウ a patient as teacher　エ as patient a teacher

(4) He suddenly saw Jane [　①　] the room. He pushed his way [　②　] the crowd of people to get to her.

ア ① over　② toward　イ ① across　② through
ウ ① across　② along　エ ① over　② across

(☆☆☆◎◎◎)

【４】(1)～(4)について，それぞれの日本語の内容を表すように，[　　]内の語句を並べかえよ。

(1) 突然，茂みから1匹の猫が私の自転車の前の路上に飛び出してきた。

All [out / of / a cat / onto / a sudden / the bush / of / jumped] the road in front of my bike.

(2) 彼は枯れ木を救えるかもしれない方法を思いついた。

He thought of a way [trees / perishing / by / might / the / be / which] saved.

(3) 近隣の学校では生徒の個々の能力を効果的に伸ばすために，英語と数学の授業を習熟度別学級にしているところもある。

English and mathematics classes are [each / as / according / ability / so / student's / formed / to] to have them develop their ability efficiently in some schools around here.

(4) すでに数社がシャーロット王女フィーバーを利用して製品を発表している。

Some companies [products / to / in / already / cash / released / on / designed / have] the Princess Charlotte frenzy.

(☆☆☆◎◎◎)

【5】次の(1)，(2)の内容について，あなたが教師として，中学校第3学年の英語の授業で生徒に対して指示することを想定し，それぞれ英語で書け。

(1) 生徒が何人かスピーチをする。それぞれのスピーチを聞き終わった後に，1分間でシートに英語で質問，感想を言うためのキーワードを書く。

(2) はじめにペアで対話文の音読練習をする。教科書を見ないで言えるようになったら，ペアで教師の点検を受ける。

(☆☆☆◎◎◎)

【6】授業の打合せの時間が合わないALTに対して，英語担当教員(JTE)であるあなたは，メモにメッセージを残すことにしました。英語の授業で行う次の活動 "Who is he / she?" について，下の内容を伝えるために次の書き出しから始め，100語程度の英語で書け。

(書き出し) I will tell you how to do an activity called "Who is he / she?"

・ねらいは，関係代名詞を使って，生徒が好きな有名人を説明する英文を作ること。

・初めにALTが説明し，次にALTとJTEがやり方を実演する。

・隣同士がペアになり，好きな有名人を決め，15分以内で3～4文の英文を書かせる。
・英文が完成したら生徒に挙手をさせ，ALT又はJTEがチェックする。
・全てのペアがチェックを受けた後，生徒同士で "Who is he / she?" を行う。

(☆☆☆◎◎◎)

【高等学校】

【1】次のCahokia(カホキア)についての英文を読んで，各設問に答えよ。

Cahokia was a pretty big deal in the 1100s. Founded by a complex cultural group that built tall mounds and sweeping plazas, the city near present-day St Louis, Missouri, was home to tens of thousands of people. But its population began declining around 1200, and by 1350, Cahokia was a ghost town.

The cause of the settlement's decline is a historical puzzle. But research published this week in the *Proceedings of the National Academy of Sciences* suggests that a major Mississippi River flood around 1200 hastened Cahokia's end.

Samuel Munoz, a geographer at the University of Wisconsin-Madison, and his colleagues based $_{(A)}$this finding on analysis of sediments from Horseshoe Lake, just 5 kilometres from Cahokia. The team extracted sediment cores up to 5.5 metres in length from the lakebed, representing 2,000 years of deposition.

A series of light bands of fine sediment in the core "popped out to us immediately" , Munoz says. A student dubbed the bands "lake butter" because of their unusually fine and silky texture.

Munoz says that this sediment would have entered the lake during major floods along the Mississippi River. "We call the river the 'Big Muddy' for a reason," he adds. "This sediment is essentially the sediment that makes the water muddy and brown."

The team dated the buttery bands using radiocarbon techniques, and confirmed and refined many of these dates by examining cores from another lake about 200 kilometres down the river. They concluded that major floods occurred around AD 280, 490, 580, 1200, 1400, 1510, 1590 and 1800.

Cahokia's heyday, which began when residents started to farm maize (corn) on its rich river bottomlands, (B) neatly inside the longest flood-free period, from 600 to 1200. Climatic conditions across North America were particularly arid then.

Flooding might have been one of many environmental and social factors that played a part in the city's decline, says Munoz. "Can we say that this flood at 1200 caused the abandonment of Cahokia? No. We can't say that with any certainty," he adds. "All we can show is that there is a correspondence in time."

Larry Benson, adjunct curator of anthropology at the University of Colorado Boulder's Natural History Museum, has published analyses of tree-ring data that suggest that drought doomed Cahokia. But he says that flooding also could have contributed by shifting agriculture from the city's floodplains to higher ground. (C)<u>That would have made Cahokia's harvest more dependent on rainfall.</u>

Benson would like to see precise estimates of when historical floods occurred, noting that dates offered in the latest paper have margins of error extending over many decades. "If we had a better idea of timing, (D)<u>the puzzle</u> would be put together much more perfectly," he says.

George Milner, an archaeologist at Pennsylvania State University in University Park, finds the analysis convincing, and thinks that floods on the Mississippi and Missouri rivers could have affected many smaller prehistoric cities as well. What is now the US Midwest began to depopulate around 1200, he says, and floods, droughts, cold years and hot years could all have triggered social instability. "The real problem of these kinds of societies is when people experience back-to-back failures," he says.

Munoz sees a lesson for present-day communities in the Midwest, which still rely on the region's great rivers to transport goods and supply water to rich, riverside croplands. "Rivers are very sensitive to climate change," he says. "We need to keep a close eye on them."

【出典　NATURE, 04 May 2015 http://www.nature.com】

(1)　下線部(A)が表す内容を日本語で答えよ。

(2)　空所(　B　)に入る最も適切な語を，次のア～エから選び，その記号を書け。

ア　draws　　イ　falls　　ウ　lies　　エ　puts

(3)　下線部(C)をThatの内容を明らかにして，日本語に直せ。

(4)　下線部(D)が指す内容を英文中から6語でそのまま抜き出せ。

(5)　現代の中西部の社会の状況と，それに対するMunozの考えを，80字程度の日本語で書け。

(6)　次の英文の中で，本文の内容と一致するものをア～キから二つ選び，記号を書け。

ア　Cahokia is the well-known ruins which prospered around 600 years ago in the US Midwest.

イ　Samuel Munoz and his colleagues extracted sediment cores from the bottom of a lake, which enabled them to examine the region's soil conditions for the past 2000 years.

ウ　When examined carefully and closely, the series of light bands in the sediment cores turned out to be unusually fine and silky.

エ　Climatic conditions of North America from 600 to 1200 inspired the residents of Cahokia to farm maize on the highlands.

オ　Munoz took for granted the fact that flooding around 1200 caused the decline of Cahokia.

カ　Larry Benson concluded that based on the analysis of tree-ring data, regardless of some margins of errors, he would be able to prove the cause of Cahokia's end.

キ　George Milner thinks that societies come to decline when people go through successive failures such as bad harvests caused by unsettled weather.

(☆☆☆◎◎◎)

【2】次の(1)，(2)について，日本語で答えよ。

(1)　英語の授業で，ある単元のまとめとして教科書の内容に基づいたテーマについて，自分の考えなどを生徒一人一人がクラスで英語で発表する活動を行うことにした。その際，①準備における指導の留意点と②発表に際しての指導の留意点について，箇条書きで答えよ。

(2)　英語の研究会で，次のような発言があった。

「英語を苦手としている生徒や嫌いな生徒が多い学校では，英語で授業を行ったり英語で言語活動をさせたりするのは無理だ。」

この発言について①あなたはどのように考えるか，また，②あなたなら苦手としている生徒や嫌いな生徒が多いクラスに，具体的にどのように対応するか，日本語で答えよ。

(☆☆☆◎◎◎)

【3】次の(1)～(5)の(　　)に当てはまる最も適切な語をそれぞれア～エから一つ選び，記号を書け。

(1) As long as you (　　) to a single perspective, it'll be impossible to achieve a breakthrough on the issue.

ア adhere　イ dominate　ウ clog　エ stab

(2) The new bypass is expected to alleviate the traffic (　　) in the business district.

ア contention　イ conversion　ウ concession　エ congestion

(3) According to the weather forecast, a typhoon was approaching; (　　), he went out to work.

ア but　イ nevertheless　ウ despite　エ although

(4) The governor couldn't attend the party (　　) person, so his secretary read his message for him.

ア for　イ of　ウ in　エ to

(5) It's difficult to (　　) between what should be changed and what cannot be changed.

ア distract　イ discharge　ウ disclaim　エ discern

(☆☆☆◎◎◎)

【4】次の(1)～(5)の各英文には，1か所誤りがある。その部分の記号を書き，正しい英語に直せ。

(1) Professor Williams assigned $_{\text{A}}$a term paper to us instead of holding the term exam, so I had to $_{\text{B}}$spend a lot of days reading $_{\text{C}}$many Shakespeare's works $_{\text{D}}$to write it during the summer vacation.

(2) If you $_{\text{A}}$had devoted half as much time $_{\text{B}}$to preparing for the test $_{\text{C}}$as you did $_{\text{D}}$to spend on web surfing, you wouldn't have failed.

(3) At the age of thirty, he $_{\text{A}}$decided to be a lawyer and took an entrance exam to the university.

He couldn't $_{\text{B}}$get a desired result, but later, he was admitted to $_{\text{C}}$enter the university to $_{\text{D}}$fill a vacancy.

(4) The pharmaceutical company succeeded $_{A}$in the development of new medicine $_{B}$with less side effects $_{C}$in collaboration with ABC University $_{D}$over a long period of years.

(5) It $_{A}$can be true that many a man $_{B}$satisfied with the current situation $_{C}$have lost opportunities $_{D}$to grow as a human being.

(☆☆☆◎◎◎)

【5】次の英文を読んで，100語程度の英語で答えよ。

A new ALT, who came to Japan for the first time, asks you what “Shugaku Ryoko” is. Please explain to him/her what it is, referring to the purpose of the event.

(☆☆☆◎◎◎)

解答・解説

【中高共通】

【1】Part A (1) (B) (2) (C) (3) (A) (4) (C) (5) (B) (6) (A) Part B (1) (A) (2) (C) (3) (B) (4) (D)

Part C (1) I should refrain from taking photos and videos.

(2) I should include a list of all medications I am taking.

Part D (1) 若い年齢で結婚を強いられることはない，夫の許可なく外出できる，教育を求めることができる，陪審員を務めることができる，投票できる (2) ・アフガニスタンを含む約84パーセントの国は憲法で男女の平等を保障している。 ・アメリカを含むわずか4か国が有給の産休を保障していない。

〈解説〉Part A (1)「この授業の評価表を持っていますか」と聞かれているので，(B)の「すみません。部屋に置き忘れました」が適切。(A)は「空欄を埋めてください」という意味である。 (2) 質問文の疑問詞はwhenなので，(C)の「だいたい1時間後に」が適切。(B)はwhereに対する答えになる。　(3)「私は10分間休みます」に対して，(A)の「わかりました。私はあなたに加わります(私も休みます)」が適切。
(4)「誰が会議室のカギを持っているか知っていますか」に対して，(C)の「タケダさんが持っているに違いない」が正解。　(5)「集会のために体育館を準備しましょう」に対して，(B)の「悪い考えではないね。どのくらいかかるの」が適切。Why don't we …? は「…しましょう」といった意味で，原因・理由を聞いているわけではないので，becauseでは答えない。　(6)「もう少し多くのボランティアを探し始めるべきだと思わない？」に対して，(A)の「はい，そうすべきだと私も思います」が適切。(B)は同じlooking forを使っているが，異なる仕事を探すわけではない。　Part B　(1)　質問は「なぜ女性はもっと遅い時間に彼女の外国語補助教員に会うことができないのですか」という意味であり，女性の最後のセリフにhe has classes all day todayとあり，(A)が同じ内容を表す。ALTはheで受けているので，男性だと判断する。be supposed to doは「…することになっている」という意味である。
(2)　父と娘の会話。友人からメールが来て，娘は返事しなければならないといっているので，(C)の「それ(スマートフォン)が彼女の勉強を邪魔するから」が適切。interfere with …は「…を邪魔する」，like＋目＋doingは「～に…してほしいと思う」といった意味になる。
(3)　最初のやりとりから，図書館での会話と判断する。最後に女性が，「図書館カードを登録するためには運転免許証かほかの身分証が必要です」と言っているので，(B)の「運転免許証を図書館員に提示する」が適切。男性の2番目のセリフに「ここの図書館は初めてです。カードを作るのに時間はかかりますか」とあることから，男性が図書館カードを持っていないことがわかり，(A)と(C)は不適と判断する。
(4)　男性(乗客)は接続便に乗り遅れ，女性(航空会社の社員)はラスベガス行き最終便のエコノミークラスは満席で，ビジネスクラスは座席が取れる。その場合は追加料金がかかる，と提案する。遅れは自分の過失ではなく，フライトが遅れたからであると主張した男性に対し，女性は「追加料金なしで(ラスベガス行き最終便のビジネスクラスの)座席が取れるかどうか確認する」とあるので，(D)の「(ラスベガス行き)最終便(のビジネスクラス)に彼を乗せる」が適切。inboundは「入ってくる，到着する」，refundは「払い戻し」といった意味である。Part C　I shouldで書き始めるので，劇場やクリニックにいたとしたら，自分はどうすべきなのか考えながら書く。　(1)　質問文は「このアナウンスの後，公演が進行中にあなたは何をすべきですか」であり，we ask that all guests refrain from taking photos and videos throughout「公演中，お客様は写真やビデオを撮ることを控えるようお願いします」とあることから判断する。throughoutはWhile the performance is in progressに言い換えられているが同じ内容を表す。　(2)　質問文は「問診票に何の情報を含めるべきですか」。3文目にPlease remember to include a list of all medications you are taking.「あなたが服用しているすべての薬のリストを忘れずに入れてください」とあることから判断する。interview sheetは「問診票」のことである。　Part D　(1)　第1段落で「社会において男女は同じ機会や権利を有し，性別によって差別されない」とあるので，2段落目の1文目はその男女間の平等という点で「世界の多くの女性より，米国の女性のほうが有利である」，つまり「米国のほうが男女間で平等である」と考える。2文目以降にその具体例が列挙されている。gender equalityは「男女の平等」，have it better than …は「…より有利である」，serve on a juryは「陪審員を務める」という意味である。　(2)　第3段落の1文目に「米国が他国に遅れをとる点がいくつかある」とあり，2文目以降と第4段落に2つの例が挙がっている。lag behindは「…に遅れをとる」といった意味である。

【2】(1)　2〜3年に1度起き上がり，人間の生け贄を要求し，そのあと洞穴に戻っていく神話上の怪物　(2)　①　イ　②　ア　③　エ　(3)　エボラはリベリアやギニア，シエラレオネ，ナイジェリア，マリ，スペイン，ドイツ，アメリカにまで広がった。エボラは医者や看護婦を襲い，脆弱な公衆衛生施設を全滅させ，また合併症を理由に病院が

入院させなかった妊婦は赤ん坊を失った。　(4)　infected
(5)　エボラの治療に対していまだに力不足だが,「行動しないことは一種の恥である」と考え,力不足にあがない治療に当たることで,向上したいとしている。

〈解説〉(1)　like「〜のような」の後に例えがあるのでまとめればよい。
(2)　①の直後に「なぜなら医者は治療法がないから」とあるので,その気持ちを表すdespair「絶望する」が適当。なお,ウは「だます」といった意味である。　②　第4段落の2文目に「その病気(エボラ)がさらに拡大するのを抑える手段はほとんどなかった」とあり,その実例として「政府は対応の体制が整っておらず,WHOは現実から目を背け,お役所仕事に阻まれていた」と考え,in denial「現実を否定して」が適切と考える。イはin prospectで「予想して」,ウはin progressで「進行中の」,エはin detailで「詳細に」といった意味になる。
③　第5段落の2文目に「感染を切り抜けて生き残った救急車の運転手のFoday Gallahは彼の…を聖なる恵みと呼んでいる」とあり,感染の中を生き残ったのは,彼の免疫力がエボラを感染させなかったからだと考え,immunity「免疫」が適切。　(3)　whichは関係代名詞で,この場合,前に出てきた内容を先行詞にして「そのこと(前に出てきた内容)が私たちを勇敢な心にする」という意味になる。第3段落の3文目の「それ(エボラ)は未曽有の数で医者や看護婦を襲い,脆弱な公衆衛生施設を全滅させた」や,次の文の「合併症が理由で病院が入院させなかったので6人の妊婦が赤ん坊を失った」などの具体例を100字程度でまとめる。　(4)　下線部を含む文は「小さな子どもたちは家族が死ぬのを見守った。そして誰も彼らを抱きしめることすらできなかった。なぜなら…」という意味。エボラで家族を亡くした子どもを慰めようと抱きしめたくても,その人が感染していたら,子どももエボラに感染して死ぬかもしれないという意味にする。cannot so much as …は「…すらできない」といった意味である。　(5)　第7段落の5文目に「私(Dr. Kent Brantly)には依然として前と同じ欠点がある。」とあり,エボラの治療に対しいまだに力不足で,患者を死なせていることを認めて

いる。6文目に「私が受けているような衝撃的な経験をするときはいつでも，人はそれをすばらしいあがないの機会とする。」とあり，力不足をあがない，治療に当たるいい機会だととらえている。7文目に「私が経験したことで，私はどれだけよりよくなれるか。行動しないことは一種の恥である」とあり，力不足をあがないながら向上したいと述べている。これらを70字程度でまとめるとよい。

【中学校】

【1】(1)　高校2年ごろに，成績が低下する現象が特に男子に多く見られること。　(2)　①　オ　②　イ　③　ウ　(3)　Ⅰ　エ　Ⅱ　ウ　Ⅲ　ア　Ⅳ　イ　(4)　semester is a consequence of not turning in his homework　(5)　shoulders　(6)　イ

〈解説〉(1)　Jamesに何かがあり，Rendon先生の2つ目のセリフに「正直，多くの子ども，特に男子が2，3年生の頃に成績が落ちます」とJamesだけではなく同じ年代の子どもも抱える問題だと言って慰めている。それを受け，Mrs. Beckは「そのことによって慰められるかどうかわからないけど」と応答していることから判断する。　(2)　①「子どもたちの中には，大学に行く前に…する時間が少し必要だ」といった意味であり，universityの前のjunior collegeに行くことを勧めていることからmature「成熟する」が適切。　②　空所の直後の文で「彼から何も得ることができない」，つまり「彼のことがわからない」と言っているので，「彼はただあいまいな返答しかしない」と考え，vague responseが適切と考える。　③　Rendon先生は「成績が落ちている以外は，彼はいい優秀な子どもです」といっているので，concern「心配」は一過性のものだと考え，passingが適切。　(3)　Ⅰ　Mrs. Beckは「Jamesの父親と私は2人ともストレートで(短期大学に行かずに)大学に行きました」とあり，それを受けRendon先生は「(両親と同じようにストレートに大学に行くためには)Jamesは(最近)宿題をしていないので，それが1つの問題です」と続くと考えられる。したがって，「私たちはJamesに同じこと(ストレートで大学に行く)をするよう期待する」

が適切。 Ⅱ Rendon先生は「宿題をやってくる子はそんなに多くない」とあり，さらに「(宿題をやっていない)Jamesの試験の点数は以前よりも少し下がっている」と続いている。したがって，Rendon先生は宿題と試験の関連性について言及しており，ウの「宿題は子どもたちに試験の準備をさせる」が適切と考える。 Ⅲ 前の文からJamesの問題となりそうなものを列挙している。「それは授業や教材でもない。…な教科でもないし，授業がよくできるからでもない」とあるので，「生徒に興味をなくさせる(教科)」と考える。 Ⅳ 後で「この年頃の子どもは自分たちの問題を胸に秘め始める」と説明しているので，問題を親に隠しているかもしれないと考え，「あなた(Mrs. Beck)が知らないかもしれない問題が，彼(James)の人生で起こっているかもしれない」が適切。 (4) His lower grade this semester「今学期の彼の下がった成績」，turning in his homework「彼の宿題を提出すること」，a consequence of …「…の結果」をそれぞれ意味のまとまりとしてとらえて考えるとよい。 (5) Rendon先生は「私は彼に成績が下がっていることをたずねた」とあり，後で「それで私は問題が何なのかわからない」と続くので，Jamesがあいまいな態度をとったから問題がわからないと考え，shrug one's shoulders「肩をすくめる」が適切と考える。 (6) Rendon先生は「もし彼(James)が私に話さないで，彼があなた(Mrs. Beck)にも話さないなら」といっているので，別の手段として「あなた(Mrs. Beck)は彼のカウンセラーに話したほうがいいかもしれません」と考える。

【2】(1) ・授業中，先生の話を書き留めることを好む視覚学習者 ・人とよく話し，聞いて覚える聴覚学習者 ・衝動的で我慢せず，動き回って直接学習活動に参加する運動感覚学習者 (2) ① notes ② leaning (3) 生徒には視覚，聴覚，運動感覚を組み合わせて効率的に学習する人もいれば，1つのスタイルで学習することを好む人もおり，それぞれの生徒が好む学習スタイルでできるようにするため。 (4) 学び方…生徒は基本から学ぶより，直接的で具体的体験に関わる

ことで学習する方法を好むようになった。　背景…今日の生徒は，出来事が目まぐるしく起こり，多くの選択肢が提示される世界で育っている。

〈解説〉(1)　(A)以後に，3つの学習スタイルが斜体で目立つように記されているので，それらをまとめればよい。　(2)　①　聴覚学習者の説明であり，「わざわざ先生がすることを見たり，…したりしない」とあるので，書き留めて視覚化することはしないと考え，take notes「書き留める」が適切。なお，bother to do …は「わざわざ…する」といった意味である。　②　第3段落の1文目に「教育者たちはまた生徒の…スタイルの変化に気づいている」とあり，その理由として「この15年間，学習過程における個々の要素の役割を理解するときに役立つMBTIを使って調べると，60％の新入生が理論的学習に取り組むよりも実践的に取り組みたい」とあるので，学習の取り組み方，つまりstudents' learning styles「生徒の学習スタイル」と判断する。

(3)　(B)は「教えられるものは多感覚に働きかけ，豊富な種類が必要である」という意味。第2段落の2文目以降に，30人のグループのうち約7割(22人)は視覚，聴覚，運動感覚を組み合わせた活動を提供すると効率的に学習でき，約3割(8人)は1つのスタイルで学習することを好む，とある。そのため，多感覚に働きかけ，それぞれの生徒が好む学習スタイルで学習できるように豊富な種類が必要だと考えている。

(4)　第3段落の6文目と第4段落の2文目に，その学び方と背景が示されている。

【3】(1)　ウ　(2)　ア　(3)　エ　(4)　イ

〈解説〉(1)　空所の直前に副詞のveryがあるので，叙述用法の形容詞が入ると考える。ウのdistractingは「注意をそらす」という意味の形容詞で，他は動詞のing形である。なお，アのrestrictは「制限する」，イのdetractは「減ずる」，エのdismissは「解雇する」といった意味がある。

(2)　コンマ以降の後半の節のwould not have wonは助動詞の過去形＋(not)＋have＋過去分詞なので，仮定法過去完了の文だと見当をつける。

文の意味は「(過去のある時に)彼が私たちのチームにいなかったならば，私たちは今年のペナントを制覇しなかっただろう」。実際は，彼が私たちのチームに入っていたので，今年のペナントを制覇したというのが過去の事実で，その過去の事実に反して仮定しているのでIf he had not been in our teamとなる。さらにif節のifが省略されheとhadが倒置されたHad he not been …という文になる。　(3)　as＋形容詞＋(a/an)＋名詞＋asの文である。問題文は「彼はだれも持ち得ないくらい忍耐強い教師だった」という意味である。　(4)　問題文の意味は「彼は突然，部屋の向こうに人を見た。彼は人込みを押しのけて前に進み彼女にたどり着いた」である。see …(人) across a room「部屋の向こうに…を見る」，push one's way through「…を押し開けて前へ進む」なのでイが適切。

【4】(1)　of a sudden a cat jumped out of the bush onto　(2)　by which the perishing trees might be　(3)　formed according to each student's ability so as　(4)　have already released products designed to cash in on

〈解説〉(1)「突然」はall of a sudden,「…から飛び出す」はjump out of …,「路上に(飛び出す)」はonto the roadと，それぞれ意味のまとまりごとに組み合わせる。　(2)　問題の文はHe thought of a way「彼はその方法を思いついた」とthe perishing trees might be saved by a way「その方法によって枯れ木は救われるかもしれない」の2つに分ける。a wayを先行詞にし，whichを使ってHe thought of a way which the perishing trees might be saved by.にし，byを関係代名詞の前に持ってきてby which …にする。　(3)　問題文を「英語と数学の授業は構成される」と考え，English and mathematics classes are formedとする。「習熟度別」は「それぞれの生徒の能力に応じて」と置き換え，according to each student's abilityとする。また,「伸ばすために」は目的を表すso as to developにする。　(4)「～を利用して製品」は「利用するために設計された製品」と置き換え，products designed to cash in onに,「(今や)すでに～を発表している」は現在完了時制を使って，have already released …にする。

【5】(1)　(例)　After each speech, you have one minute to write down keywords and phrases for asking questions or giving feedback about their speech.　(2)　(例)　Make pairs and practice reading a dialogue aloud with a partner. After practicing, I will check if you can say the dialogue aloud without looking at the text.

〈解説〉「書く」はwrite down,「ペアになって」はmake pairs,「音読する」はread aloudとする。英語の授業などでよく使われる平易な表現を軸に作文するとよい。

【6】(例)　I will tell you how to do an activity called "Who is he / she?" The aim of the activity is to have students describe their favorite famous people using relative pronouns properly. You explain how to do the activity to students and then we demonstrate it for them. After that, get the students to make pairs and write three to four sentences describing the famous person they pick up within fifteen minutes. After completing it, have the students raise their hands and either you or I check if the sentences they write make sense. Then get the students to do "Who is he / she?"

〈解説〉伝える相手はALTなので内容が正確に伝わればよく，単語や文章表現の難易度は気にする必要はないだろう。ただし語数制限があるので，日頃から語数を決めて，短時間での英作文の練習をしておくとよい。

【高等学校】

【1】(1)　1200年ごろに起きたミシシッピ川の大洪水がカホキアの終焉を速めた。　(2)　イ　(3)　洪水によって氾濫原より高地に移行したことで，カホキアの穀物収穫を降雨により依存することになっただろう。　(4)　The cause of the settlement's decline　(5)　今日の中西部の地域は大河に依存して物資を輸送し，水を肥沃な河岸の農耕地へ供給しており，Munozは川は気候の変動に敏感で，注視する必要があると考えた。　(6)　イ，キ

〈解説〉(1)　第2段落に「研究は示唆している」としてthat以下に示されている。　(2)　空所を含む文は「住民が肥沃なミシシッピ川の沖積層低地でトウモロコシを栽培し始めた時にカホキアの最盛期は始まり，最も長く洪水がない期間内に～である」という意味。その次の文に「その時(最も長く洪水がない期間)，北米の気候条件は特に乾燥状態にあった」とあるので，乾燥してトウモロコシが育たず没落すると考え，イのfallsが正解。　(3)　第9段落の2文目に「洪水はまた農業を都市の氾濫原からより高地へ移行させることに寄与したかもしれない」とあり，もともとカホキアは肥沃なミシシッピ川の沖積層低地にあり，川の水を利用してトウモロコシを栽培していたが，高地へ移ったことで，「カホキアの穀物の収穫がもっと降雨に依存することになったのだろう」という流れをつかんでおく。floodplain「氾濫原(洪水の時に水浸しになる川辺の土地)」。　(4)　第2段落の1文目にthe cause of the settlement's decline is a historical puzzleとあることからpuzzleがさす内容を考える。　(5)　第12段落の1文目に「今日の中西部の地域は大河に依存して物資を輸送し，水を肥沃な河岸の農耕地へ供給している」とMunozは中西部の社会の状況を考えていて，さらに「川は気候の変動に敏感で，(川を)注視する必要がある」と状況に対する自分の考えを述べていることをまとめる。　(6)　第3段落は「Samuel Munozと同僚はHorseshoe Lakeの堆積物の分析に基づいてこの発見をした。彼らのチームは，湖底から長さ(高さ)5.5メートルに及ぶ2000年分の堆積物を掘り出した」という意味で，イの「Samuel Munozと彼の同僚は湖の底から堆積物コアを掘り出し，この2000年にわたるその地域の土壌の状態を調査することができた」と一致する。また，第11段落の2文目に「現在のアメリカ中西部にあたる所は1200年頃に人口が激減し，洪水や干ばつ，寒冷や猛暑などはすべて社会の不安定を引き起こしたかも知れなかった」とあり，キの「不安定な天候によって引き起こされた凶作のような不運を立て続けに経験すると社会は衰退するとGeorge Milnerは考えている」と内容が一致する。

【2】(1) ① ・準備の際はテーマに関連した書物などを日本語で読んで内容に熟知する。 ・自分の知っている正しい英語で話す。
・段落ごとに内容を分け，論理的で説得力のある英語で話す。
② ・発表の際は後ろの人にも聞こえる適切な音量で，意味のまとまりごとに話す。 ・身振り手振りを交え，しっかりと聴衆の目を見て話す。 (2) ① 自分の英語力に対し自信がない生徒も多く，そのため英語を使ってコミュニケーションすることに不安を抱きがちである。また，ほかの学生から自分の英語力がどう評価されるのか不安に思うことが多いので，それらの不安を軽減するよう授業を工夫して組み立てる必要がある。 ② ペアワークやグループワークを多用して，ほかの生徒と協力することで不安を軽減させ，また可能な限り平易な英語を使用し，適切な時や場面で日本語を使用して生徒の学習不安を軽減し，学習意欲を出させる。

〈解説〉英語と日本語のギャップに苦しみ，自信を持てない生徒に対しては，間違っていても許容される雰囲気作りが重要になる。例えば，話すことを試みたこと自体が称賛される等があげられる。スピーチについては十分な準備を行い，内容に確信を持たせることも大事であろう。そのためには，授業時の会話は英語であっても，資料は日本語で読ませるなど柔軟な対応が必要になる。

【3】(1) ア (2) エ (3) イ (4) ウ (5) エ

〈解説〉(1) 問題文の意味は「1つの見方にこだわる限り，その問題で大きく進展することは不可能だろう」である。空所の直後にtoがあるのでadhere to「…にこだわる」が適切。イのdominateは「支配する」，ウのclogは「詰まる」，エのstab「突き刺す」といった意味である。
(2) 問題文の意味は「新しい迂回路はビジネス地区の交通～を緩和することを期待される」であるので，エの「渋滞」が適切。アのcontentionは「争い，議論」，イのconversionは「転換」，ウのconcession「譲歩」といった意味である。 (3) 選択肢はどれも「しかし，だけれども」という意味だが，ウのdespiteは前置詞なので，直後にコンマではなく目的語の名詞句がくる。エはalthough a typhoon was approaching, he went out to work.という語順ならよい。空所の直前をセミコロンで区切っているので，接続副詞であるイのneverthelessが適切。(4)　in personで「本人自ら」という意味。　(5)　discern between A and Bで「AとBを識別する」という意味である。アのdistractは「そらす，紛らす」，イのdischargeは「解放する，降ろす」，ウのdisclaimは「否認する」という意味である。

【4】(記号；正しい英語の順)　(1)　C；many works of Shakespeare's　(2)　D；to spending on　(3)　C；the university　(4)　B；with fewer side effects　(5)　C；has lost

〈解説〉(1)　問題文は「ウィリアム教授は学期末試験を行う代わりに学期末レポートを私たちに課した。それで夏休みの間，私はレポートを書くためにシェークスピアの作品の多くを読むことに多くの日数を費やした」という意味である。Cはa friend of mine「私の友だちの1人」のように，many works of Shakespeare'sの語順になる。　(2)　問題文は「もしあなたがネットサーフィンに費やす時間の半分をテストの準備に使ったなら，あなたは落第しなかっただろうに」といった意味である。didは代動詞でas you devotedとなり，Dのtoは前置詞なので動詞はspendingにする。なお，devote 〜 to …で「〜を…に捧げる」という意味である。　(3)　問題文は「30歳の時，彼は弁護士になることに決め，大学の入学試験を受けた。彼は望んだ結果を得られなかったが，のちに，欠員を埋めるために大学への入学が認められた」という意味である。be admitted to .…は「…への入学を認められる」という意味であり，enterは不要。　(4)　問題文は「製薬会社は長年かけてABC大学と共同で，副作用のより少ない新薬の開発に成功した」という意味である。Bのside effects「(いくつかの)副作用」は可算名詞なので，lessではなくfewの比較級のfewerが適切。　(5)　問題文は「現状に満足する多くの人は人間として成長する機会を失ってしまうというのは事実かもしれない」という意味である。many＋a＋名詞単数形で「多数の…」という意味。単数形は単数扱いなのでhaveではなくhasにする。

【5】Shugaku Ryoko is a short-term school trip and conducted as part of school events at Japanese schools, typically during the months of May, June, October and November. Students visit places of cultural heritage value like Kyoto and Nara or famous places like Disneyland, together with teachers and stay at least overnight without being attended by their parents.

The purpose of Shugaku Ryoko is to give students an opportunity for learning something about Japan and broadening their understanding and knowledge of it through firsthand experience. Shugaku Ryoko will also help students foster their own independence and learn cooperation through living together for a short time. (104words)

〈解説〉伝える相手はALTなので内容が正確に伝わればよく，単語や文章表現の難易度は気にする必要はないだろう。ただし語数制限があるので，日頃から語数を決めて，短時間での英作文の練習をしておくとよい。

2015年度　実施問題

【中高共通】

【１】リスニングテスト

Part A

In Part A, you will hear a question followed by three responses. Choose the best response to each question. The question and the responses will be spoken only once.

(3秒)

(1) When did you last visit the library?

(A) No, I didn't.

(B) Last Saturday, with my friends.

(C) It'll last about a month.

(5秒)

(2) Don't you think we need more time to finish our new program?

(A) Yes, I'm afraid we do.

(B) Because we really did.

(C) No, it starts this afternoon.

(5秒)

(3) How did you get such a pretty piece of stationery?

(A) I got to the office.

(B) I took a taxi to the station.

(C) I found it on a web site.

(5秒)

(4) Why don't we check the document one more time before the meeting?

(A) I've already looked it over three times.

(B) Yes, the meeting was very successful.

(C) He'll also attend the meeting again.

(5秒)

(5) Did Ms. Sato finish planning her demonstration class?

(A) No, her class hasn't started yet.

(B) Yes, it's in the classroom.

(C) She's still working on it.

(5秒)

(6) Do you know who will be replacing our ALT when he returns to his country?

(A) Yes, he replaced some old furniture.

(B) I hear it hasn't been decided yet.

(C) His town is a nice place to live.

(10秒)

Part B

In Part B, you will hear four short conversations between two people. Each conversation will be followed by one question. Choose the best answer from among the four choices written on your test sheet. Conversations and questions will be spoken only once.

(3秒)

(1) M : Hi, is this Ace Clinic? It's Ken Smith. I'd like to make an appointment for tomorrow.

W : Hello, Mr. Smith. Well, we have openings at 11:15, 11:30 and 11:45.

M : OK. I'll take 11:30.

W : Sure. Please make sure to check in fifteen minutes in advance.

Question : By what time should the man come to the clinic?

(10秒)

(A) By 11:00.

(B) By 11:15.

(C) By 11:30.

(D) By 11:45.

(2) W : You're interested in this Shakespeare class, aren't you? You should take it.

M : Well, I looked over the syllabus. It has a lot of homework.

W : What are you talking about? Most other classes do anyway.

M : You're right. Either way, I'll attend the first class and then decide.

Question : How does the man feel about the Shakespeare class?

(10秒)

(A) He's excited about taking it.

(B) He's decided not to take it.

(C) He'd rather take history.

(D) He's wondering if he should take it.

(3) M : Isn't the tennis tournament coming up soon?

W : Yes, Dad. But I'm having some trouble. Kate and I had been practicing together for over three months, but she left the team the other day.

M : Oh, my! I guess it's difficult for you to find a new partner at this point. Can you do that by yourself?

W : Well, I suppose I could. But we don't have enough time to practice together before the tournament.

Question : What is the girl's problem?

(10秒)

(A) She hasn't joined the tennis team yet.

(B) She doesn't want to play in the tournament.

(C) She had no choice but to give up on her partner.

(D) She and Kate hadn't been practicing together until then.

(4) M : Hello, I'm looking for a simple model. I just make phone calls and exchange some text messages. I don't need too many functions on my phone.

W : Well, how about this one? It's not our latest model, but it's easy to use.

M : Looks good. How long does the battery last?

W : With it fully charged, you can talk four hours straight. Actually, we have a good offer. If you sign up for a two-year contract now, you'll get this phone free of charge.

Question : What does the man have to do to get the phone for free?

(10秒)

(A) Talk on the phone for four hours or longer.

(B) Sign up for a two-month contract.

(C) Pay a deposit.

(D) Start a contract to use the phone for 24 months.

Part C

In Part C, you will hear two short passages. Each passage will be followed by one question. Write the answer to each question in English. Both answers should begin with "I should." Passages and questions will be read twice.

(3秒)

(1) Starting next month, our office will be introducing a new computer network system. It will help us especially with group tasks. But please remember that the new "shared folder" will not store all the files from the old folder, so it is important that you back up the necessary files and folders by the end of this month, otherwise they could be lost.

Question : What should you do before you start using the new computer network system?

(15秒)

(2回目) (20秒)

Write your answer on your answer sheet.

(2) Thank you for coming to the 2014 English Teachers' Skill Development Conference. We are offering various workshops. Workshops for jr. high school teachers will be held in Rooms 301 and 302. Those for sr. high school teachers will be held in Rooms 201 and 202. Those on elementary school activities will be held in Room 101. The workshops will start at 10:00, except for the ones on elementary school activities, which will start 30 minutes later. For a detailed schedule, please refer to the brochure you got at the registration desk. Please enjoy your day.

Question : If you join the workshops on elementary school activities, what are you supposed to do?

(15秒)

(2回目) (20秒)

Write your answer on your answer sheet.

Part D

In Part D, you will hear a passage. Two questions are written in Japanese on your test sheet. Answer these questions in Japanese. The passage will be read twice.

(3秒)

M : Julia Fine, a senior at a high school in Maryland, wrote an essay. It was the winning entry from among hundreds submitted in a contest. It was chosen by Malala Yousafzai, the Pakistani girl who made a miraculous recovery after being shot in the head by the Taliban. This is part of Julia's essay.

W : Malala stood up for herself, for her education and for her fundamental rights when confronted by a fearsome terrorist group. Malala has created a chain reaction all around the world, bringing change, light and hope to girls across all continents.

Being teenage girls in the United States, so many times, we forget the opportunities we have been given. We roll our eyes and joke about dropping out of school, a right we take for granted in this country. I don't know if I speak for all girls when I say this, but I know for me that after hearing about Malala's fight for education, I cannot take mine so lightly any longer.

I plan to continue my education so that I can fight for those who cannot. Malala has inspired me to study politics, gender studies, social justice and peace so that I am equipped with the tools I need to help others, the tools so many girls are not given.

(15秒)

(2回目) (30秒)

This is the end of the listening test.

(1) アメリカの高校生の考え方で，エッセイの筆者が問題視していることを日本語で書け。

(2) マララさんに触発されて，エッセイの筆者がしようとしていることを，具体的に日本語で書け。

(☆☆☆☆◎◎◎◎)

【2】次の英文は，南アフリカ共和国のネルソン・マンデラ元大統領(2013年12月没)について書かれた記事の抜粋である。英文を読んで，(1)～(5)の各設問に答えよ。

"Fellow South Africans, our beloved Nelson Rolihlahla Mandela, the founding president of our democratic nation, has departed. He passed on peacefully in the company of his family around 20:50 on the 5th of December, 2013." (Jacob Zuma, South African President)

Nelson Mandela's struggle for freedom defined his life. He was born in the remote hills of South Africa's Eastern Cape. He was given the name

Rolihlahla, which means "troublemaker." He was only given the name Nelson by a schoolteacher later on.

After moving to Johannesburg and studying law, Mandela's troublemaking politics began. And as a boxer, he became (①) at picking fights and sparring with the apartheid authorities, which had increased its oppression against the black population.

It was then that Mandela made the crucial decision to take up an armed struggle, launching the African National Congress's armed wing. He was (A)<u>militant and a firebrand</u>, defiantly burning his passbook, a dreaded document the apartheid authorities used to control the movement of South Africa's black population.

"The Africans require... want the (②) on the basis of one man, one vote. They want political independence." (Nelson Mandela, in 1961)

That simple demand and the methods Mandela took to fight for democracy eventually saw him and others (B)<u>tried for treason and sabotage</u> by the apartheid government, acts punishable by death. But they got life imprisonment instead, banished to Robben Island, one of the country's most brutal and isolated prisons. Mandela was released 27 years later.

"I have spoken about freedom in my lifetime. Your struggle, your (C)<u>commitment</u> and your discipline has released me to stand before you today." (Nelson Mandela, upon his release)

And his lack of bitterness towards the apartheid authorities helped him to lead one of the most remarkable political transitions of the 20th century. Mandela, the trained lawyer and lifelong rebel, outmaneuvered the apartheid leaders, and he steered South Africa's peaceful transition to democracy. He won a Nobel Peace Prize together with his former enemy, the apartheid leader F.W.de Klerk.

And then he became South Africa's first black president, in 1994.

His retirement years were busy, with fundraising for charities close to his heart. He celebrated his 90th birthday with much fanfare and told CNN in a rare interview that, looking back, he wouldn't do anything (③).

"I don't regret it, because the things that attracted me were things that pleased my soul." (Nelson Mandela)

Now, those who loved and respected him look to his legacy.

(December 6, 2013)

【出典　CNN ENGLISH EXPRESS 2014年3月号】

(1) (①)～(③)に入る最も適切な語を，次のア～エからそれぞれ一つずつ選び，その記号を書け。

① ア passive　イ cordia1　ウ adept
　エ devastating

② ア judiciary　イ welfare　ウ patent
　エ franchise

③ ア separately　イ differently　ウ exactly
　エ similarly

(2) 下線部(A)のような気質から出たマンデラ氏の具体的な行動を，50字程度の日本語で書け。

(3) 下線部(B)について，マンデラ氏は当局によってどのような処罰を受けたのか，具体的に50字程度の日本語で書け。

(4) 下線部(C)とほぼ同義である語を，次のア～オから一つ選び，その記号を書け。

ア devotion　イ betrayal　ウ respect　エ disdain
オ affinity

(5) マンデラ氏のノーベル賞受賞について，①受賞した理由と，②受賞における特筆すべきことを，それぞれ30字程度の日本語で書け。

(☆☆☆☆◎◎◎◎)

【中学校】

【1】次の会話文を読んで，(1)～(5)の設問に答えよ。

Manuel: It's time to talk about benefits. Does anyone have a concern?

Rosita : I am concerned about day care for my children. I must drive ten miles across town to take my children to a day-care center. If they get sick, I must drive back to get them. I lose working time and pay. I would like to [Ⅰ] about day care.

Angela : Not all of us have children. I don't. I care about Rosita's problem, because she is my friend. But I don't want all the company benefits to go to other people. Those who don't need day care shouldn't have to pay for it.

Ming : I am concerned about day care, but I am also concerned about (A)<u>working conditions</u>.

: No one else mentions any concerns. They all agree to discuss these topics.

Manuel : Since Rosita mentioned day care first, let's start with that.

Rosita : I have a suggestion about day care that will not cost much. There is empty space in the building. I (B)[<u>to / someone / wants / of / open / know / who</u>] a day-care service. Maybe the boss would rent her space. Then we could bring the children to work with us. Those of us who want to use the service could pay for it. It would be convenient to [Ⅱ].

Mousa : This sounds like a good possibility. It would benefit people who need day care, but it wouldn't cost the company money. Those who do not need day care would not be receiving a (①) benefit.

Manuel : Well, this is something that I need to talk about with the other supervisors. We'll see how many other employees are interested in day care. If the number is (②) enough, I think the boss will consider it.... Who else wants to talk? Ming, didn't you mention working conditions?

Ming : My eyes aren't as good as they once were. I'm worried that I might not be finding all of the bad nuts and bolts when I make my inspections. I would like brighter lighting so I can see better.

Rosita : Yes, I think it needs to be (③) in our work area, too. I sometimes get headaches.

Manuel: I agree that is an important point. I'll talk to the boss about that (④) away. Is there any more input? No? All right. I will talk to (C)<u>the other supervisors</u> about day care. And I will talk to the boss about lighting. You have had good suggestions. I am sure we can work these things out. I know you all want to [Ⅲ]. I'll see you all tomorrow. Goodbye!

【出典 Sheila Henderson, *Learning English Made Simple*, DOUBLEDAY】

(1) [Ⅰ]～[Ⅲ]に入る最も適切なものを，次のア～エから一つずつ選び，その記号を書け。

ア have our children nearby　　イ see the company do something

ウ head for home now　　エ hire about a dozen new people

(2) 下線部(A)について，具体的に求める改善の内容を，30字程度の日本語で書け。

(3) 下線部(B)の語を，意味が通るように並べかえよ。

(4) (①)～(④)に入る最も適切な語を，次のア～カから1つずつ選び，その記号を書け。

ア right　イ useful　ウ brighter　エ useless

オ bigger　カ large

(5) Manuelが下線部(C)に対して実際に発話することを想定するとき，次の言い出しに続く英文を書け。

I have a suggestion from one of my workers about day care. Before talking to the boss about it, there's something I'd like to know.

(☆☆☆☆◎◎◎◎)

【2】次の英文を読んで，(1)～(4)の設問に答えよ。

Perhaps the most important development concerning English in Japan in the past 20 years is the gradual spread of English teaching and the use of English as a medium of instruction in schools — both public and private — throughout the educational system. Although Japan has no colonial heritage involving English, nor is the Japanese language inadequate for science, technology and business, (A)state support for English teaching and for English-medium education has intensified since the 1990s. Accordingly, the Ministry of Education, Culture, Sports, Science and Technology (MEXT) has adopted a series of policies applicable to elementary, secondary and tertiary education, and worked to implement these policies through its regulation of the school system and through a public relations campaign to build support for its policies and programmes (Hashimoto, 2007).

As in many countries around the world, in Japan a common rationale for this development is that English is the most important international language of science, technology and economic competitiveness, and therefore English language ability is essential for individual participation in these areas of 'globalized' human activity and for the economic well-being of the society. In this sense, the discourse of English promotion in Japan resembles that of many other countries, where English is viewed as essential for participation in the global economy (Crystal, 1997).

Yet a closer look at English promotion in Japan reveals (B)a rather more complicated relationship between language and globalization. First, the promotion of English is often linked directly with reinvigorated programmes supporting the national language (Japanese). For example, in the MEXT document 'Developing a Strategic Plan to Cultivate "Japanese with English Abilities"' (MEXT, 2002), the promotion of English is linked with improvements in Japanese language education: '[T]he English-speaking abilities of a large percentage of the population are inadequate... However, it is not possible to state that Japanese people have sufficient ability to express their opinions on a firm grasp of their own language' (Hashimoto, 2009, p.28). That is, the complaint that Japanese citizens generally do not speak English well is articulated alongside the less common view that Japanese also do not speak Japanese well. As we will see, MEXT made this rather odd suggestion that Japanese citizens speak neither English nor Japanese adequately as part of a discursive programme that promotes English within strict social limits as well as a reinvigorated programme of Japanese national cultural identity.

As in many countries, such as Singapore and South Korea, government documents in Japan generally represent learning English (and technical skills) as the key to reaping the benefits of globalization, but in Japan globalization is also often represented in government documents as a threat to the country's unity, its values and its security. Thus the promotion of English in Japan is mediated by official uncertainty and hesitation about globalization itself. Indeed, government policies and the wider public debate offer competing representations of globalization: as a challenge with great opportunity and as a profound threat to Japan's future. Central to these ambivalent discourses of globalization is that language policies in Japan are discursively linked with debates about immigration policies (as well as the ageing of the Japanese citizenry and other important public policy issues). Like the United States, the United Kingdom and much of Europe, public discourse about immigration in Japan often includes dramatic and disturbing representations of immigrants, and language policies are often debated in conjunction with these representations.

Accordingly, analysis of English promotion in Japan reveals tensions in the discourse of language and globalization. Two competing representations of globalization can be identified: globalization as (①), and globalization as (②).

【出典 Philip Seargeant, *English in Japan in the Era of Globalization*, Palgrave Macmillan】

(1)　下線部(A)により具体的に行われたことを，70字程度の日本語で書け。

(2)　日本における英語教育推進の根拠となっている考え方を，70字程度の日本語で書け。

(3)　下線部(B)について，その具体的な内容二つを，それぞれ40字程度の日本語で書け。

(4)　文中の(　①　)，(　②　)に入る最も適切な英語1語を，それぞれ文中から抜き出して書け。

(☆☆☆☆☆◎◎◎◎)

【3】(1)～(4)について，それぞれの英文の[　　]内に入る適切なものを，ア～エからそれぞれ一つずつ選び，その記号を書け。

(1)　I lost [　　] little money saved for a rainy day.

ア　how　　イ　what　　ウ　that　　エ　which

(2)　My condition is, [　　], better than last night.

ア　if not　　イ　if any　　ウ　if only　　エ　if anything

(3)　[　　] of the three students took part in the hometown event.

ア　Each　　イ　Both　　ウ　Every　　エ　Any

(4)　We expected our new song to be a great hit, but it was [　　] from being a success.

ア　opposite　　イ　away　　ウ　distant　　エ　far

(☆☆☆☆◎◎◎◎)

【4】(1)～(4)について，それぞれの日本語の内容を表すように，[　　]内の語句を並べかえよ。ただし，文頭にくる語も小文字にしてある。

(1)　君の長髪はなんとかしなければならない。

[be / your / something / about / done / hair / must / long].

(2)　マイクは私たちを失望させるような人間ではない。

Mike [man / disappoint / us / would / to / last / be / the].

(3)　加藤先生の教え方は学習の遅い生徒たちに合わせたものであっ

た。

[method / learners / adapted / Ms.Kato / to / teaching / slow / her / her].

(4) 彼の机の上は，雑誌や文房具がめちゃくちゃな状態で散らかっていた。

[desk / and stationery / on / of / chaotic / magazines / a / lay / mess / his].

(☆☆☆☆☆◎◎◎◎)

【5】次の(1)，(2)の内容を，中学校第3学年の授業で指示することを想定し，それぞれ英語で書け。

(1) 机を移動し6人のグループになり，最初の発表者を決める。

(2) 3分間インタビューをし，自分と同一の意見の人をできるだけ多く見付ける。

(☆☆☆☆◎◎◎◎)

【6】あなたが勤務する学校に週2回訪問しているALT(Jack)に対して，次の内容を伝えるEメールを60語程度の英語で書け。

＜伝えたい内容＞

・打合せの日時　　　：来週月曜日の午後3時半

・準備してほしいもの：前時の復習用アクティビティ数例

・検討したいこと　　：過去形を導入する際のALTとJTEのインタラクション

(☆☆☆◎◎◎◎)

【高等学校】

【1】次の文章を読んで，(1)～(6)の設問に答えよ。

Why worry that we are moving toward a society in which everything is up for sale?

For two reasons: one is about inequality; the other is about corruption. Consider inequality. In a society where everything is for sale, life is harder for those of modest means. The more money can buy, the more affluence (or the lack of it) matters.

If the only advantage of affluence were the ability to buy yachts, sports cars, and fancy vacations, inequalities of income and wealth would not matter very much. But as money comes to buy more and more — political influence, good medical care, a home in a safe neighborhood rather than a crime — ridden one, access to elite schools rather than failing ones — the distribution of income and wealth looms larger and larger. Where all good things are bought and sold, having money makes all the difference in the world.

This explains why the last few decades have been especially hard on poor and middle-class families. Not only has the gap between rich and poor widened, (A)the commodification of everything has sharpened the sting of inequality by making money matter more.

The second reason we should hesitate to put everything up for sale is more difficult to describe. It is not about inequality and fairness but about the corrosive tendency of markets. (B)Putting a price on the good things in life can corrupt them. That's because markets don't only allocate goods; they also express and promote certain attitudes toward the goods being exchanged. Paying kids to read books might get them to read more, but also teach them to regard reading as a chore rather than a source of intrinsic satisfaction. Auctioning seats in the freshman class to the highest bidders might raise revenue but also erode the integrity of the college and the value of its diploma. Hiring foreign mercenaries to fight our wars might spare the lives of our citizens but corrupt the meaning of citizenship.

Economists often assume that markets are inert, that they do not affect the goods they exchange. But this is untrue. Markets leave their mark. Sometimes, (C)market values crowd out nonmarket values worth caring about.

Of course, people disagree about what values are worth caring about, and why. So to decide what money should — and should not — be able to buy, we have to decide what values should govern the various domains of social and civic life. How to think this through is the subject of this book.

Here is a preview of the answer I hope to offer: when we decide that certain goods may be bought and sold, we decide, at least implicitly, that it is appropriate to treat them as commodities, as instruments of profit and use. But not all goods are properly valued in this way. The most obvious example is human beings. Slavery was appalling because it treated human beings as commodities, to be bought and sold at auction. Such treatment fails to value human beings in the appropriate way — as persons worthy of dignity and respect, rather than as instruments of gain and objects of use.

Something similar can be said of other cherished goods and practices. We don't allow children to be bought and sold on the market. Even if buyers did not mistreat the children they purchased, a market in children would express and promote the wrong way of valuing them. Children are not properly regarded as consumer goods but as beings worthy of love and care. Or consider (D)the rights and obligations of citizenship. If you are called to jury duty, you may not hire a substitute to take your place. Nor do we allow citizens to sell their votes, even though others might be eager to buy them. Why not? Because we believe that civic duties should not be regarded as private property but should be viewed instead as public responsibilities. To outsource them is to demean them, to value them in the wrong way.

These examples illustrate a broader point: some of the good things in life are corrupted or degraded if turned into commodities. So to decide where the market belongs, and where it should be kept at a distance, we have to decide how to value the goods in question — health, education, family life, nature, art, civic duties, and so on. These are moral and political questions, not merely economic ones. To resolve them, we have to debate, case by case, the moral meaning of these goods and the proper way of valuing them.

This is a debate we didn't have during the era of market triumphalism. As a result, without quite realizing it, without ever deciding to do so, we drifted from *having* a market economy to *being* (E)a market society.

The difference is this: A market economy is a tool — a valuable and effective tool — for organizing productive activity. A market society is a way of life in which market values seep into every aspect of human endeavor. It's a place where social relations are made over in the image of the market.

【出典　MICHAEL J.SANDEL, *WHAT MONEY CAN'T BUY, FARRAR, STRAUS AND GIROUX*】

(1)　下線部(A)の具体例として直前のパラグラフで挙げられているものの中から，三つを日本語で記せ。

(2)　下線部(B)の具体例として挙げられているものの中から，一つを日本語で答えよ。

(3)　下線部(C)の意味として最も適切なものを次のア～エのうちから選び，その記号を記せ。

ア　市場価値が，本来金銭で売買すべきでないが大事にしなければいけない価値とは無関係に消えていく。

イ　市場価値が，本来金銭で売買すべきでないが大事にしなければいけない価値を駆逐する。

ウ　市場価値の方を，本来金銭で売買すべきでない価値よりも大事にしなければいけない。

エ　市場価値の多くが，本来金銭で売買すべきでないが大事にしなければいけない価値に内容的に近付いていく。

(4)　下線部(D)を筆者はどのように説明しているか。日本語で答えよ。

(5)　下線部(E)を筆者はどのように説明しているか。日本語で答えよ。

(6)　次の英文の中で，本文の内容と一致するものを二つ選び，その記号を記せ。

ア　In a society in which everything is up for sale, inequality and the corrosive tendency of markets are unavoidable.

イ　In a society where the gap between the rich and the poor is all about the affordability of yachts, sports cars, and fancy vacations, life is hard for poor and middle-class families.

ウ　Over the last few decades the gap between the rich and the poor has not widened, and inequalities of income and wealth did not matter very much.

エ　Economists seldom agree with the idea that markets are inert and do not affect any good things turned into commodities.

オ　Slavery did not necessarily treat human beings as instruments of gain and objects of use.

カ　Where the market belongs ought not to be up for public debate.

キ　The era of market triumphalism did not see public discussion about the role and reach of markets.

(☆☆☆☆◎◎◎◎)

【2】次の(1)，(2)について，日本語で答えよ。

(1)　「コミュニケーション英語Ⅰ」の授業で①音読の活動を行う際の注意点，また②音読の活動の具体的な種類を三つ挙げ，それぞれの活動における留意点を箇条書きで答えよ。

(2)　発信力を測るためのライティングテストを複数の教員で評価する際，留意すべき点について具体的に箇条書きで答えよ。

(☆☆☆☆◎◎◎◎◎)

【3】次の(1)～(5)の(　　)に当てはまる最も適切な語句をそれぞれア～エから一つ選び，記号で答えよ。

(1)　He negotiated a new deal with a major publisher, only to find it difficult to (　　) his ideals with reality.

ア　recant　　イ　recast　　ウ　reconcile　　エ　rectify

(2)　A special meeting was (　　) to discuss further developments in English language teaching in Akita.

ア　convened　　イ　converted　　ウ　converged　　エ　conversed

(3)　More and more people tend to live a (　　) life because of the tax increase.

ア　wasteful　　イ　public　　ウ　frugal　　エ　subjective

(4) With our courage and wisdom, we must find a peaceful solution to the deterioration of the two countries no matter how (　　) the crisis seems to be.

ア　blatant　　イ　formidable　　ウ　aggressive　　エ　defiant

(5) The applicants who scored high in liberal arts last year can be (　　) from the first exam this year.

ア　resulted　　イ　eliminated　　ウ　passed　　エ　exempted

(☆☆☆☆◎◎◎◎)

【４】次の(1)～(3)の各英文には，1か所誤りがある。その部分の記号を答え，正しい英語に直せ。

(1) Either billiards or darts $_{A}$<u>is</u> available to play $_{B}$<u>with</u> free $_{C}$<u>for</u> anyone $_{D}$<u>who</u> stays at the hotel overnight.

(2) He is such a good tennis player $_{A}$<u>so</u> he may $_{B}$<u>well</u> $_{C}$<u>enter</u> the tournament $_{D}$<u>instead</u> of me.

(3) $_{A}$<u>That</u> the students didn't understand $_{B}$<u>that</u> the professor referred $_{C}$<u>to</u> in his lecture was completely $_{D}$<u>against</u> his expectations.

(☆☆☆☆◎◎◎◎)

【５】次の質問に，100語程度の英語で答えよ。

According to "English Education Reform Plan corresponding to Globalization," English is going to be taught as a formal subject at elementary school and classes will be conducted, in principle, in English at junior high school as well as senior high school. High-level language activities are to be required at senior high school. What is your opinion about this trend as a future English teacher?

(☆☆☆☆◎◎◎◎◎)

解答・解説

【中高共通】

【1】Part A (1) (B) (2) (A) (3) (C) (4) (A) (5) (C) (6) (B) Part B (1) (B) (2) (D) (3) (C) (4) (D)

Part C (1) (I should) back up the necessary files and folders.

(2) (I should) go to Room 101 by 10:30.

Part D (1) 解答略 (2) 解答略

〈解説〉Part A (1) 問は「あなたが最後に図書館を訪れたのはいつか」である。 (2) 問は「新しい計画を完成させるのにさらに時間が必要だと思わないか」である。 (3) 問は「そんなにかわいらしい文房具をどうやって手に入れたのか」である。 (4) 問は「なぜ報告書を会議の前にもう一度点検しないのか」である。 (5) 問は「サトウさんは教育実習の指導案を完成させたか」である。 (6) 問は「今の指導助手が帰国した後の後任は誰だか知っているか」である。

Part B (1) スミスさんは11：30に予約をしたが，担当者からは15分前に来院するように言われた。 (2) 男性は講座自体には興味があるが，宿題を心配している。 (3) 彼女は，相手を探すことは問題ないと言っている。 (4) その場で2年間の契約を交わすことが無料で使用する条件である。 Part C (1) 必要なファイルとフォルダーのバックアップを今月末までにとることが必要である。 (2) 小学校教員の会場は101である。ただし，時刻は中学高校の30分遅れの10時30分である。 Part D (1) 今まで当然のこととして考えてきた学校での勉強や，場合によっては退学ということについての反省を述べている。 (2) 今，自分に与えられている権利を今後は軽々しく考えずに，勉強を続けて，勉強の機会が得られない人々のために尽くすことがひとつ。また，政治や社会，平和についても勉強して他の人の役に立つと述べている。

【2】(1)　①　ウ　　②　エ　　③　イ　　(2)　解答略　　(3)　解答略　(4)　ア　　(5)　①　アパルトヘイト体制に穏便な態度で臨み民主政府を築いたこと。　②　旧体制と新体制双方の代表が共同で受賞したこと。

〈解説〉(1)　①　第3パラグラフにヒントがある。相手がアパルトヘイトの当局者という点がポイントである。　②　イと誤りやすいので要注意。直後のon the basis of one man, one voteがポイントである。あくまでも法律的に保障を求めたのである。　③　「何も特別なことはしなかった」の意味である。　(2)　直後のdefiantlyから最後までがヒントである。この中のpassbookとa dreaded documentが同格で，the apartheid以下がdocumentを説明している。　(3)　第6パラグラフ2文目にマンデラ氏が受けた処罰が書いてあるので，その点を訳せばよい。life imprisonmentは「終身刑」という意味である。　(4)　第7パラグラフ2文目の内容が現在のマンデラを築いたという意味である。したがって「関係する，参加する」の意味である。　(5)　①　第8パラグラフ2文目にpeaceful transition to democracyとある。　②　第8パラグラフ最後の文にtogether with his former enemy …とある。2014年の平和賞も協同受賞であった。

【中学校】

【1】(1)　Ⅰ　イ　　Ⅱ　ア　　Ⅲ　ウ　　(2)　解答略　　(3)　know of someone who wants to open　　(4)　①　エ　　②　カ　　③　ウ　④　ア　　(5)　Do you know how many workers are interested in day care? I think it possible if the number is large enough.

〈解説〉(1)　Ⅰ　Rositaは勤務しているので，会社に対して何かをしてほしいと思っているのである。　Ⅱ　Rositaの2回目の発言5文目がヒントになる。　Ⅲ　議論も煮詰まったので，そろそろお開きだと言っている。　(2)　Mingの2回目の発言の照明関係についてまとめればよい。(3)　「託児所を開設したがっている人のことを知っている」という意味である。　(4)　①　託児所不要の人々は受益者負担の論理からすれば，利益は「不要」という考え方である。 ② 託児所を設置するにしても，一定の需要があれば可能という考え方である。 ③ Mingの発言を受けて，「今よりも明るく」と言っているのである。
④ 「すぐに」という意味である。immediatelyまたはwithout delayでもよいだろう。 (5) 言い出しの部分は「職場の仲間から社内の託児所新設の可能性について相談を受けた。社長に話をする前に，いくつか知りたいことがあるのだが」という意味である。Manuelの3回目の発言がヒントである。

【2】(1) 小学校，中学校，高等学校，大学等を通じて英語教育を一連のものとして行うことと，学校制度にかかる法律を通じてこれらの政策を実行してきたこと。 (2) 英語は科学や技術や経済的な競争分野で最も重要な国際言語であり，よって，英語運用能力は，これらの分野の人的国際化と社会の経済的繁栄には必須である。 (3) ・自国語の教育は国際化と表裏一体の関係であり，英語教育と日本語教育は微妙な関係である。 ・日本の国際化は利益と安全の二面性があり，国の政策も不確かで揺れ動いている点がある。 (4) ① opportunity
② threat(※①，②は順不同)
〈解説〉(1) 第1パラグラフ3文目，a series ofからschool systemまでがヒントである。and worked以下は2つ目の内容になる。 (2) ヒントは第2パラグラフ1文目のEnglishからsocietyまでである。この内容をまとめればよい。 (3) 下線部(B)の意味は，「言語と国際化のむしろもっと複雑な関係」である。1つ目は第3パラグラフの内容であり，2つ目は第4パラグラフの内容である。 (4) 第4パラグラフ3文目のas a challengeからJapan's futureの部分が，①，②を含む文と呼応している。

【3】(1) イ (2) エ (3) ア (4) エ
〈解説〉(1) 「万が一の時のために蓄えた金をすべて失った」の意味である。whatは関係形容詞で「わずかながらもすべて」の意味がある。なお，a rainy dayは「逆境，不測の事態」という意味である。

(2)「私の状況は，どちらかと言えば，昨晩よりはよくなっている」の意味である。　(3)「3人の生徒が各自の故郷の行事に参加した」の意味である。take part in …は「…に参加する」という意味である。(4)「私たちは新曲が大ヒットになると期待したが，結果は程遠いものだった」の意味である。far from …は「…からは程遠い」という意味である。

【4】(1)　Something must be done about your long hair.　(2)　(Mike) would be the last man to disappoint us.　(3)　Ms.Kato adapted her teaching method to her slow learners.　(4)　A chaotic mess of magazines and stationery lay on his desk.

〈解説〉(1)　日本語を直訳風にして「あなたの長髪について何かが措置されねばならない」と考えればよい。　(2)　日本語を直訳風にして「マイクは私たちを失望させるとすれば最後の人間だ」と考えればよい。wouldは仮定法過去の用法で「～するとすれば」の意味である。(3)　日本語を直訳風にして「加藤先生は自分の教え方を学習の遅い生徒たちに合わせた」と考えればよい。　(4)　日本語を直訳風にして「彼の机の上には，(多くの)雑誌や文房具がごちゃごちゃの状態で存在していた」と考えればよい。layはlieの過去形で自動詞である。他動詞lay-laid-laidの活用と間違えないこと。

【5】(1)　All students, listen to me. Ok, listen carefully. Now, make groups of six members each and set the desks. Then tell me who the first speaker will be. Ok, let's start.　(2)　Well, listen to me again. Now, this time, I want you to make a three-minute interview. Please find the student(s) who has the same opinion with you as many as possible.

〈解説〉中学校の第3学年なので，語いの範囲と文法事項について留意しなければならない。(1)「決める」は，「私に教えてください」と考えればよい。　(2)　three-minutesと複数形にはしないこと。数詞が形容詞の働きをする場合は単数形である。また，student(s)は，グループ全体に呼びかければ複数形，単独のグループの場合は単数形である。

【6】Dear Jack,

Thank you for your lesson at the school.

Now we are to have a meeting at 15:30, next Monday in the school. You are expected to have some sample activities to review the last lesson. The theme is to discuss the interaction between ALT and JTE when we introduce the past form.

〈解説〉ALTのJackに対して，打合せを行うための依頼のEメールである。場所が明記されていないが，当然校内と考えてよいだろう。民間会社で日常的に通信される内容としては，このような場合には，「日時」，「場所」，「持ち物」，「その他」があげられる。本問では，「打合せ」はmeeting，「日時」はthe time and date，「準備してほしいもの」は「持ち物」と考えて，materials to be prepared，「検討したいこと」はthemeなどと考えればよい。別解として，次のように記述することも考えられる。

Dear Jack,

Thank you for your lesson at the school.

We'll have a meeting as bellow, appreciate your participation.

1 Date and time:at 15:30, next Monday.

2 Materials to be prepared:some sample activities already done last lesson.

3 Theme:interactions between ALT and JTE for introduction of the past form.

【高等学校】

【1】(1) 解答略　(2) 解答略　(3) イ　(4) 解答略　(5) 解答略　(6) ア，キ

〈解説〉(1) 第3パラグラフ2文目に政治関係，健康福祉関係，住環境の3つをあげている。 (2) 第5パラグラフの5から7文目までに述べられている。5文目のPaying以下，6文目のAuctioning以下，7文目のHiring以下が該当する。 (3) crowd outは「排除する」である。意味を取り違

えないようにすること。worth …ingは「…する価値がある」という意味である。　(4)　第9パラグラフ9文目のcivicからresponsibilitiesまでがヒントである。citizenshipをcivic dutiesと言い換えて説明していることに注意する。　(5)　下線部の直前の部分を踏まえる必要がある。つまり，having a market economy　　とbeing a market societyをあげて，第12パラグラフで説明している。第12パラグラフ2文目がヒントである。なお，seepは「浸透する」という意味である。　(6)　ア　第2パラグラフ全体がヒントであり，corrosiveは「浸食する，むしばむ」という意味である。　イ　第3パラグラフ最初の文がヒントである。本文ではwould not matter very muchとある。　ウ　第4パラグラフ2文目がヒントである。選択肢にはhas not widenedとある。　エ　第6パラグラフ冒頭にEconomists often assume …とある。選択肢にはseldom agreeとある。
オ　第8パラグラフ4文目にSlavery … treatedがヒントになる。選択肢にはdid not necessarily treatとある。　カ　第10パラグラフ2文目以下がヒントである。同パラグラフ最後の文で，… we have to debate, …と述べられている。選択肢にはought not to be up for public debateとある。
キ　第11パラグラフ1文目の内容と一致している。

【2】(1)　①　・聞き手が的確に内容を理解できるように反応を確かめること　・リズムやイントネーションなどの英語の音声的な特徴，話す速度，声の大きさなどに注意して音声で表現すること　・指導項目の特徴を踏まえ，状況に応じて柔軟に指導すること　②(種類…留意点の順)　・個人…十分な声の大きさで読むこと，発音やリズムなどに注意しながら読むこと　・ペア…聞き手のリズムやイントネーションなどに注意すること，聞き手の反応に注意しながら読むこと　・グループまたはクラス全体…トピック・センテンスや繰り返しの表現に注意して読むこと，5W1Hに注意して読むこと，つながりを示す語句に注意を払いながら読むこと　(2)　論理の一貫性及び段落のつながりがあるか，対象者・目的がはっきりしているか，根拠となる段落や部分が含まれているか，あいまいな表現や内容と関係ないことが書かれ

ていないか，語句の使用や文法などの間違いはないか

〈解説〉(1)　①「コミュニケーション英語Ⅰ」の目標は2つあり，「英語を通じて，積極的にコミュニケーションを図ろうとする態度を育成すること」と「英語を通じて，情報や考えなどを的確に理解したり適切に伝えたりする基礎的な能力を養うこと」である。これを踏まえて，内容に関しては，「説明や物語などを読んで，情報や考えなどを理解したり，概要や要点をとらえたりする。また，聞き手に伝わるように音読する」である。　②　実際の指導においては，活動の目的に沿った形態での音読が必要となる。　(2)「書くこと」に関する指導内容が含まれていることが必要である。解答例以外に，大文字と小文字の区別，いわゆる「iの点を打ち，tの横棒を書く」というように，表記自体の正確さなどがあげられる。

【3】(1)　ウ　(2)　ア　(3)　ウ　(4)　イ　(5)　エ

〈解説〉(1)「彼は大手の出版社と新しい取引について交渉したが，結局は彼の考えが現実とはおりあわなかった」という意味である。to findは結果の不定詞である。　(2)「秋田県の英語教育をさらに進めるための特別な会議が招集された」という意味である。　(3)「増税のせいでますます多くの人々が質素な生活を送る傾向がある」という意味である。live a frugal life=live frugallyであり，lifeは同族目的語と呼ばれる。　(4)「私たちの勇気と知恵で，2つの国の混乱を平和的な解決に導かなくてはならない。たとえ危険がどんなに恐ろしいと思われようとも」という意味である。no matter howはhoweverでもよい。

(5)「教養科目で去年高得点を取った学生は今年最初の試験は免除される」の意味である。

【4】(記号：正しい英語の順)　(1)　B : for　(2)　A : that

(3)　B : what

〈解説〉(1)「ホテルの宿泊者はビリヤードかダーツが無料で遊べる」の意味である。for freeで「無料で」という意味である。　(2)「彼は私

に代わってその試合に出場できるほどのテニスの名手である」の意味である。such＋名詞＋thatの構文に注意すること。　(3)　まず，全体の構文を把握する必要がある。Thatからlectureまでが名詞節で主語，文頭のthatは接続詞である。主語の部分の動詞understandは，「教授が授業で言及したこと」が目的語の意味なのでBは誤りである。文全体の意味は，「教授が授業で言及したことを学生たちが理解しないのは，教授の完全な想定外である」の意味である。

【5】解答略

〈解説〉問題文の意味は，「『グローバル化に対応する英語教育改革計画』では，英語を小学校で正式な教科として教え，中学校及び高等学校では原則として英語を用いて授業を行うものとする，となっており，高度な言語活動が高等学校では求められている。この流れに対して，未来の英語教師としてあなたはどのように考えるか」である。まずは設問の意味を整理する必要がある。つまり，小学校での正式な教科としての導入，および中・高等学校では「原則として」英語を用いての授業の実施について，さらに，高等学校での「高度な言語活動」についてどのように考えるか，ということになる。正式な教科となれば，「免許，検定教科書，評価評定」が必要となる。また，「原則として」とは，必ずしも授業のすべてを英語で行わなければならないということではないことを踏まえなくてはならない。さらに，「高度な言語活動」とは，相手との議論やディベート等の言語活動を含む。これらの要素を踏まえて記述する必要がある。全体の論調の例としては，「小学校の外国語活動が一定の成果を見せたので，組織的に英語を教えることによって，中学校の授業との円滑な接続を目指す。また，高等学校では，中学校でのコミュニケーション活動の基礎を踏まえて，議論やディベート等のより高い発信能力の育成を目指すことと同時に，自国文化の認識もあわせて教育する必要がある」などと記述すればよい。コミュニケーションの道具としての英語という観点も大切である。

2014年度　実施問題

【中高共通】

【1】リスニングテスト

Part A

In Part A, you will hear a question followed by three responses. Choose the best response to each question. The question and the responses will be spoken only once.

(1) What do you think of my lesson plan?
 (A) I don't think so.
 (B) It'll work well.
 (C) I'm pretty good.

(2) Would you mind if we take a break now?
 (A) No, not at all.
 (B) That's an emergency brake.
 (C) Yes, we should.

(3) Who will be presenting a short lesson at the workshop?
 (A) I can't participate in the lesson.
 (B) Ted already bought her a present.
 (C) I suppose Ted and Mr. Suzuki will.

(4) You're launching a new program, aren't you?
 (A) Lunchtime is convenient for me.
 (B) I'm not very good at programming.
 (C) It'll start in a couple of weeks.

(5) Did you submit the report to your supervisor?
 (A) Yes, he was a good reporter.
 (B) No, I'll do that by Friday.

(C) Of course, I'll be able to meet the deadline.

(6) Could you show me the handouts of today's meeting?

(A) I'll send them to you by e-mail later.

(B) I'll adjust the meeting schedule.

(C) The meeting will be held on the third floor.

Part B

In Part B, you will hear four short conversations between two people. Each conversation will be followed by one question. Choose the best answer from among the four choices written on your test sheet. Conversations and questions will be spoken only once.

(1) W : Let's start putting up posters of our school festival. We should do it by tomorrow.

M : How many should we put up? Do you think fifty posters will be enough?

W : I'd say we need thirty more at least. I want to cover a larger area.

M : OK. I'll print out one hundred. I hope more people will come this year.

Question: How many posters does the woman say she wants?

(A) Less than 30.

(B) Less than 50.

(C) Not less than 80.

(D) More than 100.

(2) W : Excuse me. I got this jacket as a birthday gift last week, but I don't care for the color. I can exchange this for another one, can't I?

M : Certainly. The jacket comes in a darker gray than the one you now have. It also comes in black, beige and brown.

W : Well, let me take a look at them.... The brown is nice. Do you have it in a size 6?

M : I'm sorry, we sold the last one this Sunday. I can call our branch store to see if they have the brown in a 6.

Question: What does the woman want to do?

(A) Have a gift wrapped.

(B) Have a jacket exchanged.

(C) Buy a brown jacket.

(D) Buy a birthday present.

(3) M : I need to submit a purchase order before the end of the day today, but there's a problem. I forgot to ask my boss to sign it, and he's already left. Can we put the order through just the same?

W : No, a signature is necessary. There's nothing we can do without it.

M : Then we do have a problem. Is there any way I could sign it for him?

W : I'm afraid not. You need to get him to sign it tomorrow morning, and deliver it straight to my desk.

Question: What does the man find out?

(A) The purchase order has already been sent to his boss.

(B) The purchase order has been approved by his boss.

(C) He can deliver the purchase order today.

(D) He cannot sign the purchase order for his boss.

(4) M : Hello, I'm calling to reserve some seats of the Super Komachi in August. I heard they're usually full two months in advance, and it's already mid-July. Do you still have any seats during the second weekend of August?

W : Let me see. There's a chance that a few seats might still be available. Do you want me to check the availability?

M : Yes, please. I want four seats in the first-class car, if possible.

W : Just a moment while I check. You're in luck. A group canceled their reservation, and five seats are available.

Question: What will the man do next?

(A) Make a reservation.

(B) Call the woman back.

(C) Hang up the phone.

(D) Check the availability.

Part C

In Part C, you will hear two short passages. Each passage will be followed by one question. Write the answer to each question in English. Both answers should begin with "I should". Passages and questions will be read twice.

(1) Welcome to the new Akita Prefectural Museum of Art. The building was completed last year. The museum's core collection will include numerous artworks by Fujita Tsuguharu, one of the most famous Japanese painters in France. Especially, the main feature will be his great work painted on the huge canvas as large as the wall of the venue. We would suggest that you see this. Its grand opening will be on Saturday, September 28th.

Question: If you go to this museum after its grand opening, what should you do?

(2) Good afternoon. Here's the traffic news for Friday, July 26th. The bypass of Route 46 is still closed between Smith Town and Gordon Town, because a livestock trailer fell over at the Smith Town entrance this afternoon. The section will be opened as soon as it's cleaned, but taking the bypass should be avoided for a while. Drive safely.

Question: If you want to drive from Smith Town to Gordon Town, what should you do?

Part D

In Part D, you will hear a passage. Two questions are written in Japanese on your test sheet. Answer these questions in Japanese. The passage will be read twice.

On the surface, the Morgan Center might look like any other preschool: colorful toys, shelves lined with books, walls adorned with educational posters, children gleefully engrossed in activities. But it's different in many ways. Because of the children's delicate immune systems, they are required to sanitize their hands throughout the day. They also have individualized supply boxes with their own crayons and glues. They never share supplies, and all items are meticulously cleaned by teachers after each use. Exposure to a simple childhood cold or illness can become life-threatening to these children.

Three times a week, students learn to read, sing and create arts and crafts. On Fridays, they have show-and-tell. There are parties during the holidays. And a few times a year, there are organized field trips. “It's wonderful to see my daughter be like a normal kid,” said one of the parents. The Morgan Center is the only program of its kind in America.

(1)　この施設で子どもを活動させる際に，教員が留意しなくてはならないことは何か，日本語で書け。

(2)　この施設に入所している子どもの保護者は，何を「すばらしい」と言っているのか，日本語で書け。

This is the end of the listening test.

(☆☆☆◎◎◎)

【2】次の英文は，ミャンマー(ビルマ)の政治家アウン・サン・スー・チー氏が，2012年にノーベル平和賞受賞演説を行ったことについての記事の抜粋である。英文を読んで，(1)～(5)の設問に答えよ。

“I heard the news on the radio one evening. I've tried very hard to remember what my immediate reaction to the announcement of the award had been. I think it was something like: ‘Oh ... so they've decided to give it to me’.”

Aung San Suu Kyi arrived in Norway from Switzerland, her first stop on a two-week tour of Europe. The journey is her first in Europe since 1988, when she left her husband and two young sons in England to visit her ill mother in Burma and became the focal point for the nascent democracy movement.

She made a wide-ranging, deeply personal lecture, which touched on her feelings of isolation under house arrest, the Buddhist concept of suffering, human rights and her hopes and fears for her country's future, and the importance of the peace prize itself.

"It did not seem quite real because in a sense I did not feel myself to be quite real at that time," she said. "Often during my days of house arrest it felt as though I were no longer a part of the real world.

"There was the (①) which was my world, there was the world of others who also were not free but were together in (②) as a community, and there was the world of the free; each was a different (③) pursuing its own separate course in an indifferent (④).

"What the Nobel peace prize did was to draw me once again into the world of other human beings outside the isolated area in which I lived, to restore a sense of reality to me. (A)<u>This</u> did not happen instantly, of course, but as the days and months went by, and news of reactions to the award came over the airwaves, I began to understand the significance of the Nobel prize. It had made me real once again.

"What was more important, the prize had drawn the attention of the world to the struggle for democracy and human rights in Burma. We were not going to be forgotten. When the Nobel committee awarded the peace prize to me, they were recognising that the oppressed and the isolated in Burma were also a part of the world, they were recognising the oneness of humanity ... The Nobel peace prize opened up a door in my heart."

Talking about the motivation in a period during which she was separated from her family and her British husband, the academic Michael Aris, died, she said: "If I am asked why I am fighting for democracy in Burma, it is because I believe that democratic (B)<u>institutions</u> and practices are necessary for the guarantee of human rights.

"When I joined the democracy movement in Burma, it never occurred to me that I might ever be the recipient of any prize or honour. The prize we were working for was a free, secure and just society where our people might be able to realise their full potential."

Aung San Suu Kyi appeared impossibly small, entering the City Hall wearing a purple jacket and flowing lilac scarf to the sound of a trumpet fanfare.

(C)Thorbjørn Jagland, chairman of the Nobel committee, who introduced her, said: "Today's event is one of the most remarkable in the entire history of the Nobel prizes ... We hope that Liu Xiaobo [the Chinese political activist] will not have to wait as long as you have before he can come to Oslo."

Jagland recalled how, when the peace prize celebrated its 100th anniversary in 2001 with more than 30 laureates in attendance, "we left one chair empty [for her]".

【出典　http://www.guardian.co.uk/world/2012/jun/16/aung-san-suu-kyi-nobel-peace-prize?INTCMP=SRCH】

(1) 文中の(　①　)～(　④　)に入る最も適切な語を，次のア～オから一つずつ選び，その記号を書け。

ア　universe　イ　house　ウ　court　エ　prison
オ　planet

(2) 下線部(A)が表す内容を，60字程度の日本語で書け。

(3) スー・チー氏は，自身がノーベル平和賞を受賞したことで，世界にどのような変化があったと考えているか，35字程度の日本語で書け。

(4) 本文の内容から判断して，下線部(B)とほぼ同義である語を，次のア～オから一つ選び，その記号を書け。

ア　buildings　イ　systems　ウ　offices　エ　platforms
オ　actions

(5) 下線部(C)の人物の言葉から分かる，2人のノーベル平和賞受賞者の共通点を日本語で書け。

(☆☆☆◎◎◎)

【中学校】

【1】次の会話文を読んで，(1)～(5)の設問に答えよ。

Melinda Kinkaid: I never thought I'd become a natto aficionado, but I have, thanks to Yoko. She gave me some edamame and natto

(①) a goodbye gift when she left to join Great Lakes' leadership development program.

Ron Walker: Edamame I've heard of, but what on earth is natto? Some new kind of decaf coffee?

Jack Wakimoto: [I] you're a natto newbie, Ron. Natto is the Japanese term for fermented soybeans, which are an incredibly nutritious food. I've been eating natto ever since I was a kid, and it's (②) a regular part of my diet.

Kinkaid: It's become one of my faves too, but I admit natto is an acquired taste. Many people are turned off by its gooey stringiness and musky odor. My daughter Rebecca can't stand the stuff, (A)<u>[my / to / try / efforts / best / her / despite / to / it / get]</u>.

Wakimoto: When I was growing up, my mom used to remind me that a serving of natto has the same amount of protein as a similar serving of beef — (③) the cholesterol.

Kinkaid: Try telling that to Rebecca. She just turns her nose up whenever I try to serve it to her. But her natto aversion aside, she keeps to a very balanced diet. [Ⅱ] ever since she was a toddler.

Walker: Good for you, Melinda. As my doctor is always telling me, food is at the center of health and illness. To be well, you've got to eat well. There's a lot of truth in the old saying, " (B)[________] "

Kinkaid: But while I make sure Rebecca has a balanced diet, [Ⅲ] my husband and I aren't good role models. Lots of times I'll be so preoccupied (④) making breakfasts and lunches that I'll skip eating or just snack.

【出典　実践ビジネス英語】

(1) (①)～(④)に入る最も適切な語を，次のア～カから一つずつ選んで，その記号を書け。

ア with　イ to　ウ without　エ off　オ as

カ still

(2) [Ⅰ]～[Ⅲ]に入る最も適切なものを，次のア～エから一つずつ選んで，その記号を書け。

ア I'm ashamed to admit that　イ I've made sure of that

ウ I might not admit that　エ Sounds like

(3) 下線部(A)の語を，意味が通るように並べかえよ。

(4) 次の(a)～(c)の説明にそれぞれ該当する1語を，会話文中から抜き出して書け。

(a) a strong feeling of not liking something

(b) soft and sticky

(c) a person who likes a particular sport, activity or subject very much and knows a lot about it

(5) 下線部(B)に入る最も適切なものを，次のア～エから一つ選んで，その記号を書け。

ア A good medicine tastes bitter.

イ An apple a day keeps the doctor away.

ウ A good appetite is the best sauce.

エ Man shall not live by bread alone.

(☆☆☆◎◎◎)

【2】次の英文を読んで，(1)～(4)の設問に答えよ。

One principal of an inner-city school in Tennessee created (A)a "neighborhood watch" program to promote accountability and safety as his students walked to and from school each day. He met with the neighbors in the community and asked them to stand in their yards or on their porches from 7:45 to 8:15 each morning and from 2:45 to 3:15 each afternoon to greet kids and make sure they arrived to school and back home safely. This proved to be a very successful collaboration that contributed to the welfare of children and the community. The program helped form bonds among the neighbors, the school, and families. It also helped enhance safety and deter students from getting into mischief on their way to and from school.

(B)*Lunch Mentors* is an example of a community partnership program where senior citizens visit a local elementary school each week and partner with teachers and students. The senior citizens become mentors with students who are chosen by classroom teachers as having low self-esteem or self-confidence, having limited social skills, or struggling with one or more academic areas. Seniors from a local assisted-living center meet with students in various grade levels once a week, have lunch with their buddies, and engage in reading a book or another fun learning activity. This type of partnership has the potential to enhance the education of children who are struggling with some area of formal schooling and offers one-on-one adult interactions.

Stevenson Elementary School in Long Beach, California, has found success partnering with the local YMCA. The YMCA operates inside the school, and the YMCA staff work with teachers and administrators to organize the after-school program and link the program's content and activities with the school curriculum. In addition, YMCA staff members educate parents in literacy skills and send them out into the community to teach other families in their homes.

In the book *The Freedom Writers Diary*(1999), (C)teacher Erin Gruwell discusses how she taught her high school English students how to take action, fight stereotypes, and reach their fullest academic potential as writers. After a racial caricature of one of the students with huge exaggerated lips was passed around in class, Gruwell decided to throw out her lesson plans and make tolerance the core of the curriculum that year. She brought history to life by accessing books, taking field trips, and inviting a variety of guest speakers to the classroom. She made a personal commitment to learn more about her students, their lives, their hobbies, their strengths, and their fears. She encouraged and motivated them to express their ideas, thoughts, and vexations through writing. Her students were invited to meet Steven Spielberg at Universal Studios to discuss the movie *Schindler's List*. They corresponded and met with a Holocaust survivor and hosted Zlata Filipovic, a child author from Bosnia. These types of experiences are at the core of culturally relevant teaching and provide students with the power, the insight, and the motivation to extend education beyond the four walls of the classroom. Gruwell's experiences are highlighted in the movie *Freedom Writers*, starring Hilary Swank. It should be noted that Gruwell formed a partnership with her students first; then, empowered, they reached out together to form partnerships with the broader community.

(D)Community resources are only resources if accessed by schools, family, and community members. Teachers in an educational partnerships class arranged for a former major league baseball player to visit their university class to discuss his job responsibilities and partnerships with local schools. Because the teachers contacted him and *asked* him to provide information about his role as an educational community leader, he made an appearance and made a huge impact on teachers as they pursued partnership possibilities. He discussed his organization's commitment to the community and schools and the importance of seeking role models in the community. He also discussed the untapped partnership opportunities that exist. The teachers were very surprised that this sports organization had a community outreach program about 10 miles away and that they had never heard about it or prepared activities to collaborate with it.

【出典　Amy Cox-Petersen, *Educational Partnerships Connecting Schools, Families, and the Community*, SAGE】

(1)　下線部(A)の具体的な成果を二つ，それぞれ20字程度の日本語で書け。

(2)　下線部(B)に期待されることを，50字程度の日本語で書け。

(3)　下線部(C)の人物が行った実践的な体験活動により，結果的に生徒にどんなことが身に付くと述べられているか，30字程度の日本語で書け。

(4)　下線部(D)の事例を，80字程度の日本語で書け。

(☆☆☆◎◎◎)

【３】(1)～(5)について，それぞれの日本語の内容を表すように，[　　]内の語句を並べかえよ。ただし，文頭にくる語も小文字にしてある。

(1)　あなたの寄付は，これらの歴史的遺産や重要文化財を維持するための費用をまかなうのに役立つだろう。

Your [the cost / will / donation / preserving / help / of / cover] these historical remains and important cultural assets.

(2)　熟練した職人でさえ，これらの部品を完成させるには数か月かかる。

It [to / complete / a / takes / even / several months / skilled craftsman / these parts].

(3)　私は新聞を読んで，初めて我が社が直面している危機に気が付いた。

Not [I / the crisis / is / read / facing / recognize / until / did / the newspaper / I / our company].

(4)　日本の死亡事故のおよそ1/4がスピード違反に起因することを統計が示している。

Statistics show that about [in / fatal / accidents / Japan / due / one-fourth / are / of / to] speeding.

(5)　円の面積は，πr^2である。

[the radius / of / pi / a circle / equal / to / the area / is / times] squared.

(☆☆◎◎◎)

【4】次の英文は,「中学校学習指導要領　第2章　各教科　第9節　外国語」(文部科学省　平成20年9月)の英訳版(仮訳)からの抜粋である。このことについて,あなたは中学校教師としてどのように指導を工夫していくか,例を挙げて50語程度の英語で述べよ。

【Ⅱ. 2. (2) B.】

(a) Language activities in Grade 1

A certain extent of the foundation of communication abilities, such as a positive attitude toward communication focusing on speech sounds, is formed through foreign language activities in elementary schools. In light of this, language activities should be carried out with familiar language-use situations and functions of language taken into account.

(☆☆☆◎◎◎)

【5】学習指導要領に基づき,生徒に求められる英語力を達成するための目標(学習到達目標)を「CAN—DOリスト」の形で具体的に設定することが,各中学校・高等学校に求められている。これにより,どのような指導上の改善が期待できるか,100語程度の英語で書け。

(☆☆☆◎◎◎)

【高等学校】

【1】次の世界遺産に関する英文を読んで,(1)~(6)の設問に答えよ。

The historic center of Hoi An looks just how Vietnam is supposed to look: narrow lanes, wooden shop houses, a charming covered bridge. Hoi An's well-preserved architecture — from the 16th century onward, the port attracted traders from as far away as Portugal and Persia — led UNESCO to deem it a World Heritage site in 1999, praising it as an "outstanding material manifestation of the fusion of cultures over time in an international commercial port." Last month, I took a family holiday there, if not to enjoy an "outstanding material manifestation," then simply to visit a historic place. I was not the only one.

Thirteen years ago, when Hoi An was first inscribed on the World Heritage list, the city welcomed 160,300 visitors. In 2011, 1.5 million tourists arrived. Today, tour buses crowd the edge of Hoi An's old town, (A)disgorging sunburned foreigners. Hundreds of nearly identical storefronts — catering to tourists and selling the same tailored clothes, shoes and lanterns — colonize the 1,254 heritage structures. Cyclos prowl the perimeter of the historic center, even as locals complain they can no longer afford the bicycle rickshaws because tourists have driven up the prices. In the rush to squeeze tourism revenue from the area, a hospital has been evicted. The building now houses a tailoring business.

There are 725 World Heritage cultural sites in the world today, an eclectic list that ranges from the old quarters of Istanbul and Rome to the less-heralded town center of Gjirokastra, Albania, and the walled city of Shibam, Yemen. UNESCO says these sites boast "outstanding universal value," and descriptions of them often employ the same adjectives: ***unique, authentic, well preserved.***

It's true that a World Heritage designation can save a historic urban center from becoming yet another undifferentiated, concrete-and-glass dystopia. But many cash－poor countries are fixated on World Heritage because they believe that making the list will unlock tourism riches. A 2008 UNESCO report that sounded the alarm over (B)Hoi An's development could be applied to any number of World Heritage sites. "While local government officials and business owners view ... changes in the old quarter positively, tourists are beginning to notice the loss of authenticity in Hoi An," it warned. "Unless tourism management can be improved, the economic success generated by tourism will not be sustainable in the long term."

It's a fine calculus: How do you lure travelers to historic locales without destroying their integrity in the process? Those places that succeed best tend to be large enough to absorb all the wide-eyed sightseers.

(C)Paris may be touristy, but it's still Paris. (Although it should be noted that the only parts of the French capital designated a World Heritage site are on the banks of the Seine.)

The biggest disappointments arise in countries where World Heritage status is used as a tourist honey trap rather than a tool to preserve a national treasure. (D)Take Lijiang, home to the Naxi minority in southwestern China. I first visited in 1994. There were plenty of backpackers converging on the town back then — as a foreign student in China, I was one of them — but the town had a soul. Three years (and one devastating earthquake) later, the old town of Lijiang gained World Heritage status. Walking its lanes today, crammed with tour groups and assaulted by the techno blaring from bars, it's hard to imagine what "outstanding universal value" existed there. Many historic buildings have been gutted and replaced with replicas. The bulk of costumed maidens posing for tourists aren't even Naxi; they're migrants from elsewhere in China. Half the original residents have left.

Conversely, there's also (E)the danger that World Heritage recognition preserves a place in amber, forcing it to become a theme park instead of a living landmark. In recent months, historic parts of Liverpool (listed as a "Maritime Mercantile City") and Seville (whose sites "perfectly epitomize the Spanish 'Golden Age'") have both been threatened with delisting because of plans for skyscrapers. (The Dresden Elbe Valley was booted off the list in 2009 "due to the building of a four-lane bridge in the heart of the cultural landscape.") Yes, skyscrapers can puncture an urban fabric. But these are magnificent cities with real residents going about their real business.

Compare that with Lijiang or Hoi An, which may adhere to World Heritage rules but feel increasingly like outposts of Disney. And there is more to come. Beijing, for instance, hopes to turn what it has snappily designated as the five "Sites for Liquor Making in China" into a future World Heritage spot. Imagine the tourist potential in a multiprovince pub crawl.

【出典　TIME, February 6, 2012】

(1)　下線部(A)とほぼ同義である語句を次のア～エから一つ選び，その記号を書け。

ア　guiding　　イ　attracting　　ウ　pushing out

エ　disappointing

(2)　下線部(B)について，Hoi Anの状況の推移とは具体的にはどういうことか，日本語で説明せよ。

(3)　下線部(C)は具体的にはどういうことか，日本語で説明せよ。

(4)　下線部(D)について，今日Lijiangを訪れて失望するのはなぜか，その理由を三つ日本語で記せ。

(5)　下線部(E)は，ある地区が世界遺産に登録されることで望ましくない状態になる危険性を比喩的に述べているが，どのような危険性か，日本語で具体的に説明せよ。

(6)　次の英文の中で，本文の内容と一致するものを次のア～キから二つ選び，記号で答えよ。

ア　The writer recently spent a holiday in Hoi An and found that it was losing some of its appeal as a historic center.

イ　A tailor shop opened next to a hospital in the city center of Hoi An.

ウ　UNESCO describes some of the World Heritage sites today as having "outstanding universal value."

エ　Few cash-poor countries which want World Heritage status for some of their cities are interested in a surge of tourism.

オ　A UNESCO report warns that the improvement of tourism management will destroy the economic success of Hoi An in the long term.

カ　It is not easy to attract many tourists to a World Heritage site and maintain its authenticity at the same time.

キ　Beijing believes that the five "Sites for Liquor Making in China" are highly unlikely to gain a World Heritage designation because they are just a tourist honey trap.

(☆☆☆◎◎◎)

【2】次の(1)，(2)について，日本語で答えよ。

(1) 各校において，CAN—DOリスト形式で学習到達目標を作成し活用する際，①作成時に留意すべき点と，②作成後に留意すべき点について具体的に箇条書きで答えよ。

(2) あなた(JTE)が主導して，外国語指導助手(ALT)とティーム・ティーチングでコミュニケーション英語Ⅰの授業をする際，①授業の計画時に留意すべき点と，②授業の展開時に留意すべき点について具体的に箇条書きで答えよ。

(☆☆☆◎◎◎)

【3】次の(1)～(5)の(　　)に当てはまる最も適切な語句をそれぞれア～エから一つ選び，記号で答えよ。

(1) He advised the candidates that the application handbook (　　) carefully before submitting their résumés.

ア read　イ was read　ウ be read　エ reading

(2) The secretary suggested his coming back later, but Bob resented (　　) away and persuaded her to let him wait.

ア to be turned　イ to being turned　ウ turning

エ being turned

(3) North European furniture is known for (　　) yet functional design.

ア simple　イ simplify　ウ simply　エ simplistically

(4) The team, (　　) at the bottom of the league, finally achieved a hard-earned victory.

ア decreasing　イ wondering　ウ floundering

エ overwhelming

(5) The ceremonial event (　　) the choral singing of the prefecture song.

ア elaborated on　イ culminated in　ウ resided in

エ deferred to

(☆☆☆◎◎◎)

【４】次の(1)～(3)の各英文には，1か所誤りがある。その部分の記号を答え，正しい英語に直せ。

(1) If you $_A$<u>had not been</u> asleep last night when we $_B$<u>had arrived</u>, I $_C$<u>would have asked</u> you to go with us, but I $_D$<u>didn't want</u> to bother you.

(2) He said something $_A$<u>on the effect</u> that Japanese $_B$<u>reluctance to</u> $_C$<u>communicate with</u> others was an unfortunate quality since it $_D$<u>tended to give</u> the impression of lacking of confidence.

(3) The trade unions are concerned $_A$<u>about</u> the unemployment that may result $_B$<u>in</u> displacement $_C$<u>of</u> jobs $_D$<u>by</u> new technology.

(☆☆☆◎◎◎)

【５】次の英文を読んで，高校生にグローバル社会における英語の必要性について理解を促し，英語学習のモチベーション向上を図るために，あなたならどのようなプランを提案するか。理由も含めて，100語程度の英語で書け。

Globalization brings about unprecedented necessity of English in universities and enterprises; on the other hand, it is pointed out that students have few opportunities to feel the necessity of English.

According to a survey on curriculum implementation held in 2003, third-year junior high school students who believed that they could not follow English classes amounted to about 30 percent, the proportion being high as compared to other subjects. In addition, more than 60 percent of students liked English learning in the first year of junior high school but this proportion decreased over time dropping below 50% in the third year; again, this decrease was high as compared to other subjects. Therefore, it is important to reduce the number of students who believe that they do not understand English, or who do not like English, while enhancing the skill of those who possess advanced English skills.

【出典　Five Proposals and Specific Measures for Developing Proficiency in English for International Communication, 2011】

(☆☆☆◎◎◎)

解答・解説

【中高共通】

【1】Part A (1) (B) (2) (A) (3) (C) (4) (C) (5) (B) (6) (A) Part B (1) (C) (2) (B) (3) (D) (4) (A) Part C (解答例) (1) I should see Fujita Tsuguharu's great work. (2) I should take a different route. Part D (解答例) (1) 教員は一日中子どもに手を消毒させ，支給されるものはすべて個人用として，決して他の子どもとの共有をさせず，使用ごとに教員が丁寧にふき清める。 (2) 休日にはパーティーが催されて年に数回の遠足もあり，親たちの一人は「娘が普通の子どものように過ごすのを見るのは素晴らしい」と言っている。

〈解説〉Part A 放送は1度しか聞くことができないが，読まれる内容は初級会話レベルであり，落ち着いて疑問代名詞や助動詞をきちんと聞き取れば答えることが出来るはずである。聞き取りが特に苦手な人はTOEIC教材などで聞き取り問題に慣れておくとよい。 Part B この問題も1度しか読まれないが，会話と質問を聞いたあと選択する答えはテスト用紙に書かれているので，ある程度予測しながら聞くことができるだろう。こちらも，聞き取り教材で練習しておくことは効果があるだろう。 Part C 短いパラグラフを聞き，設問に対する答えを記述する問題。放送は2回流れるので落ち着いてメモを取りながら内容を把握することである。シンプルな解答でよいので，文法やスペルミスをしないよう，よく注意してほしい。 Part D 内容に関する日本語の質問に対する答えを日本語で記述する問題。日本語である分まとめやすい反面，内容をしっかり聞き取って訳すことが出来なければならない点，ハードルが高いとも言える。文は2回読まれるので，きちんとメモを取り，聞きのがした個所にはこだわらずに簡潔にまとめるようにする。

【2】(1) ① イ　② エ　③ オ　④ ア　(2) (解答例) 私を再度，それまで私が住んでいた隔絶された空間の外の，他の人間たちの世界に引き戻し，私に現実感覚を取り戻させること。

(3) (解答例) 賞はビルマにおける民主化と人権を求める闘争に対して世界に目を向けさせた。　(4) イ　(5) (解答例) 活動家として政府の弾圧を受けて国外に出ることが許されず，ノーベル平和賞授賞式に出席できない状態だったこと。

〈解説〉(1) ① 軟禁状態だった当時のことについて述べており，空欄前の文にも my days of house arrest という表現があるので house が適切と判断できる。　② in prison で「獄中に幽閉されて」。house arrest / not free 等の表現から，家でありながら刑務所と同じ機能とわかる。

③④ 幽閉されている家と，それらの集合である community を，惑星と宇宙に例えている。　(2) This は指示代名詞であり，指し示す名詞(語または句，節)が，通常は直前に置かれているはずなので，遡って指し示している内容を訳せばよい。　(3) 第7段落に，スー・チー氏の言葉で the prize had drawn the attention --- と，賞を主語としたコメントがあるのでそこを引いてまとめる。　(4) institution には「機関，制度，施設」等いくつかの意味があるが，democratic institution で「民主主義的な制度」。　(5) スー・チー氏がノーベル平和賞を受賞したことが文のテーマであり，下線部の人物がノーベル賞委員会の議長であること，Liu Xiaobo 氏が政治活動家であるとの文中の記載，最後の段落の "we left one chair empty [for her]" とのコメントなどから考え，まとめる。

【中学校】

【1】(1) ① オ　② カ　③ ウ　④ ア　(2) Ⅰ エ　Ⅱ イ　Ⅲ ア　(3) (解答例) despite my best efforts to get her to try it　(4) (解答例) (a) aversion　(b) gooey　(c) aficionado　(5) イ

〈解説〉(1) ① give as a gift で「贈り物としてあげる」。「彼女はエダマメと納豆をお別れのプレゼントにくれた」　② 空欄前に「子どもの頃から納豆をずっと食べてきた」とあるのを受け，「そして[今もなお]私の日常の食生活の一部だ」と言っている。　③ 前のせりふで蛋白質の含有量について「牛肉とほぼ同じ」と言っており，さらに「コレステロール[なしで]」と言い添えている。　④ be preoccupied with で「～に気を取られる，いつも頭にある」。「朝食やランチを作ることばかり頭にあって，食べる方は抜いたりおやつで済ましたりしてしまう」　(2)　Ⅰ　Sounds like で「～のように聞こえる，話を聞いていると～のようだね」。Ron が納豆について的外れな事を聞くので，「どうやら納豆初心者のようだね」と言った。　Ⅱ　前の文は「彼女はバランスの良い食事を続けている」。Melindaは「彼女」の母親なので，「彼女がよちよち歩きの頃から[私が気を付けてきた]」と言っている。Ⅲ　娘の食事のことは気を付けているのに自分は「食事を抜いたりおやつで済ませたりする」と言っているので「恥ずかしながら認めるけど」と言うせりふがあてはまる。　(3)　語群から，[get 人 to 動詞の原型 (人に～させる)]というかたちを思いつければ「レベッカに試させる」という意味で get her to try it のかたまりが出来る。Kinkaid は娘に納豆を食べさせようとしているので efforts to get her to --- と続く。「私の努力にもかかわらず」で despite my effort to と繋がり，余った best は effort の前に置いて「最善の努力」とする。　(4)　(a)「何かを好まないという強い感情」で，「強い反感・嫌悪」のaversion が適切。
(b)「やわらかくてネバネバする」で「ネバネバした」の gooey があてはまる。　(c)「あるスポーツや活動，教科(または対象になる人，主題)をとても好み，それについて非常に詳しい人」で，「熱狂的なファン」の aficionado が適切である。　(5)　前の文に，To be well, you've got to eat well. とあり，「食べることにより健康を保つ」という主旨が，イ「毎日一つのりんごで医者いらず」と共通している。他選択肢はそれぞれ，ア「良薬口に苦し」，ウ「空腹にまずいものなし」，エ「人はパンのみにて生きるにあらず」。

【２】(解答例)　(1)　・地域，学校，および家庭の結びつきの強化　・安全性向上と通学中の生徒へのいたずら防止　(2)　正規の学校教育のある分野で困難を抱えている生徒の学びを支援し，大人との一対一のやりとりの場を与える。　(3)　生徒に力，洞察力，教室の壁を超えて教育を広げる意欲を与えた。　(4)　コミュニティー・リーダーの役割に関する情報提供を依頼して初めて，組織がすでに地域での連携に取り組んでおり，役割モデルについても準備が進んでいることがわかった。

〈解説〉(1)　段落単位で見ると，問題提起，例示，結論という構造になっている。下線部の後には事例紹介が続くので目を通していくと，段落最後に，得られた成果についての言及がある。　(2)　上記(1)と同様，段落の構造として最後に結論部分がある。下線部の後に事例紹介が続くので目を通していくと，段落最後に，紹介された取り組みに期待されることについての言及がある。　(3)　段落中央近くの She encouraged and motivated 以下，four walls of the classroom. までが，Gruwell の取り組みについての実際的な説明となっている。実例に続いて取り組みの成果についての言及がある。　(4)　段落中央近くに asked「依頼した」という語があり，イタリック体になっていることから，「依頼したことでやっとその情報が得られた」という意味合いがわかる。段落最後にも「教師は組織がすでに連携の準備を進めていることを知って驚いた」とあり，アクセスすることで初めて得られた情報であったことがわかるので，その点をまとめる。

【３】(1)　(Your) donation will help cover the cost of preserving (these historical remains and important cultural assets.)　(2)　(It) takes even a skilled craftsman several months to complete these parts (.)　(3)　(Not) until I read the newspaper did I recognize the crisis our company is facing (.)　(4)　(Statistics show that about) one-fourth of fatal accidents in Japan are due to (speeding.)　(5)　The area of a circle is equal to pi times the radius (squared.)

〈解説〉(1) 「維持するための費用をまかなうのに役立つだろう」という部分を組み立てる。主語が「あなたの寄付」なので，Your に続くのは donation，続いて will help が述部の「役立つだろう」にあてはまる。「維持するための費用」は the cost of preserving で，help のあとの動詞 cover は原型不定詞であることを確認する。 (2) 「職人でさえ」は even a skilled craftsman となり，take 人 期間，という順序で並べていき，「～するために」の部分に to complete these parts をあてる。
(3) 語群に until があるので[Not until S V 倒置]で「～して初めて～した」の構文を思いついてほしい。そこに気付ければ，the crisis のあとに形容詞節 our company is facing を置けばよい。 (4) 「スピード違反に起因する」は due to speeding，Statistics show で「統計が示している」，one-fourth の前に「およそ」の about を置く，などによりまとめる。
(5) pi「π」，area「面積」，circle「円」，radius「半径」，equal to「～に等しい」，times「～倍である」 などの表現は，もし知らなかったならぜひ常識として覚えておいてほしい。

【4】(解答例) As the students have formed positive attitude toward communication focusing on speech sounds, it will be a good idea to involve ALT to class activities as much as possible. It will be also effective, in teaching grammar, to utilize expressions the students have been familiar with through language activities in elementary school.
〈解説〉小学校での言語活動を踏まえ，それを無駄にしないように中学での学習に結び付ける，という点を中心に，自由に考えを述べる。

【5】(解答例) By setting up specific learning attainment targets in the form of Can-Do list, it will become easier for teachers to asses students' progress and know in what area and how they should enhance teaching. The faculty members can also give and get advice and ideas on teaching methods and any other issues to and from one another by sharing the lists among members, which will greatly help teachers who generally teach alone in classes and have to face any problem matters alone. Students can also set up learning attainment targets by Can-Do list to know their achievement, which will fuel students' motivation to shore up their weaknesses.

〈解説〉自由に考えを述べてよいが，指導要領および英語教育の現状を大きく逸脱してはならないのは言うまでもない。文法的な誤りを避けるためには，自分が展開できる範囲の論理・テーマで簡潔に書くこと。今後どのようなテーマで出題されるかはわからないので，昨今教育現場や文科省の方針で問題になってきたこと，変更された・されようとしている点などについては常に情報を得ておく努力が必要である。

【高等学校】

【1】(1)　ウ　　(2)　(解答例)　世界文化遺産指定を受けてから10数年を経た今，旅行者は満載のツアーバスから吐き出され，世界遺産指定区域内には旅行者への飲食を提供する店や，服や靴，提灯などの土産物を売る店がひしめいている。旅行者を受け入れるためには古くからある景観を取り壊して施設を新設せざるをえない。　(3)　(解答例)　パリは都市として広大であり，世界遺産指定地区を訪れる人を十分受け入れることができ，同時に景観を維持することができる。

(4)　(解答例)　団体の旅行客があふれ，バーから大音量のテクノ・ポップが流れて「素晴らしい普遍的な価値」とはどのようなものかさえ想像できない状況。 /　歴史的建造物は取り壊されて複製に置き換えられている。　/　写真に収まる民族衣装の少女たちは，少数民族のナシーですらなく，中国の他の地域から流れてきた移住者で，先住民の半分はすでにこの地を去ったあとだ。　(5)　(解答例)　世界文化遺産地区の中心に超高層ビルを建てる計画により，指定が取り消される恐れがある。　(6)　ア　カ

〈解説〉(1)　disgorgeは「吐き出す」。バスからたくさんの観光客が押し出されてくる光景を描写した語で，pushing out「押し出している」と同義。　(2)　1999年に世界遺産指定された場所が2011年にはすっかり変貌したさまが，第2段落に詳述されている。　(3)　下線部は直前の

段落の主旨をまとめたものなので，その段落を解説する。 (4) 下線部に続く個所に，その例が述べられているのでそこを引いてまとめる。 (5) 下線部に続く個所に説明が述べられている。 (6) 第1段落最後から2つ目の文に「その地を訪れた」とあり，アと一致。 第5段落に，How do you lure travelers to historic locales without destroying their integrity in the process?「歴史的な舞台の全体性を破壊することなく，その舞台に旅行者を誘い込むことがどうやってできるだろうか？」とあり，「世界遺産に多くの旅行者をひきつけつつ，その場所の真の価値を保つのは難しい」とするカと趣旨一致。

【2】(解答例) (1) ① ・生徒の現状について，感覚的にではなく，客観的データを活用して確認すること。 ・リストの作成とともにその成果の検証などについては，学習指導要領に沿って整理すること。
・Can-Doリストを作成するメンバー相互で，言語学習観や現状認識を整理し，共通認識をもって作成すること。 ② ・Can-Doリスト形式による学習到達目標については，学校単位，担当教師グループ単位等で検討し，各学校の事情によって書き換えられるべきであると認識する。 ・リストに沿った学習の結果をフィードバックし，目標事項，レベル，方法等を常に改訂していくべきであることを確認する。
(2) ① ・指導要領内容に基づいて逸脱のないよう，計画の大筋をおさえる。 ・4技能を総合的に育成することをねらいとして内容を計画するうえで，そうした活動に適した題材の選択等については，文化の違いなどを踏まえ，ALTの意見を引き出すようにする。
② ・内容の展開については，JTEとALTの役割分担を確認しあい，それぞれの特徴が生かされるよう配慮する。 ・指導要領のねらいをおさえつつ，ALTの自然な反応やコミュニケーション態度が生かされるよう，授業外でのコミュニケーションを続けていく。
〈解説〉指導要領の方向性として，実践的なコミュニケーション能力育成，具体的な教育計画の作成や成果のフィードバックなどは重視すべき点であることを踏まえ，常に具体的な教室活動についての考察を行い，

自分なりの授業計画作成をいろいろなレベル，状況を想定して練っておくことが必要である。

【3】(1)　ウ　(2)　エ　(3)　ア　(4)　ウ　(5)　イ

〈解説〉(1)　空欄は直前の handbook を主語としての補語の役割をしているので，handbook[が]「読まれる」とするウがあてはまる。

(2)　coming back later は「戻ってくること」，すなわち今は対応できないので一旦退出してほしいと秘書が言ったわけである。Bob にとっては部屋に通すこと，あるいは対応することを「断られた」ということになるのでbeing turned away のエ。　(3)　空欄と後の functional という語が yet でつながっており，「---でありながら，functional」という構造になっている。functionalは形容詞なので，このように並列でつなぐには空欄も形容詞でなければならないので，アを入れて「シンプルでありながら機能的な」とする。　(4)　文後半で「最終的に苦労の末勝利を達成した」とあるので，それに矛盾しない表現を探す。アは「減少していた」，イ「不思議に思っていた」，ウは「もがき苦しんでいた」，エは「圧倒していた」で，ウがあてはまる。「リーグ最下位で苦しんでいたチームが，最終的には苦労の末勝利を勝ち取った」　(5)　選択肢は，ア「詳しく述べた」，イ「最高潮になった」，ウ「～に滞在した」，エ 「意見に従った」。「セレモニーのイベントは，県の歌の合唱で最高潮に達した」とするイがあてはまる。

【4】(1)　記号…B　正しい英語…arrived　(2)　記号…A　正しい英語…to the effect　(3)　記号…B　正しい英語…from

〈解説〉(1)　過去完了はある時点を基準とし，その一段階過去のことを表す。問題文の場合，「私たち」が「到着した」時点で「あなた」は「その前にすでに眠っていた」という状況なので，「到着した」は過去形になる。「私たちが到着したときにあなたが(すでに)眠ってしまっていなかったなら，一緒に行こうと頼んだでしょうが，あなたを煩わせたくなかったのです」　(2)「彼は，日本人の他の人とのコミュニケーションへの消極性は，自信の欠如という印象を与える傾向があるため，残念な性質である，という主旨のことを述べた」で，to the effect が適切。on the effect は「～に基づいている」という意味。

(3)　unemployment that may result in displacement of jobs by new technology だと，「失業が，新技術による仕事の置換という結果を招くかもしれない」ということになるが，常識的に言えば技術革新によって人員が不要になり失業が起こるのがふつう。従って result in ではなく result from とし，「新技術導入の結果引き起こされるかもしれない失業(について懸念している)」としなければならない。

【5】(解答例)　Today, English-speaking world has been broadened to large area including Asia, Africa and other developing countries. Under such a situation, it is crucial to have the English communication skills for securing the safety in overseas, for business use, for understanding other cultures and for understanding one another in private basis. In order to have students realize the importance of English communication skills, I suggest that role-playing be frequently used in classroom. The point is, to have students go through mock foreign travel, mock business negotiation, mock situations in which foreign travelers are in trouble in Japan, and so forth.

〈解説〉英語を教える立場として，英語を学ぶ必要性についての生徒の疑問には常に対応できるよう準備しておくことは必須である。教師が必要を感じていない教科を積極的に学ぼうと思う生徒はまず非常に少ないと考えられるからである。日本語でも英語でも，説得力をもって説明できるだけの英語学習に対するモチベーションを，自分自身，常に持っていてほしい。

2013年度　実施問題

【中高共通】

【１】リスニングテスト

Part A

In Part A, you will hear a question followed by three responses. Choose the best response to each question. The question and the responses will be spoken only once.

(1) Have you ever used an electronic dictionary?

(A) Yes, I've had one since last month.

(B) Sure, I'll try it someday.

(C) No, I don't know much about electronic banking.

(2) How did the demonstration class go?

(A) Not so soon, I believe.

(B) Everything went well.

(C) I went there by bus.

(3) Where will the new education office building be located?

(A) The new office was on the third floor.

(B) It'll be on the next corner beside the prefectural office building.

(C) It'll be more comfortable than the old one.

(4) Is it possible to reschedule the English teachers'meeting for the same time on Friday?

(A) I'm sorry, Friday is more convenient for me.

(B) Until the same time on Friday.

(C) Sure, no problem.

(5) Do you think the new kind of virus threatens our life?

(A) Yes, I surely do, and I'm scared.

(B) No, you always sweat it out.

(C) Yes, I have a bias toward you.

(6) How long will it take for this gift to get to New York?

(A) Since this weekend.

(B) Yes, I'll take you there in a few days.

(C) About a week if you send it by air.

Part B

In Part B, you will hear four short conversations between two people. Each conversation will be followed by one question. Choose the best answer from among the four choices written on your test sheet. Conversations and questions will be spoken only once.

(1)

W : Can I help you find something?

M : Yes, I'm looking for a general book on computers, nothing too technical, just an introductory text.

W : Well, let me look up what we have on our computer.... Here's one, "Basic Computing for Beginners."

M : That sounds good. Where can I find that on the shelves?

Question : What will the woman probably do next?

(A) Recommend the man to take her class.

(B) Order a book on computers.

(C) Tell the man where the book is.

(D) Return the books to the shelves.

(2)

W : Why don't we clean up the garage? I want to be able to get two cars in there.

M : Can't you wait until next weekend?

W : You remember what you said last week, don't you?

M : Of course, I do, but I'm so busy this week. Let's do that next weekend.

Question : What is the man trying to do?

(A) Clean up the garage today.

(B) Put off the work for one more week.

(C) Put away another car in the garage today.

(D) Ask the woman to clean up the garage.

(3)

M : Hello. Pete speaking.

W : Hi, Pete. It's Naomi. Can you come to the party we're having on Friday evening?

M : Of course, I can.

W : Great. We're having a birthday party for Kate, but she doesn't know anything about this. So everybody's meeting at my house at 6:30. Kate will probably come over around 7:00.

M : That sounds interesting. I'm going to see her later, but I promise I'll keep it secret.

Question : What is the most important thing about Kate's birthday party?

(A) That Pete should say something to Kate.

(B) That Pete should come to Naomi's at 7:00.

(C) That Kate will be twenty years old.

(D) That it is a surprise.

(4)

M : I'm sorry I'm late. I heard on the car radio that the highway was closed by last night's snow, so I took back roads to come in.

W : You're not the only one. Everybody's stuck in traffic. Actually, you're the third person to come to the office.

M : I'm sure the snow did a lot of damage. Traffic is a mess. I wouldn't expect anyone for quite a while.

W : No, and that's okay. We don't have any important business today.

Question : What does the man probably expect next?

(A) His coworkers will be late.

(B) His office building will be destroyed.

(C) His coworkers will charge their cell phones.

(D) His coworkers'cars will not start.

Part C

In Part C, you will hear two short passages. Each passage will be followed by one question. Write the answer to each question in English. Both answers should begin with "I should." Passages and questions will be read twice.

(1) Welcome to Tropical Beach Resort. We would like to announce a side trip which is available from now. It's a boat trip which takes you to an island off the shore. It will make you feel like you are on a tropical island. Reservations for that can be made at the front desk at any time. I hope you enjoy your visit to our resort. Thank you.

Question : If you want to take part in the boat trip, what should you do?

(2) Now I'm going to give you feedback on your class performance. I've read over your paper. It's excellent, but your midterm grade is still a B. You seem to understand the course material very well, but, as this is a seminar, it is necessary for you to express your opinions actively during class. This will be an important part of grading.

Question : What should you do to improve your class grade?

Part D

In Part D, you will hear a passage. Two questions are written in Japanese on your test sheet. Answer these questions in Japanese. The passage will be read twice.

Cyclones are actually very important, even though, of course, they can be deadly. Essentially they help to balance out the temperature across the globe. They are an equalizer, so they take the heat energy from the tropics and transfer it to where it is needed in colder climates.

The generic term for this is tropical cyclone. That can refer to any cyclone that has a closed center of circulation anywhere in the world, like in the Atlantic. When they reach a certain wind strength, we call them hurricanes. But if you're in the western Pacific, a hurricane is called a typhoon. There's no difference between a hurricane and a typhoon except in the name. They're both tropical cyclones.

問い

(1)　サイクロンが重要である理由を日本語で書け。

(2)　大西洋でサイクロンをハリケーンと呼ぶのはどのような場合か，日本語で書け。

This is the end of the listening test.

(☆☆☆☆◎◎◎)

【2】次の英文は，アメリカの実業家スティーブ・ジョブズ氏が，スタンフォード大学の卒業式で学生たちに行ったスピーチの抜粋である。英文を読んで，(1)～(5)の各設問に答えよ。

About a year ago I was diagnosed with cancer. I had a scan at 7:30 in the morning, and it clearly showed a tumor on my pancreas. I didn't even know what a pancreas was. The doctors told me this was almost certainly a type of cancer that is incurable, and that I should expect to live no longer than three to six months. My doctor advised me 〔　　〕, which is doctor's code for prepare to die. It means to try to tell your kids everything you thought you'd have the next 10 years to tell them in just a few months. It means to make sure everything is buttoned up so that it will be as easy as possible for your family. It means to say your goodbyes.

I lived with that diagnosis all day. Later that evening I had a biopsy, where they stuck an endoscope down my throat, through my stomach and into my intestines, put a needle into my pancreas and got a few cells from the tumor. I was sedated, but my wife, who was there, told me that when they viewed the cells under a microscope the doctors started crying because it turned out to be a very rare form of pancreatic cancer that is curable with surgery. I had the surgery and I'm fine now.

(A)<u>This</u> was the closest I've been to facing death, and I hope it's the closest I get for a few more decades. Having lived through it, I can now say this to you with a bit more certainty than when death was a useful but purely intellectual concept :

No one wants to die. Even people who want to go to heaven don't want to die to get there. And yet death is the destination we all share. No one has ever escaped it. And that is as it should be, because (a) is very likely the single best invention of (b). It is Life's change agent. It clears out the old to make way for the new. Right now the new is you, but someday not too long from now, you will gradually become the old and be cleared away. Sorry to be so dramatic, but (B)<u>it</u> is quite true.

Your time is limited, so don't waste it living someone else's life. Don't be trapped by dogma — which is living with the results of other people's thinking. Don't let the noise of others'opinions drown out your own inner voice. And most important, have the courage to follow your heart and intuition. They somehow already know what you truly want to become. Everything else is secondary.

【出典スタンフォード大学ホームページ(http : //news. stanford. edu/news/)】

(1) 文中の〔　　〕に入る最も適切なものを，次のア～オから一つ選び，その記号を書け。

ア　to fight against cancer and go back to business

イ　to have an operation for cancer and live in peace with my family

ウ　to go home and get my affairs in order

エ　to make my will and enjoy the remainder of my life

オ　to call a funeral company and tell them my wishes

(2) 下線部(A)が表す内容を，50字程度の日本語で書け。

(3) 文中の(　a　)，(　b　)に入る最も適切な語を，次のア～オから一つずつ選び，その記号を書け。

ア　Life　　イ　Heaven　　ウ　Future　　エ　Death　　オ　Past

(4)　下線部(B)の内容を，20字程度の日本語で書け。

(5)　第5パラグラフで述べられているジョブズ氏のメッセージの内容を，50字程度の日本語で書け。

(☆☆☆☆◎◎◎)

【中学校】

【１】次の会話文を読んで，(1)～(5)の設問に応えよ。

Here are two conversations about parties. In the first one a woman is calling a friend to accept an invitation to a potluck dinner party.

JEAN : Hello?

ROBERTA : Hello, Jean? This is Roberta.

JEAN : Oh, hi!

ROBERTA : I got your invitation and it says R.S.V.P., so that's what I'm doing.

JEAN : Oh, good. Can you come?

ROBERTA : Yes, I think so, but Tony can't. He's got to go to his parents' and (A)[their / them / work / on / help / house] this weekend.

JEAN : Oh, that's too bad. It'd be fun to see you both.

ROBERTA : Yeah, well, some other time I guess ... Uh, Jean, I won't have any transportation that night. (B)I think I can get a lift over, but it's going to be a hassle getting home. Think somebody could give me a ride?

JEAN : Oh, sure! [　Ⅰ　] I'm sure one of them would be glad to. If that doesn't work (　①　), I'll drive you.

ROBERTA : Great! Thanks, Jean. Uh, what will people be wearing?

JEAN : Oh, most anything. [　Ⅱ　] We'll be in the yard, you know.

ROBERTA : Good! I can wear my new pants and sweater. Uh, it says "potluck." What can I bring?

JEAN : Well, a side dish would be good and a bottle of wine, maybe, but that's not really necessary cause there'll be plenty (　②　) drink and we're making punch.

ROBERTA : Okay, see you then!

JEAN : Bye!

The second conversation takes place at a cocktail party. Lois and Patrick work for the same company.

PATRICK : Lois, I'd like to introduce you to Alan Bernard, who's down here from company headquarters in Indianapolis. Alan, this is Lois McGrath from our marketing department here in Memphis.

ALAN : Pleased to meet you.

LOIS : How do you do, Alan. I hope you're enjoying your stay here.

ALAN : Yes, I am very much.

LOIS : What are you doing here?

ALAN : Well, I'm getting more familiar with our branches around the country. [Ⅲ] I'd like to see more, but I have to be in Phoenix tomorrow.

LOIS : That's too bad! Where have you been staying?

ALAN : At the Morrison Hotel near here. It's small, but very nice. Great Southern hospitality! And the airport shuttle's just two blocks away.

LOIS : That's convenient! [Ⅳ]

ALAN : Yes. The company'd pick up the tab, but I don't mind the shuttle at all.

LOIS : Do you feel like something to drink?

ALAN : Thanks, but I'm afraid I'll have to take a rain check. But I'll be back in Memphis in five weeks. Maybe I could collect (③) the rain check then?

LOIS : Oh, I'd like that! Here, let me give you my card.

ALAN : That's great. Thanks!

LOIS : You're welcome!

【出典　Nancy Church and Anne Moss, *How to Survive in the USA.*, CAMBRIDGE UNIVERSITY PRESS】

(1) [　Ⅰ　]～[　Ⅳ　]に入る最も適切なものを，次のア～オから一つずつ選んで，その記号を書け。

ア　I noticed your office is very well run.

イ　It's a fairly casual party.

ウ　I think I'd be tempted to give it some more.

エ　Taxis are so expensive these days.

オ　There's a bunch of people coming who live near you.

(2) (　①　)～(　③　)に入る最も適切な語を，次のア～カから一つずつ選んで，その記号を書け。

ア　for　　イ　with　　ウ　on　　エ　to　　オ　at　　カ　out

(3) 下線部(A)の語を意味が通るように並べかえよ。

(4) 下線部(B)を日本語に直せ。

(5) 次の(a)，(b)の説明にそれぞれ該当する1語を，会話文中から抜き出して書け。

(a)　a section of a business specializing in a particular product or service

(b)　friendly and generous behavior towards guests

(☆☆☆☆◎◎◎)

【2】次の英文を読んで，(1)～(4)の設問に答えよ。

Classroom-based assessment of English language learners must begin with what we know about the second language acquisition process, including how students acquire skills in reading, writing, and the content areas. For example, if we know that writing is a process of revising multiple drafts of work after getting feedback on them, why do we test this construct differently (product only) from what the research suggests? Acquiring literacy skills in a second language means tapping prior knowledge, actively using reading and writing strategies, knowing something about text structure or how texts are organized, relating the topic to students' interests, and having students work collaboratively on reading-related activities. Do our classroom assessment tools capture student learning on any or all of these processes?

To inform teaching and improve learning, classroom assessment must be conducted on a regular, systematic basis, not just at the end of a unit of study. Effective teachers use assessment to collect baseline data or information on students' background knowledge and experiences prior to launching into a new unit of study. Teachers assess students weekly or biweekly to keep tabs on how they are progressing with regard to learning objectives. Teachers who are not able to judge student progress must resort to either teaching without feedback, in a void, with no basis for judging the effectiveness of their teaching or following a scripted curriculum or specific teaching method.

Classroom assessment also calls for collecting data from multiple sources in order to make a reliable judgement about student progress. The sources should be varied in format, a combination of assessments ranging from multiple-choice and fill-in-the blank tests to performance assessments such as written essays, oral reports, self-assessments, reading logs, and portfolios. The use of multiple sources is especially important when working with English language learners and special needs learners because it provides individual snapshots of student learning under a variety of conditions and skill requirements.

Classroom-based assessment must also be (A)<u>culturally and developmentally appropriate</u> to yield valid results. Culturally appropriate assessment begins with instruction. First, the language of the assessment should be the same as that of the instruction. So, for example, a student learning to read in Spanish would also be assessed in Spanish reading. In addition, students from traditional cultural backgrounds may not value competition with peers, and students from these cultures (including Latino students) may not respond to calls for individual achievement but instead may be more motivated to work as a team to help members attain a learning goal. Teachers can encourage group work while also showing students that individual competition in school is a highly valued American principle. Developmentally appropriate assessment refers to using materials and tasks that have been designed for the age, interest levels and language proficiency of the student. For example, in the state of Virginia, much controversy has revolved around standards for Grade 3 Social Studies calling for detailed knowledge of Egyptian kings and queens and forms of government. Many educators believe this topic is not developmentally appropriate for third graders. A much more appropriate topic might be "My Community," where students learn about people and places in the community in which they live.

A final assumption about (B)classroom-based assessment is that it has *content* and *consequential validity*. Students are assessed on the instructional principles and activities presented in class (content validity), and assessment results are used by the teacher to improve teaching and learning (consequential validity). Fairness is achieved when teachers assess students on the material and formats that have been presented in class. Assessments are unfair when teachers ask students to do something that has not been part of instruction, such as asking students to apply synthesis or evaluation skills when only knowledge and comprehension skills have been practiced in class. Assessment is also unfair when teachers show bias in their scoring or grading toward students whom they know to be "A" students or "F" students, based on previous performance.

【出典　Carlos, J.O., & Mary, C. C. , & Virginia, P.C., *BILINGUAL AND ESL CLASSROOMS*, McGraw-Hill】

(1)　第1パラグラフを読んで，次の英文の(　①　)，(　②　)に当てはまる語をそれぞれ1語ずつ書け。

Classroom-based assessment of English language learners must be based on what we know about how language learners learn, in particular how they acquire (　①　) and (　②　) processes.

(2)　生徒の進歩を正しく評価するために大切なことは何か，20字程度の日本語で書け。

(3)　下線部(A)とはどのような状態を表しているか，60字程度の日本語で書け。

(4)　下線部(B)が公正に行われない例について，60字程度の日本語で書け。

(☆☆☆☆◎◎◎◎)

【3】(1)～(5)について，それぞれの日本語の内容を表すように，[　　]内の語句を並べかえよ。ただし，文頭にくる語も小文字にしてある。

(1)　その博物館まで駅から歩いて15分もかからないだろう。

It [than / you / walk / will / take / less / to / fifteen minutes] from the station to the museum.

(2)　子どもたちを両親が望むようにさせるのは決して容易ではない。

It is [do / make / no means / easy / to / their parents / children / by / as / wish].

(3)　そのとき彼に真実を告げなかったことを悔やまない日は一日もない。

Not a day passes [I / regret / not / him / the truth / having / told / when / don't] then.

(4)　厚かましいと思われるのは本意ではないが，私を議長に推薦していただけないだろうか。

[to / without / immodest / wanting / sound], could you put me forward as a chairman?

(5)　個人情報を知られるよりは，参加者名簿を配らない方がよいと考える人もいる。

Some people believe that not [is / having / to / distributing / private information / preferable / their / the attendance list] known.

(☆☆☆☆◎◎◎◎)

【4】次の英文を読んで，そのあとの問いに50語程度の英語で答えよ。

A new ALT has come to your school. While he is at school, he usually dresses casually in a hooded sweat shirt or a printed T-shirt and even wears jeans. He says he likes this style because he wants to move around in class.

This tendency is also true of his way of managing classes. Students are encouraged to ask questions at any time in his class, so they rarely sit quietly listening to the lecture. He seems to feel that informal atmosphere is effective for students to discuss their ideas and express themselves.

Question : What do you think about this ALT?

(☆☆☆☆◎◎◎◎)

【5】秋田県では，公の場で自分の考えを積極的に発言することができる"「問い」を発する子ども"の育成を進めている。このことについて，あなたは英語の授業の中でどのように指導を工夫していくか，100語程度の英語で書け。

(☆☆☆☆◎◎◎◎◎)

【高等学校】

【1】次の英文を読んで，各設問に答えよ。

THE MORNING I spotted Tony Gardner sitting among the tourists, spring was just arriving here in Venice. We'd completed our first full week outside in the piazza — a relief, let me tell you, after all those stuffy hours performing from the back of the cafe, getting in the way of customers wanting to use the staircase. There was quite a breeze that morning, and our brand-new marquee was flapping all around us, but we were all feeling a little bit brighter and fresher, and (A)I guess it showed in our music.

But here I am talking like I'm a regular band member. Actually, (B)I'm one of the 'gypsies', as the other musicians call us, one of the guys who move around the piazza, helping out whichever of the three cafe orchestras needs us. Mostly I play here at the Caffè Lavena, but on a busy afternoon, I might do a set with the Quadri boys, go over to the Florian, then back across the square to the Lavena. I get on fine with them all — and with the waiters too — and in any other city I'd have a regular position by now. But in this place, so obsessed with tradition and the past, (C)everything's upside down. Anywhere else, being a guitar player would go in a guy's favour. But here? A guitar! The cafe managers get uneasy. It looks too modern, the tourists won't like it. Last autumn I got myself a vintage jazz model with an oval sound-hole, the kind of thing Django Reinhardt might have played, so there was no way anyone would mistake me for a rock-and-roller. That made things a little easier, but the cafe managers, they still don't like it. The truth is, if you're a guitarist, you can be Joe Pass, they still wouldn't give you a regular job in this square.

There's also, of course, the small matter of my not being Italian, never mind Venetian. It's the same for that big Czech guy with the alto sax. We're well liked, we're needed by the other musicians, but we don't quite fit the official bill. Just play and keep your mouth shut, that's what the cafe managers always say. That way the tourists won't know you're not Italian. Wear your suit, sunglasses, keep the hair combed back, no one will know the difference, just don't start talking.

But I don't do too bad. All three cafe orchestras, especially when they have to play at the same time from their rival tents, they need a guitar — something soft, solid, but amplified, thumping out the chords from the back. I guess you're thinking, three bands playing at the same time in the same square, that would sound like a real mess. But the Piazza San Marco's big enough to take it. A tourist strolling across the square will hear one tune fade out, another fade in, like he's shifting the dial on a radio. What tourists can't take too much of is the classical stuff, all these instrumental versions of famous arias. Okay, this is San Marco, they don't want the latest pop hits. But every few minutes they want something they recognise, maybe an old Julie Andrews number, or the theme from a famous movie. I remember once last summer, going from band to band and playing 'The Godfather' nine times in one afternoon.

Anyway there we were that spring morning, playing in front of a good crowd of tourists, when I saw Tony Gardner, sitting alone with his coffee, almost directly in front of us, maybe six metres back from our (D)<u>marquee</u>. We get famous people in the (E)<u>square</u> all the time, we never make a fuss. At the end of a number, maybe a quiet word will go around the band members. Look, there's Warren Beatty. Look, it's Kissinger. That woman, she's the one who was in the movie about the men who swap their faces. We're used to it. This is the Piazza San Marco after all. But when I realised it was Tony Gardner sitting there, (F)that was different. I *did* get excited.

Tony Gardner had been my mother's favourite. Back home, back in the communist days, it had been really hard to get records like that, but my mother had pretty much his whole collection. Once when I was a boy, I scratched one of those precious records. The apartment was so cramped, and a boy my age, you just had to move around sometimes, especially during those cold months when you couldn't go outside. So I was playing this game jumping from our little sofa to the armchair, and one time I misjudged it and hit the record player. The needle went across the record with a zip — this was long before CDs — and my mother came in from the kitchen and began shouting at me. I felt so bad, not just because she was shouting at me, but because I knew it was one of Tony Gardner's records, and I knew how much it meant to her. And (G)I knew that this one too would now have those popping noises going through it while he crooned those American songs. Years later, when I was working in Warsaw and I got to know about black-market records, I gave my mother replacements of all her worn-out Tony Gardner albums, including that one I scratched. It took me over three years, but I kept getting them, one by one, and each time I went back to see her I'd bring her another.

【出典　Kazuo Ishiguro, *Nocturnes*, faber and faber】

(1)　下線部(A)の理由を，itを具体的に説明しながら答えよ。

(2)　下線部(B)の意味を本文の内容に沿って，日本語で説明せよ。

(3)　下線部(C)について，具体的に日本語で説明せよ。

(4)　下線部(D)，(E)とほぼ同じ意味を示す語を本文中から見つけよ。ただし，下線部(D)についてはその前の段落から，下線部(E)については第一段落からそれぞれ1語を抜き出して答えよ。

(5) 下線部(F)のように感じたのはなぜか，本文の内容に沿って日本語で理由を答えよ。

(6) 下線部(G)を日本語に直せ。

(7) 次の英文の中で，本文の内容と一致するものを一つ選び，記号で答えよ。

(ア) I am not a regular member of the band although I am a guitarist born in Venice.

(イ) Last autumn I bought a jazz guitar, which makes the cafe managers all the more uneasy.

(ウ) The cafe managers in the Piazza San Marco would like some of their band players to keep their mouths shut since they haven't paid their utility bills.

(エ) Tourists coming to the Piazza San Marco enjoy not classical music but some kind of old popular film music they know.

(オ) Every time the band members finish their tunes, they enjoy talking a lot about celebrities coming here as tourists.

(☆☆☆☆☆◎◎)

【2】次の(1)，(2)に答えよ。

(1) 英語の授業後の校内研修会で，ある先生が次のような発言をした。これについてあなたはどのように思うか，日本語で述べよ。

「生徒に，間違った英語でもいいからコミュニケーション活動をさせろと言うけれど，うちの高校の場合はほとんどの生徒が大学入試を受けるので，まずしっかりと文法を教えなければならない。コミュニケーション活動と文法指導を両立させるのは無理がある。」

(2) 英語Ⅰの教科書で，ある単元末に文法事項について次のような記述があり，授業の中で，この文法事項について，ドリル活動まで終わったとする。この後で，15分程度を使い，コミュニケーション活動を行うとすると，どのような活動が考えられるか。活動の内容と形態やその活動を行う際の留意点について日本語で述べ，ワークシートを作成せよ。

○関係代名詞の使い方　・・・直前の名詞を修飾する

I know ***the man*** **who came to the party last night**.

The woman **(whom) you saw yesterday** is on TV.

Do you know ***the girl*** **whose smile is very cute**?

(☆☆☆◎◎◎◎)

【3】次の(1)～(5)の(　　)に当てはまる最も適切な語(句)をそれぞれ(a)～(d)から一つ選び，記号で答えよ。

(1) Childhood (　　) is one of the most serious public health problems these days. Many children eat a lot of oily food and don't take exercise. That causes the problem.

(a) rampage　(b) obesity　(c) dementia　(d) leukemia

(2) The bears used to (　　) in that area a long time ago, but now their number is dramatically decreasing.

(a) thrive　(b) populate　(c) boost　(d) prevaricate

(3) The prime minister issued a statement to the media (　　) the criticism of the new policy.

(a) in response to　(b) in collusion with　(c) in comparison with
(d) in contrast to

(4) The 9.0 magnitude earthquake set off a (　　) tsunami, and it sent walls of water washing over coastal cities and towns in the northern area.

(a) distinctive　(b) serene　(c) solemn　(d) devastating

(5) Both parties are willing to make (　　) in order to reach a settlement.

(a) recessions　(b) oppressions　(c) concessions　(d) admissions

(☆☆☆☆◎◎◎)

【4】次の(1)～(3)の各英文において，誤りのある部分の記号を答え，正しい英語に直せ。

(1) I try $_A$to reduce stress $_B$by accepting events $_C$what they are, rather than as I would like them $_D$to be.

(2) You will find a $_A$snowflake has an $_B$amazing $_C$minute structure $_D$through a magnifying glass.

(3) The parents $_A$warn their children $_B$that the river is dangerous $_C$to swim after $_D$a heavy rain fall.

(☆☆☆◎◎◎)

【5】次の英文を読んで，下線部に対するあなたの立場を明確にして，意見を100語程度の英語で書け。なお，語数を書くこと。

More companies are taking action against employees who smoke off-duty, and, in an extreme trend that some call troubling, some are now firing or banning the hiring of workers who light up even on their own time.

The outright bans raise new questions about how far companies can go in regulating workers' behavior when they are off the clock. The crackdown is coming in part as a way to curb soaring health care costs, but critics say companies are violating workers' privacy rights. <u>The zero-tolerance policies are coming as more companies adopt smoke-free workplaces</u>.

【出典 *USA TODAY*, May 11, 2005】

(☆☆☆☆◎◎)

解答・解説

【中高共通】

【1】Part A　(1)　(A)　(2)　(B)　(3)　(B)　(4)　(C)　(5)　(A)　(6)　(C)　Part B　(1)　(C)　(2)　(B)　(3)　(D)　(4)　(A)

Part C　(1)　(I should) make a reservation for it at the front desk.

(2)　(I should) express my opinions actively during class.

Part D　(1)　熱帯地方の熱エネルギーを寒い地域へと運び，地球規模で気候のバランスをとるから。　(2)　ある一定の風速に達したとき。

〈解説〉Part A　(1)「電子辞書使ったことありますか？」「はい，先月から1台持っているので」　(2)「公開授業はどうだった？」「全てうまくいったよ」　(3)「新しい教育事務所ってどこにできるの？」「県庁そばの次の角のところだよ」　(4)「英語教員のミーティングを金曜日の同じ時間にずらせますか？」「ええ，大丈夫ですよ」

(5)「新種のウィルスは私たちの生活を脅かすと思う？」「うん，そう思うし，怖いよ」　(6)「この贈り物をNYに届けるのにどれくらいの時間がかかりますか」「航空便で送れば1週間ほどです」

Part B　(1)　最後に男性が「本棚のどこにありますか？」と尋ねている。　(2)　最後に男性が「来週末にそれ(ガレージの片づけ)をしようよ」と言っている。put off ～「～を延期する」　(3)　Kateの誕生日パーティーを開こうとしていて，最後に男性が「内緒にすると約束するよ」と言っている。サプライズパーティーにしようとしているため。

(4)　男性のI wouldn't expect anyone for quite a while.はanyoneの後にto come to the officeを補って，「しばらく誰も職場に来ないと思う」という意味。　Part C　(1)「ご予約はフロントデスクでいつでもできます」とある。　(2)「ゼミなので，授業中に授業で活発に意見を出す必要があります」と言っている。　Part D　(1)　第1段落2～3文目を参照。whereは先行詞(the place, area)を含む関係副詞。　(2)　第2段落3文目を参照。

【2】(1) ウ　(2) 治療できないと思われたがんが見つかり，余命を宣告されたが，治療できるとわかり，手術によってがんを摘出したこと(54字)　(3) (a) エ　(b) ア　(4) 人はいずれ年をとり，世の中から消え去ること(21字)　(5) 人生には限りがあるのだから，他人に自分の内なる声が惑わされないよう，心と直感にしたがって行動しなさいということ(55字)

〈解説〉(1) 空欄の後に「それは死ぬ準備をせよという医師の暗号だ」とある。アとイは病いと闘う内容が入っているので×。エとオは「遺書(will)を書く」や「葬儀屋に電話する」など内容が直接的なので×。ウのget one's affairs in orderは「物事を整理する」といった意味。

(2) This was ～ facing to deathは「これが，私が死に最も近づいたときだ」の意味。よってThisは前段落までのジョブズ氏のがんとの闘病体験を指している。医師から受けた通告の内容，手術での出来事を字数制限内で簡潔に書けばよい。　(3) that is～からの訳は「それはそのとおりであるべきなのだ，なぜなら死は生命の最高の発明だからだ」。Lifeは次文の「それ(死)は生命(Life)を変えるエージェント(行為者)である」からわかる。　(4) 下線部は前文の内容を指している。今は若者である学生も，いずれ年をとり，この世から片づけられる(cleared away)といった内容を字数制限内で述べればよい。　(5) dogma「教義，定説」　drown out ～「(小さい音・声を)かき消す」　let ～ drown out …「～によって…を聞こえなくさせる」　have the courage to V「Vする勇気をもつ」

【中学校】

【1】(1) Ⅰ オ　Ⅱ イ　Ⅲ ア　Ⅳ エ　(2) ① カ　② エ　③ ウ　(3) help them work on their house　(4) 行きは送ってもらえるけど，家に帰るのが厄介になる。

(5) (a) department　(b) hospitality

〈解説〉(1) Ⅰ「誰か迎えに来れないかな？」「もちろん！」とあるので，オの「あなたの家の近くに住んでいる人ならたくさんいるよ」が正解。

Ⅱ「みんな何着ていくの？」「まぁ何でも」とあるので，イの「カジュアルなパーティーだから」が正解。　Ⅲ　「ここ(Memphis)では何をしているの？」「全国の支店にもっと詳しくなろうと思って」とあるので，アの「君の支店はよく経営されているね」が正解。　Ⅳ　空欄に続く会話で「そうだね。会社は勘定を払ってくれる(pick up the tab)と思うけど，シャトルでも全然いいよ」とある。前後の文脈から，勘定とはシャトル以外の乗り物の代金だとわかるので，エの「最近はタクシーは高いね」が正解。　(2)　①　work out「うまくいく」
②　plentyは代名詞で「たくさんのもの」の意味。to drinkはto不定詞の形容詞的用法でplentyを修飾している。　③　Alanの会話のI'm afraid I'll have to take a rain check.は「また別の機会にしようかな」という意味。rain checkとは野球の試合などが中止のときにもらえる「雨天引換券」のことで，それを使って次回の試合を観戦することができるもの。collect on the rain checkで「雨天引換券を使って次回集まる」といった意味。　(3)　help O V「OがVするのを手伝う」　work on ～「～にとりかかる，修繕する」　(4)　ここのliftはrideと同じで「車で送ってもらうこと」の意味。over「向こうへ」があるので，行きに誰かに送ってもらえることを指す。しかしit's going to be a hassle getting home「家に帰るのが厄介になる」とあるので，帰りは足がないとわかる。
(5)　(a)　特定の製品やサービスを担当とする商業の部門(department)
(b)　客に対する親切で寛大な行為，おもてなし(hospitality)

【２】(1)　①　reading　②　writing　(2)　複数の評価材料を用いてデータをとること(19字)　(3)　言語が指導とテスト間で統一され，生徒の文化的背景への配慮もあり，生徒の発達段階に応じた方法によって評価されている状態(58字)　(4)　授業で指導していないことを評価したり，生徒の学力に対して経験からくる先入観をもって採点や評価を行ってしまうこと(55字)
〈解説〉(1)　1文目の内容から。skills in reading, writing, and the content areasをreading and writing processesと言い換えているだけ。　(2)　生徒

の進歩(progress)の評価の仕方は第2・3段落に書かれている。第2段落2文目の use assessment to collect baseline data or informationや3文目のassess students weekly or biweeklyなどから,「進歩具合を見るための基準となるデータをまめにとる」必要があるとわかる。第3段落では,1文目のcollecting data from multiple sourcesから「複数の資料からデータを集める」必要があるとわかる。 (3) 第4段落の内容によると,「文化的に適切な評価(culturally appropriate assessment)」とは,指導とテストの言語が一致していることや,評価方法が学習者の文化的背景(例:個人間の競争を嫌う)に反していないかなどを指す。一方「発達的に適切な評価(developmentally appropriate assessment)」とは,評価に用いたタスクが学習者の年齢,興味,言語熟達度(language proficiency)に合っているかを指す。解答ではこれらを60字程度で簡潔にまとめればよい。 (4) 最終段落のAssessments are unfairからの文と,Assessment is also unfairからの文の,when以下に具体例が出ている。前者は,指導していないことを評価すること,後者は予断や先入観(bias)をもって生徒の学力を評価してしまうことを述べている。

【3】(1) (It) will take you less than fifteen minutes to walk (from the station to the museum.) (2) (It is) by no means easy to make children do as their parents wish (.) (3) (Not a day passes) when I don't regret not having told him the truth (then.) (4) Without wanting to sound immodest(, could you put me forward as a chairman?) (5) (Some people believe that not) distributing the attendance list is preferable to having their private information (known.)

〈解説〉(1) It takes/will take 人 時間 to V「Vするのに～かかる」
(2) by no means「決して～でない」 make は使役動詞で「～に…させる」の意味。 (3) Not a ～「ただ一つの～もない」 whenはdayにかかる関係副詞。regret having 過去分詞 で「～したことを後悔する」(完了形になるのは時制が遡るため)。 notが入ると「～しなかったことを後悔する」の意味になる。 (4) without wanting to V「Vはしたくないが」　sound「～だと思われる」(＝seem)　immodest「厚かましい」(5)　preferable to ～「～よりも好ましい」(toの後は名詞または動名詞がくることに注意)　haveは使役動詞で，目的語と動詞の過去分詞形を伴い，「…を～される」という被害の意味を表す。

【4】(解答例)　It is necessary to have the ALT understand that Japanese schools are expected to discipline students and that teachers must be a role model for students. For this reason, even an ALT should not come to school wearing casual clothes. Moreover, the ALT must have a control over students' behavior when they have to listen to others. (57語)

〈解説〉生徒が活発に活動するのはよいことだが，話を聞くべきときに落ち着いて話を聞けないのは問題である。授業におけるルール(例："Teacher, may I ask you a question?"と言って許可を得てから質問をさせる等)を設けて，生徒がめりはりをつけられるよう指導すべきである。毎回決まった教室英語(例：Make groups of four!)を用いると，英語の授業の雰囲気を保ちつつ，的確に生徒の行動を管理できる。服装も生徒の行動を管理するには重要である。教師が適切な服装をしていなければ，生徒に威厳を感じてもらえず，生徒は言うことを聞かなくなる。ALTとはいえ節度は保ってもらわなければいけない。日本の文化を説明するなどして，服装への理解を求めるべきである。

【5】(解答例)　Nowadays, the ability to express one's opinion in front of others is becoming more important, thus students should be given ample opportunity to do so in the English classroom. The primary role of the English teacher is to make students feel that they want to express their ideas. To accomplish this, the teacher should provide a topic or passage that stimulates students' interest. For this purpose, the teacher may want to give students a question that facilitates discussion on the topic or passage. This process helps the students generate their own ideas and speak in front of others. (98語)

〈解説〉自分の考えを表現する力を育てることは，学習指導要領の目標にも掲げられていること。学習指導要領の「2 内容 (1)言語活動」では，読んだり聞いたりした内容をもとに，自分の考えなどを表現させる等の活動が示されている。生徒自ら表現したい気持ちにさせるためには，まず質・量ともによいインプット，すなわち深い読みやリスニングをする機会を十分に与える必要がある。そのためには推論的質問を与えるなど発問を工夫し，個々の生徒が独自のフィルターを通して教材の内容を捉えられるようにするとよい。それをもとに原稿を書かせ，クラスやグループで発表させる機会を持つとよいだろう。

【高等学校】

【1】(1)　普段はカフェの奥で演奏していてお客の邪魔になっていたが，今は広場で明るくさわやかな気持ちで演奏できるため。　(2)　他の演奏家たちに呼ばれると，広場を移動して，3つあるカフェのオーケストラのどれかを手伝っているから。　(3)　他の場所ではギター奏者は人気があるのに，ベニスではモダンすぎると言って，カフェの経営者も観光客も敬遠してしまうということ。　(4)　(D)　tent(s)

(E)　piazza　　(5)　Tony Gardnerは母の大のお気に入りで，小さい時に誤って彼のレコードを破損し母に怒られた思い出があったから。

(6)　このレコードも，Tonyがアメリカの歌を口ずさんでいる間，あの針飛びの音を起こしてしまうとわかっていたから。　(7)　エ

〈解説〉(1)　We'd complete ～ outside in the piazza.からわかるように筆者は屋外で演奏を行った。a relief ～ to use the staircaseというのは，かつて筆者は狭い店内で演奏していたので広い屋外で演奏できることが安らぎだということ。そういった気持ちをさらに具体的に述べているのがwe were all feeling a little bit brighter and fresher「私たちはみな少し明るくさわやかな気持ちでいた」の部分。itはこのような心情を指していて，それが音楽に表れているということ。　(2)　gypsyは漂泊民族のこと。筆者らがなぜこう呼ばれているかは，本文のone of the guys ～ needs usに書かれている。すなわち，「(私がgypsiesのひとりだということは，)私たちを必要とする3つのオーケストラカフェのどれかを手伝

いながら，広場のあたりを移動している者たちのなかのひとりだということだ」。　(3)　下線部は「全ては上下逆さまだ」の意味。その理由は次文のAnywhere以降の5つの文に表れていて，「他の場所ならギターは気に入られるのに，ここではモダンすぎるといって，旅行者にもあまり人気がない」といったことが述べられている。in one's favour (favor)「～に気に入られて」　(4)　(D)のmarqueeはバンドが演奏時に使用する大きなテントのことを指している。tent(s)は前段落の2文目にある単語。(E)のsquareは広場のことをいい，第1段落では2文目にあるpiazzaがこれに近い言葉。　(5)　下線部の「それは違ったのだ」は，有名人はよく来るのでいつもなら興奮しない(we never make a fuss)のだが，Tony Gardnerは違った，つまり興奮したのだということ。その理由は次の段落に書いてあるように，Tonyは母のお気に入りの歌手で，共産主義時代で手に入れにくかったレコードに傷をつけてしまったなどの思い出があったから。　(6)　this one (record)は傷をつけてしまったTonyのレコードを指す。those popping noises「あの針飛びの音」going through it (when the needle goes through the record)「針がレコード面を通るとき」　croon「ささやくように歌う」　(7)　正解のエは第4段落に書いてある内容。古い人気映画の音楽(old popular film music)の例はThe Godfatherの曲。アについて，第3段落1文目にmy not being Italianとあるように，筆者の出身地はVeniceではないので×。イは第2段落に they still don't like it「彼らはまだギターが気にいらない」とはあるが，all the more uneasy「いっそう不安になった」とは書かれていないので×。ウについて，口をつぐんで演奏しなければいけないのは，第3段落にあるように，イタリア人ではないことがばれないようにするためなので×。オについて，第5段落に We get famous people … we never make a fuss「有名人は来るが…決して興奮しない」とあるので×。

【2】(1) (解答例) 文法指導はコミュニケーション活動と一体で行われるべきものである。文法を学ぶ意義は，相手に的確に意志を伝えるための言葉の使い方を学ぶことである。しかし，相手に意志が伝わったかどうかは，実際に意味のやりとりを行わなければわからないからである。英語によるコミュニケーションを促すために，教師は過度に生徒の誤りを正すべきではないが，間違った表現を繰り返し練習することで誤った言語知識が定着してしまう恐れもある。したがって，教師はコミュニケーション活動を通して生徒に何を学ばせたいかを明確にし，正すべき誤りと寛容であってよい誤りを区別することが肝要である。 (2) 解説参照。

〈解説〉(1) 文法は話し手の意図を正確に伝えるために学ぶべきもので，その必要性にはコミュニケーション活動などで言語をアウトプットする機会があって初めて気づくものである。よってむしろ2つは相補的な関係にあり，文法指導それ自体が目的化してはいけない。

(2) 関係代名詞の主格・目的格・所有各を使って，人物を説明するような活動を行えばよい。したがって次のような手順が考えられる。①生徒に芸能人やミュージシャンの切り抜き写真を無作為に配る，②その人物について説明する文を生徒に考えさせる，③教室を回りながら人物クイズを互いに出す。ワークシートには，説明文を書くスペース，例文，コミュニケーションのときに使う会話文などを載せるとよいだろう。指導上の留意点としては，活動前に教師がモデルを示すことなどが挙げられる。

【3】(1)　(b)　　(2)　(a)　　(3)　(a)　　(4)　(d)　　(5)　(c)

〈解説〉(1)　obesity「肥満」　「児童の肥満は，近年の最も深刻な健康問題の一つである。多くの子供が油分の多い食べ物をたくさん食べ，運動をしていない。それが問題を引き起こしている」　(2)　thrive「栄える」　「その昔クマはその地域で栄えていたが，今はその数は劇的に減少している」　(3)　in response to ～「～に応じて」　「首相は新しい政策への批判に応じてメディアに声明を出した」

(4)　devastating「破壊的な」　「マグニチュード9.0の地震が破壊的な津波を引き起こし，それは水の壁を生じさせ，北部の沿岸の都市や町に押し寄せた」　(5)　concession(s)「譲歩」　「両党は合意するために譲歩することに前向きである」

【4】(1)　C　正しい語　as　　(2)　B　正しい語　amazingly

(3)　C　正しい語　to swim in

〈解説〉(1)　accept events as they areで「出来事をそのまま受けとめる」の意味。rather thanの後にas～があるのでそれも参考に。「こうなれと思うよりも，出来事をそのまま受け止めることで私はストレスを減らすようにしている」　(2)　このminuteは「微細な」という意味の形容詞なので，それを修飾する語は副詞(amazingly)でなければならない。「拡大鏡を使えば雪が驚くほど微細な構造をしているとわかるでしょう」　(3)　to swimはthe riverを説明する語句だが，swim the riverではなくswim in the riverとしなくてはならない。同じようなto不定詞の形容詞用法の例にDo you have anything to write with?「何か書く道具を持ってない？」などがある。

【5】(解答例) Even though firing workers who are already hired may be too harsh, companies should be given a right to restrict employees' smoking habit. Smoking brings several disadvantages to the company. First, as mentioned in the passage, smoking injures employees' health thus increases health care costs. Second, it is costly to carry out the maintenance of smoking room and the purifier. Finally, smokers often cannot keep from smoking for long hours, so some of them may sneak out to smoke outside the building. This is another form of cost for the company in that the company may be able to make more benefits if the employees do not settle down to their cigarettes. (112語)

〈解説〉喫煙者の解雇と雇用制限に関する文章。勤務時間外に喫煙している者もその対象に含めてもよいのかが問題となっているが，会社側は医療保険にかかる費用を削減するための措置だとしている。下線部は「より多くの会社が職場を禁煙にすると，ゼロ容認方針は拡大するだろう」という意味。以上をふまえ，職場で喫煙者をどのように扱うべきかについて，自分の考えを述べればよい。最初に主題文を，続く支持文において具体的な根拠や解決策を述べよう。

●書籍内容の訂正等について

弊社では教員採用試験対策シリーズ（参考書，過去問，全国まるごと過去問題集），公務員試験対策シリーズ，公立幼稚園・保育士試験対策シリーズ，会社別就職試験対策シリーズについて，正誤表をホームページ（https://www.kyodo-s.jp）に掲載いたします。内容に訂正等，疑問点がございましたら，まずホームページをご確認ください。もし，正誤表に掲載されていない訂正等，疑問点がございましたら，下記項目をご記入の上，以下の送付先までお送りいただくようお願いいたします。

① **書籍名，都道府県（学校）名，年度**
（例：教員採用試験過去問シリーズ　小学校教諭 過去問　2025 年度版）
② **ページ数**（書籍に記載されているページ数をご記入ください。）
③ **訂正等，疑問点**（内容は具体的にご記入ください。）
（例：問題文では“ア～オの中から選べ”とあるが，選択肢はエまでしかない）

〔ご注意〕
○ 電話での質問や相談等につきましては，受付けておりません。ご注意ください。
○ 正誤表の更新は適宜行います。
○ いただいた疑問点につきましては，当社編集制作部で検討の上，正誤表への反映を決定させていただきます（個別回答は，原則行いませんのであしからずご了承ください）。

●情報提供のお願い

協同教育研究会では，これから教員採用試験を受験される方々に，より正確な問題を，より多くご提供できるよう情報の収集を行っております。つきましては，教員採用試験に関する次の項目の情報を，以下の送付先までお送りいただけますと幸いでございます。お送りいただきました方には謝礼を差し上げます。
（情報量があまりに少ない場合は，謝礼をご用意できかねる場合があります）。

◆あなたの受験された面接試験，論作文試験の実施方法や質問内容
◆教員採用試験の受験体験記

送付先	○電子メール：edit@kyodo-s.jp ○FAX：03-3233-1233（協同出版株式会社　編集制作部 行） ○郵送：〒101-0054　東京都千代田区神田錦町 2-5 協同出版株式会社　編集制作部 行 ○HP：https://kyodo-s.jp/provision（右記の QR コードからもアクセスできます）

※謝礼をお送りする関係から，いずれの方法でお送りいただく際にも，「お名前」「ご住所」は，必ず明記いただきますよう，よろしくお願い申し上げます。

教員採用試験「過去問」シリーズ

秋田県の
英語科 過去問

編　集	© 協同教育研究会
発　行	令和6年3月10日
発行者	小貫　輝雄
発行所	協同出版株式会社
	〒101-0054　東京都千代田区神田錦町2－5
	電話　03－3295－1341
	振替　東京00190－4－94061
印刷所	協同出版・POD工場

落丁・乱丁はお取り替えいたします。